To Carol –
who also write
passion and
with respect "93
Kathleen Cawley
April 1998

157 – The idea of therapy
Claims = a
KC's religious
nutshell
"

D0849059

LIFE'S
DAUGHTER/
DEATH'S BRIDE

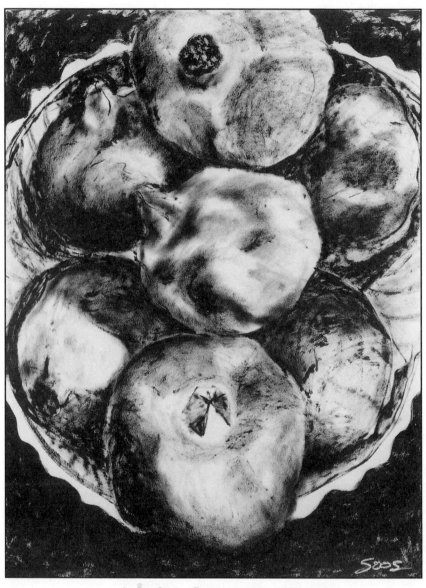

Anita Soos, *Pomegranates*, 1996.

LIFE'S DAUGHTER/ DEATH'S BRIDE

*Inner Transformations through the
Goddess Demeter/Persephone*

Kathie Carlson

Kathie Carlson [signature]

SHAMBHALA
BOSTON & LONDON
1997

Shambhala Publications, Inc.
Horticultural Hall
300 Massachusetts Avenue
Boston, Massachusetts 02115
http://www.shambhala.com

9   8   7   6   5   4   3   2   1

First Edition

Printed in the United States of America

⊗ This edition is printed on acid-free paper that meets the
American National Standards Institute Z39.48 Standard.

Distributed in the United States by Random House, Inc.,
and in Canada by Random House of Canada Ltd

Library of Congress Cataloging-in-Publication Data
Carlson, Kathie.
    Life's daughter/death's bride: inner transformations through the
goddess Demeter/Persephone / Kathie Carlson.—1st Shambhala ed.
        p.   cm.
    ISBN 0-87773-903-X (cloth)
    1. Demeter (Greek deity)   2. Persephone (Greek deity)   I. Title.
BL820.C5C37   1997   97-9007
    292.2'114—dc21   CIP

Contents

Sue MacDougall, *Persephone: Guardian of the Underworld*, 1987

Preface

LIFE'S DAUGHTER/DEATH'S BRIDE has been through many "labors" to get to its final birthing. Though I have gathered materials for this book for more than two decades, when I first began writing it in the summer of 1990, I was totally overwhelmed. Trying to comprehend the myth in its vastness and many-layered meanings felt like trying to condense the night sky into a funnel. Inevitably my approach narrowed down to the particular contribution to the ever-growing literature that I felt I had to offer. Nevertheless, writing this book is the hardest thing I have ever done.

In the background of this book stands a trinity of particularly significant influences on my intellectual development and personal and professional growth as an adult. These include Jungian psychology, which I studied extensively during my several years at the C. G. Jung Institute in New York; feminism, particularly as it came to me and affected me on a feeling level through a number of women friends; and the Old Religion of the Goddess, the study of which over the past fifteen years or so has formed the core of my passionate interest in feminine psychology and the feminine Self.

I discovered Jung back in 1966 when I was a young graduate student in psychology at the New School for Social Research in New York City; what drew me to Jung then was his inclusion of a spiritual dimension within psychology that gave weight, meaning, and real attention to the spirit and spiritual quest instead of reducing it to "nothing but" the wishful projections or sublimations of a human ego. Jung gave me a language for much of my own experience up to that point, which opened me up to myself even more deeply and companioned me in what had been a lonely self-journey; it was a deep and vital find to come upon his work at that time.

It was also through Jungian psychology that I was first introduced to the idea of a specifically feminine psychology that had a profound awakening influence on me as a young adult back in the 1960s. Here the work of several of the early women Jungians left a deep and lasting imprint. While some of this early writing on the Feminine and feminine experience seems outmoded to me now, I want to acknowledge these early contributions to the development of my perspective on women, the Goddess, and the Demeter-Persephone dynamic.

Esther Harding's *The Way of All Women* and *Women's Mysteries* left an early, indelible mark on me. Her chapter on "Friendship" in *The Way of All Women* still stands out as a little gem in the history of Jungian psychology, marking an initial focus on the value of relationships *between* women, a topic that in the early days got short shrift in a psychology so otherwise focused on the contra-sexual dynamics of masculine and feminine.[1] *Women's Mysteries* with its focus on the moon, the inner meaning of the menstrual cycle, and the prepatriarchal meaning of the "virgin" as "one-in-herself" moved me deeply, sparked my imaginal capacity, and was an initiatory experience into a whole new way of looking at my own and others' experiences of being female.[2] The "one-in-herself" woman has, I realize, continued to be a guiding image in my feeling and thinking throughout the years and forms the basis of my working hypothesis that unless and until a woman belongs to herself, she is not adequately in possession of an inner base from which she can fully relate to others or to the Self.

Other early writers influenced me as well. Irene de Castillejo's insistence in her book *Knowing Woman* that the soul image in women is feminine simply rang true and is perhaps a hidden precursor of my subsequent passion for pursuing the variety of feminine god-images in early religion as potential mirrors of the female Self today.[3]

Erich Neumann's book *The Great Mother* was extremely influential to my early thinking, and I still love the vision, expanse, and audacity (not a single clinical example!) of his "grand" style, as well as his poetic reverence for his subject.[4] Neumann's work is an extensive exploration of the Mother archetype (i.e., the Goddess) and a gold mine of mythological amplification of this image. While some of Neumann's scholarship has stood the test of time (and has been extended by the more recent work of the archaeologist and "grandmother" of the Women's Spirituality Movement, the late Marija Gimbutas), many of his theoretical formulations as applied to women, in my opinion and experience, do not.[5] Like some other male writers on the Goddess, Neumann assumes too readily that women, who in fact have also been estranged from and ignorant of the Goddess after years of patriarchal distortion and repression, have automatic and conscious access to the feminine archetypal dimension (in other words, women don't have to search for connection with the Feminine as men do; they already *have* it or *are* it).[6] In my experience, both personally and in working with women, this is far from the truth. To a great extent women have also been starving for connection with the transpersonal Feminine in their lives and, once awakened to its existence, have to make enormous efforts to push through the narrowness of cultural ignorance and stereotypes of "feminine" to make deeper contact with its bigger, more sacred dimension.

Nevertheless, some of Neumann's concepts have been and continue to be extremely useful to me, particularly his ideas of the "elementary" and "transformative" aspects of the Mother.[7] In my first book, *In Her Image*, I summarized and illustrated these concepts, applying them to women's experiences with their personal mothers.[8] In *Life's Daughter/Death's Bride*, I go a step further, amplifying Neumann's idea of the transformative aspect of the Feminine (which he tended to see largely in terms of the "anima" experience of men) and applying it to relationships between women as well as to the dynamics of a woman's intrapsychic experience, exploring the transformative element within and for herself. This transposition of Neumann's work will be most evident in chapters 6 and 7 of this book.

In contrast to my early exposure to Jung, I came to feminism rather late in my life (I was already in my thirties) and then via a particularly personal rather than initially academic or political route. I was living and practicing in East Lansing, Michigan, and at one point became part of several women's groups: a large, social/networking group that met monthly; a small women's support group; and the midwestern branch of the Society for Women in Philosophy. The several women who formed the core of my connections to each of these groups were women I was initially drawn to because of shared intellectual interests; each was also a long-standing feminist. What was remarkable about these women and different from some other feminists I met then and some I have met since was the maturity of their feminism: the breadth, flexibility, and openness to differences they embodied, a profound generosity of both vision and spirit. Through them and the reading I did later (Dorothy Dinnerstein, Carol Gilligan, and Adrienne Rich's work were especially important to me), I gained an awareness of culture and cultural conditioning (fleshing out what Jung called, amorphously, "the collective"); of the characteristics, impact, and historicity of patriarchy; and of gender differences in both cultural messages and personal experience. Even more critical for my subsequent development and interests was the awakening of an imperative to search for "origins," both personal and collective, in woman-derived experience instead of male fantasy or prescription.

As I look back now, what was affected most in me by my introduction to feminism and the way that it came to me was my *feeling*. This experience and these women left a *feeling imprint*, awakening in me a profound sense of commonality across differences between myself and other women and a deep sense of compassion, caring, and openness to a vast array of different styles and preferences in being female and to different life situations and life choices. I realized as I was thinking through these introductory comments for this book that this is congruent with and perhaps even the subjective base for much of my intellectual and spiritual apperception of the Goddess, my delight in and continuous experience of being moved and compelled by the richness and complexity of her many faces.

Feminist influences have also solidified and made more articulate my interest in women's individuation issues. The struggle to become authentic has been a driving force in my life as far back as I can remember, bringing with it the pain, estrangement, and self-fulfillment that Jung so eloquently wrote about in much of his work. Learning to look at myself and others through feminist eyes has extended my understanding of what shapes, challenges, and thwarts the development of the individual. Looking through these eyes forms much of my picture of what constitutes the "collective" for contemporary women, with the subsequent challenges and tasks it creates for the ego and the ego/Self relationship.

Feminism has also changed my perceptions of men and men's issues. For years, I had been wrenched by father and son stories I was hearing in therapy, deeply aware of unhealed wounds in the experiences of so many men with their fathers. Now I see these experiences and the deep scars they generated within a broader backdrop of patriarchal dynamics, with its emotionally constrictive definitions of masculinity and imperatives toward distancing, competition, and a drive for power over others that stultify relatedness. Although my treatment of the Masculine in this book is limited to a particular kind of shadow and its dynamics within both men and women, I will be following the myth to suggest that the healing of such a shadow—at least as the myth of Demeter and Persephone images it—comes about via a different relationship to the Feminine. My personal conviction, however, is that at this point in time, it is for many if not most men even more imperative that a new masculinity be carved out via a different relationship to the transpersonal Masculine through a reforging of the father-son dynamic.

The third major influence on my life, work, and perspective as an adult stems from my research into the imagery of the Goddess and from the Women's Spirituality Movement. I first encountered the Goddess in my early teens when I was passionate about both mythology and creative writing and wrote short stories and songs about the goddess Aphrodite. My next conscious encounter with the Goddess came in the late 1960s when (still trying to fit in to a formal religion) I became briefly involved with Vedanta Hinduism and the life of Sri Ramakrishna, who was devoted to the goddess Kali. I don't remember being especially impressed back then by the fact that Kali was a *goddess*, that is, that the Deity was imaged as *female*, but I do recall being especially moved by some of the hymns to her that I found in *The Gospel of Sri Ramakrishna*, which I still often use in my teaching. What continues to move me, after all these years, is that Ramakrishna envisioned this horrific, death-dealing goddess as also the good and benevolent Mother and often spoke of playing with her (a decidedly different approach from the hero's "slaying the Terrible Mother as Dragon"). He never denied Kali's awfulness and horror, yet approached her with the confidence and affection of a well-loved child. Ramakrishna's vision and capacity to hold together the horrific and the benevolent sides of the Goddess is one of the most complete visions of her that I have encountered and moves and teaches me still.

In spite of these and other personal touchpoints with the Goddess early in my life, my spiritual life did not gravitate toward her consciously as its center until very late. I discovered Merlin Stone's book *When God Was a Woman* sometime in the 1970s and was stunned by the recognition that the biblical Genesis was not "The Beginning," that there was a whole other religion that existed before and alongside of it and this religion was the religion of the Goddess. This opened a new world for me, one that touched a deep hunger that I was compelled to pursue.

Though I knew I was gripped intellectually and imaginally by the Goddess literature that I subsequently read and by the teaching I began to do around it, it was not until the early 1980s, when I became aware of a feminine Presence in my apple tree (which I wrote about briefly in the conclusion of *In Her Image*), that I began to get in touch with my personal connection to all of this. Around the same time, the ancient Egyptian goddess Sekhmet appeared to me in a powerful, moving, and also funny dream—she made me aware of her presence by *biting* me (an obviously nonpatriarchal "annunciation"!).

Since these early epiphanies, my personal experiences of the Goddess through dreams, fantasy, and devotion have intersected with my eager drinking in of the Goddess literature, making up the basis of my understanding and perspective regarding this powerful feminine Deity. The flowering of the Women's Spirituality Movement, of which I consider myself a modest part, has been extremely important to me and to the work I do, infusing my heart's apperception of the Goddess and my passion to transmit her images through teaching and writing. Many women and some men, both prominent and nonprominent, have enriched my thinking and my soul; they are too many to enumerate but I owe special debts to the work of Marija Gimbutas, Starhawk, Carol Christ, Chris Downing, Clysta Kinstler, Enos Benjamin, Barbara Walker, Elinor Gadon, Genia Pauli Haddon, Sylvia Perera, Ajit Mookerjee, Lex Hixon, and Merlin Stone. While our emphases and orientations sometimes differ, we are all concerned with excavating the past to unveil and make visible again the Goddess's many faces and to dream her forward into our present and our future.

All of these perspectives—Jungian, feminist, and the study of the Old Religion—are in the background of this book; their confluence makes up the threads from which much of my own perspective is woven. At the same time, I want to make clear that I do not hold any one of these points of view to be *the* comprehensive explanation or lens through which I see the world, nor am I able to be "politically correct" in any one of my various loyalties. It has been both my bane and my fate to not be able to fit in to any system of thought—religious, psychological, or ideological—no matter how much I admire and respect it. This appears to be both the often-painful price of my struggle to be authentic and the signature of my own particular path of individuation. Thus the content of this book is my own responsibility and should not be read as fully representing any of the various orientations I draw from.

Life's Daughter/Death's Bride aims at being both an accessible and multilayered treatment of the Demeter-Persephone myth. It moves from a focus on mythology in the earliest chapters to an increasing emphasis on psychological examples of mythical dynamics. Chapter 1 takes the reader into thinking about myth in general and introduces the fluidity and simultaneity of early pagan thinking and spirituality. It also outlines basic Jungian concepts and sets forth my specific perspective on the Demeter-Persephone myth. Chapter 2 is devoted to a recounting of the myth and its variants as "story," as well as a description of the Eleusinian mysteries; following the ancient material is a consideration of what of its imagery and potency remains and what has disappeared as viewed through some contemporary rural Greek funeral lamentations and customs. Included too is a relatively contemporary "saint" story that both preserved and rewrote the ancient story of the grain goddess and her daughter. This chapter lays the groundwork of imagery and interpretation for the rest of the book.

Chapters 3 through 5 focus in on the myth's three major characters—Demeter, Kore-Persephone, and Hades—interweaving mythology with psychological interpretation and examples. Chapter 3 considers the passion and power of Demeter as Mother and her appearance as a potent, initiatory archetypal force in human life. Chapter 4 takes a multifaceted look at Persephone and the power to "gestate" the death experience that lies behind her seeming helplessness in the face of Hades. Chapter 5 focuses on the Death god himself, the "death-marriage" theme and its psychological equivalents, and illustrates this shadow side of the more positive and expansive patriarchal Zeus. Each of these three chapters offers experiential examples of these dynamics.

Chapter 6 moves into a more exclusively psychological approach and centers on a subject that has absorbed me for nearly two decades: the Goddess as a representation of the transpersonal Self for women. This chapter examines the Mother-Daughter archetype as a paradigm for feminine wholeness and what it means when this wholeness has been split by experiences of Hades as patriarchal shadow in a woman's relationships with men or the culture at large or in the form of animus in other women or herself.

Chapter 7 in some ways is the heart of this book (it was the most persistently difficult to write). It concerns the plight of women who have grown up in patriarchal cultures (nearly all of us), unconnected with a transpersonal (or often, personal) "positive" powerful mother, who have taken in the patriarchal "diabolizing" of women and thus *begin* psychologically in Hades' underworld. If the underworld (characterized by experiencing oneself as unmothered, overpowered, insubstantial, and "male-identified") has been "home," the initiatory journey through this myth is likely to begin with a longing for and fighting against becoming a child of the Mother and a move toward an experience of the Goddess. This transformative journey of "living the myth backward" and its archetypal underpinnings as they constellate in therapy between women are described at length through the conscious struggles and unconscious dynamics of two female clients. Finally, in chapter 8 I explore in depth the archetype of Hades as shadow as it appeared in the psychological process of an older male client. While most of this book focuses on the dynamics and healing potential of this myth for women, this chapter includes commentary on the psychological meaningfulness and healing potential of the Eleusinian mysteries for men. The brief conclusion to this book moves back to the ancient focus on the Mother as power and Presence in the face of literal death and psychological "death equivalents."

A note about language: beginning in the first chapter and periodically throughout the book, I speak of viewing this myth through a "matriarchal" or "patriarchal" accent. I recognize that these terms are somewhat problematical but have retained them because they are more familiar to the general reader as compared to the more recent convolutions, such as androcentric/gynocentric or patristic/matristic, etc. The problem with "matriarchal" and "patriarchal" is that to some people these terms imply sociopolitical dominance, that is, a "matriarchal" society would be one ruled by women, just as a "patriarchal" society is ruled by men. Since the questions of whether any ancient societies were ever "matriarchal" in this sense or whether one can read sociopolitical arrangements in any given society from the imagery in that society's religion remain unanswered controversies, it seems imperative to clarify the way in which I am using these terms in this book. Because this book is largely concerned with collective and individual psychology, when I speak of "matriarchal" and "patriarchal" I am most often speaking of *psychological* dominants—for example, in a collective or personal mythology that is "matriarchal", images of the archetypal Feminine predominate and have supreme power while the Masculine plays a lesser role or is devalued and effaced and vice versa.

I find this to be psychologically if not politically sound, and these conceptions serve my purposes in trying to elucidate the content and consequences of both matriarchal and patriarchal psychologies.

Two other notes: I have followed the increasing trend among feminist historians, archaeologists, and others and refer to specific historical periods using the nonreligiously loaded designations BCE (before the common era) and CE (common era) instead of BC and AD with their singularly Christian connotations.

Acknowledgments

SPARKED BY A DREAM I had as a young woman, *Life's Daughter/Death's Bride* has been many years in the making and the most challenging work I have ever done. So many people offered encouragement and interest during its long gestation that it is simply impossible to thank everyone by name without inevitably overlooking someone vital. Therefore I wish to express my deepest thanks to the following groups and a few individuals:

- To all my friends, near and far, as well as my children and their partners for the love that sustains my life.
- To all of the students in my Goddess literature class for giving me a forum in which I could test out my ideas and my passions. Special thanks to those who willingly slogged through Farnell when I taught Demeter and Persephone, even though only one person could understand his frequent lapses into untranslated Greek!
- To past clients for giving permission to use portions of their therapeutic processes and life stories (with identifying referents fictionalized or disguised); their contributions bear witness to this myth as "living symbol."
- To the artists for contributing their own rich visions of this myth, adding visual dimension and beauty to this work.
- To the C. G. Jung Institute in New York for my many years of psychotherapeutic training. Special thanks to Dr. Christopher Whitmont, whose enthusiasm for my initial understanding of this myth gave me the impetus to stay with it and develop my ideas in depth.
- To the C. G. Jung Foundation, the Kristine Mann Library, and the Archive for Research in Archetypal Symbolism (ARAS) in New York for their interest, support, and resources extended to me over all the years. I am especially indebted to Annmari Ronnberg and Karen Arm of ARAS and Doris Albrecht, Michele McKee, and Steven O'Neill of the library for help with the research and the bibliography.
- To the Ann and Erlo Van Waveren Foundation and the Ludwig Vo-

gelstein Foundation for providing much-needed grants in support of my work on this book. Special thanks to Bezo Morton and Olivier Bernier, who walked me through my first grant application.

· To all the staff at Shambhala Publications who have waited patiently for me to produce this work with unflagging interest and friendship as well as professional support. Deepest thanks to my editor, Emily Hilburn Sell, for her patience, humor, empathy, and grace in fielding moments of panic.

· To several individuals who were instrumental in seeing this book through to completion: I want to thank my online "musemates," Julie Weston and Elaine Pinkerton Coleman, who read the most problematic portions of the manuscript, listened to my whines, cheered me on, and offered helpful suggestions; Sylvia Perera and Anne Hussey, who read the entire manuscript in its final draft and provided thoughtful and stimulating critique; and Anne Mitchell, N.D., whose care, challenges, and innovative work helped break a long-standing, stubborn block, literally enabling me to finish the writing.

Finally, I want to acknowledge my center in the Goddess, who, here in the form of Demeter and Persephone, has given me a vision of Her initiatory path toward creative encounter with the forces of dissolution and transformation that the ancients called Hades, a life task I learn about still. . . .

Kathie Carlson
November 1996

LIFE'S DAUGHTER/
DEATH'S BRIDE

Sue MacDougall, *Demeter Still Searching*, 1987.

~❧ 1 ❧~

Approaching the Myth

In what direction must we enlarge our thoughts in order to stand in fit relationship to the phenomenon?

—CARL KERÉNYI, *"Kore"*[1]

All that is visible must grow beyond itself, extend into the realm of the invisible. Thereby it receives its true consecration and clarity and takes firm root in the cosmic order.

—*I Ching*, Hexagram 50, The Caldron[2]

A BELOVED YOUNG DAUGHTER is snatched away from her devoted mother by a rapist known to possess his victims completely and lead them to certain death. The mother, beside herself with grief and rage, sets out to find her daughter and uncovers a collusion between the highest authorities and the rapist, a collusion that facilitated her daughter's abduction. Adding to the outrage is the fact that the rapist is the young girl's own uncle and the higher authorities are governed by her father. Incensed and determined to bring about justice, the mother stages a highly effective protest against the authorities that results in her daughter's return, traumatized but alive and possessing her own considerable strength to both survive and transform her ordeal.

This is not the stuff of contemporary newspaper headlines but the

1

central mythologem in a complex, richly layered ancient story that became the basis for a Mystery religion that lasted for at least fifteen hundred years, well into the Christian era. The setting was ancient Greece, and the mother in the mythic drama was not a human mother but the deeply benevolent grain deity, the goddess Demeter, whose gifts were vital to human survival and well-being. Her daughter was the maiden goddess Kore, destined to return from her traumatic abduction as Persephone, Queen of the Dead; the rapist was none other than Death itself, the dreaded god Hades, Lord of the Underworld. So too the triumph in this drama, made holy in the Eleusinian mysteries that grew out of this myth, was not simply a human survival and recovery from extreme violation but the overcoming of a certain vision of death, vividly evidenced not only in the daughter's return from Death's kingdom but in her transformation into Brimo, the Mystery goddess who brings forth Brimos, the luminous son.

To the ancients, this myth was seen as an intense portrayal of the seeming opposition of life and death and, in the end, the transcendence of this opposition. Death in this drama was visioned vividly as the Snatcher, the violator of life who suddenly erupts from the darkness below, snatching away not only the old and infirm, but even more poignantly the young, the still-developing, the barely begun. Human beings could find their own grief written large in the mourning and rage of the Divine Mother, follow her path of resolution and reconciliation, and through initiation into her Mysteries, participate in her power to confront the forces of death and transform them. The myth of Demeter and Persephone and the Eleusinian mysteries fulfilled a powerful, universal human need: relief from the terror of death and hope for the future even in the face of it. Thus Homer could write, of the meaning of the Mysteries, "Happy is that man among the men of earth who witnesses these things. And whoever is not initiated in the rites, whoever has no part in them, he does not share the same fate when he dies and is down in the squalid darkness."[3] So potent were these Mysteries held to be that the ancient Greeks believed that without their regular celebration, life itself would be untenable and that not only Greece but the entire world would come undone.[4] So sacred were they that in more than a millennium, not a single individual betrayed their secrets.

On one level, then, the myth of Demeter and Kore-Persephone and the Mysteries that grew out of it are the collective attempt of one culture to come to grips with the human dilemma of death. From a historical perspective, they also reflect and distill a particular historical event that took place thousands of years ago but is pivotal even for us today: the rape of Kore away from the Mother mirrors mythologically the usurpation and gradual assimilation of an older southern European religion of the Mother Goddess by the earliest forces of patriarchy, worshipers of a warring sky god, who invaded from the North. Hades was the brother of the sky god Zeus, both patriarchal imports to Greece, while Demeter and her daughter have prepatriarchal roots indigenous to southern Europe and to earlier times.

Over a period of thousands of years, the New Religion with its dominant masculine gods overcame and assimilated the Old Religion of the Mother. Mythically, this assimilation was repeatedly pictured as the Goddess being raped, dismembered, slain by a hero figure, or married (and subordinated) to the invading god. Thus the myth of Demeter and Persephone can also be seen within its ancient framework as a drama of religious tensions and opposition. Since it can be interpreted in both directions as a triumph for either the archetypal Masculine or the Feminine, the New or the Old Religion, it can both serve as a vivid demonstration of the conflict of values and visions in these two religions and offer at least two possibilities toward their resolutions.

Today we still struggle with the fear of death in many forms, both literal and psychological, as well as with the legacy of patriarchy and the destructive aspects of its claims to power. This myth can teach us much about both of these still-contemporary issues. As the work of C. G. Jung and related scholars of mythology like Joseph Campbell has pointed out and amply elucidated, the richness and relevance of ancient myths are not confined to the times or cultures in which they arose. Rising from a layer of the objective psyche that is common to us as a species and appears to transcend the boundaries of space, time, and consciousness (the layer that Jung called the collective unconscious), ancient mythic patterns, themes, and symbols appear at times in the dreams, fantasies, artistic creations, visions, relationships, life histories, and life events of modern people.[5] Jung called these images and motifs (which also appear in art, ritual, and fairy tales) archetypal; common examples of these archetypes include the Great Father, the Great Mother, the Hero, the journey to the Center, the descent to the underworld, the Wise Old Woman and Man, and the encounter with

3

the Evil One, to name but a few. Their origins and meanings are often unknown to us when they appear today, yet nevertheless these archetypes may have an impressive emotional impact: one has the sense of having had a "big" dream; of being caught up in a bigger-than-life relationship or human drama; of being awed, surprised, profoundly moved, or even filled with fear by what emerges from one's creative vision. This impact—which Rudolf Otto termed the experience of the "numinous"[6]—is the spiritual earmark of an archetype and conveys with it a sense of meaning and emotional import even if not intellectually grasped or understood.

Using the tools of depth psychology, we can discern further layers of meaning in these experiences, layers perhaps unconceived of consciously by the ancients yet inherent in their myths and surprisingly relevant and healing for people today. These layers tap us back into the deeper transformative forces that exist within and beyond all cultures and that we share in common across space and time. Thus, contemporary struggles with threats of literal death or its psychic equivalents and the current strivings of both men and women to come to terms with and transform the destructive aspects of patriarchy have much to gain from an in-depth look at a myth that not only reappears in the modern psyche but offered healing possibilities for such issues centuries ago.

Every archetypal image or pattern can appear both intrapsychically (in dream image or an emotional complex, for example) and relationally (in the psychological dynamics between people in relationship or within a group). In other words, archetypal epiphanies can be experienced both "in here," in the inner life of an individual, or "out there," as the unconscious backdrop for his or her experiences with others. This is not to suggest an either/or framework for these possibilities; the line between "inner" and "outer" is fluid at best and the same person whose innermost psyche is informed by a particular mythological drama or pattern may find himself or herself playing out precisely the same dynamics in relationship with others.

This dual possibility of archetypal manifestation is particularly important to keep in mind when exploring this myth of Demeter and Persephone. "Demeter," for example, can be seen as a unity embracing the entire complex of the myth's characters (Demeter-Kore-Persephone-Hades), which along with the myth's dynamics may open a window of perception into a particular intrapsychic constellation of

4

the Self in an individual woman. Or Demeter may be approached more simply as the mother of a daughter, her image lending itself to being seen in a particular style of mothering behavior in relationship to someone who is in a daughter role. Thus the same archetypal configuration can be seen as illustrative of Self dynamics or as a drama played out in relationship between two women (e.g., an actual mother and daughter, female friends or lovers, or between therapist and client). In subsequent chapters, I will consider both of the arenas—the intrapsychic and relational—in which this myth may manifest, focusing particularly on the realm of therapy.

A psychological approach to an ancient myth that interprets its images and drama in terms of emotional complexes and relational patterns is, of necessity, different from the original collective mind-set within which the myth arose and had meaning. Nevertheless, in order to fully appreciate the richness, nuance, and depth of its subject matter, such an approach needs to be cognizant of the original mind-set and perhaps even to some extent infused with it.

To the ancients, myths carried a fullness of spiritual reality, continuous with the religious beliefs and important ritual practices of the time. We in contemporary Western culture are used to thinking of "myth" as something one-dimensional and, by definition, inherently false. Contemporary dictionaries still define myth from this perspective: thus *Webster's Ninth New Collegiate Dictionary*, for example, lists among its several meanings for the word myth "a usually traditional story of *ostensibly* historical events that serves to unfold part of the world view of a people or explain a practice, belief, or natural phenomenon; an *unfounded* or *false* notion; [or] a person or thing having only an *imaginary* or *unverifiable* existence" (emphasis mine). Similarly, the descent to and return of Persephone from the underworld has often been seen merely as a story made up to explain the seasons or account for agricultural dynamics. It is assumed that the ancients, lacking scientific knowledge, invented fanciful explanations out of their ignorance (and that our modern thinking, is, of course, vastly superior and carries the truth).

Myth, in our habitual thinking, is not only contrasted with the truth of science but also with the claims of a different orientation: the perspective of religion. Religion (stemming from a root word meaning "reverence"), in contrast to myth, is defined by *Webster's* as "the service and worship of God or the supernatural; a personal set or institu-

5

tionalized system of religious attitudes, beliefs, and practices; or a cause, principle, or system of beliefs held to with ardor and with faith"—not a mention of "unfounded," "unverifiable," "false." Religion is assumed to be about something transcendent—God and the supernatural—to be expressed in worship, to be held with passionate belief, with reverence and with faith. But Zeus, Demeter, Persephone, and Hades were all worshiped in ancient times; the ritual celebration of the Eleusinian mysteries was believed to be so spiritually potent that the fate of the entire world depended on it; and the essence of these practices was held with such reverence and deemed so holy that no one *ever* betrayed its secrets. What we have learned to dismiss as myth was once religion, naming divinity and the supernatural and holding a depth and breadth of spiritual apperception to the people for whom it was not merely story but living experience.

It is even more difficult for many of us to be aware of nuance and depth in Greek myth or to easily imagine ourselves into its numinosity. The goddesses and gods, as they have come down to us, seem little more than rather quarrelsome and one-dimensional extensions of human beings; most of us, familiar with Greek myth through our general educations, have no idea that the versions most readily available to us bear only thin resemblances to their original potency and fullness. Nor are we aware that the sources of these versions (the author of the Homeric hymns, for example) reshaped the myths by screening out their most archaic (and often richest) elements.[7] The Greek culture we most readily identify with as precursor to our own thinking and ideals flourished around 500 BCE. But the Mysteries had already been practiced for hundreds of years prior to this time and elements of the myth stretch back even further than that.

The goddesses and gods were not originally the paper-thin analogues that populate our storybooks today but rather were rich and multifaceted figures of spiritual dimension. The goddess Demeter was not simply "the mother," as she tends to be labeled now in modern commentaries, but richly layered, her dimensionality stretching even beyond her humanlike form. She was expressed not only as Mother (and even this was multifaceted, since she was not only mother of a daughter but also of the grain—and even mother of the dead) but she was also the Maiden, a spring goddess known as Demeter Chloe, and an underworld figure, Demeter Chthonia. Moreover, in an exquisite example of the fullness of early pagan spirituality, she was continuous with the plants whose tending she taught and governed; she was not only Maiden, Mother, and Crone but also the life force within the plant itself.[8] This continuity with Nature is especially important in appreciating the depth and spiritual richness of this myth, its origins in nonpatriarchal thinking, and the nature of the pagan vision that engendered it.

To approach this myth adequately, then, we need to gather whatever versions and fragments of it we can and interweave them in an imaginal attempt to re-create the fullness of their origins (I will do this in the following chapters). We must put aside not only the biases of our educational conditioning around Greek myth but also seek to lower the barriers created by some of the structure of our modern consciousness, attempting instead to dream our way back to a pagan fluidity of mind. Thus the classicist Jane Harrison, writing in 1903 about ancient Greek religion, asserted

> There is no greater bar to that realizing of mythology which is the first condition of its being understood, than our modern habit of clear analytic thought. The very terms we use are sharpened to an over-nice discrimination. The first necessity is that, by an effort of the sympathetic imagination, we should think back the "many" we have so sharply and strenuously divided, into the haze of the primitive "one." Nor must we regard this haze of the early morning as a deleterious fog, as a sign of disorder, weakness, oscillation. It is not confusion or even synthesis; rather it is as it were a protoplasmic fullness and forcefulness not yet articulate into the diverse forms of its ultimate births. It may even happen, as in the case of the Olympian divinities, that articulation and discrimination sound the note of approaching decadence.[9]

To dream our way back to the "protoplasmic fullness and forcefulness" that infuse early pagan religion is a first necessity in approaching an understanding of this myth. We need to take on something of a "lunar consciousness," as Erich Neumann called it, a consciousness that can be diffuse, permeable, flow with the transformations, the fullness, and even the contradiction of the imagery.[10] We need to enter into the myth via an empathic "feeling into," a "participation mystique" that allows us to experience numinosity and mystery and to enter the pagan mind-set so different from our own. It is this kind of consciousness we need to hold alongside our more conceptual attempts at "making psychology" out of ancient myth. In this way, we can participate as well as understand: with this myth, which was essentially an entrée into participation in a numinous and secret mystery celebration, such a both/and approach is particularly appropriate.

Pagan spirituality, as we know it in the present and can reconstruct it from the past, was centered in a profound relationship with Nature (as has been true of other nonpatriarchal religions as well, like those of various Native Americans). The vision of Nature and beliefs about human life in relationship to Nature were markedly different from those more familiar to us from our own patriarchal religions. Nature was seen as infused with Spirit; Spirit was found in and through Nature rather than being outside and above it. Human life was essentially a part of Nature and continuous with it, and Nature was to be empathetically participated with, rather than transcended, for all hope and meaning for human life could be drawn by analogy from what happened in the natural world. (Dominion over Nature, Nature as the property of human beings, would have been unthinkable, a sacrilege, a violation of continuity. This is perhaps why Demeter's agricultural teachings were seen as her gift; people were taught how to work with Nature, allowed to learn how to augment the natural process and co-create with it for the benefit of both the gods and humankind.) The life of the human body and bodily process—our obvious touchpoint with Nature—was not seen as carnal flesh, opposed to Spirit and to be transcended and overcome; its naturalness, stages, vulnerability, and even its aging toward certain death were not approached with intent to fixate the body into one condition or one stage of life (unlike, for example, our culture's cultivation of perpetual youth). The vicissitudes of human bodily life were seen as mirroring the life of the body in Nature, in animals and plants, to be essentially and continually transforming; from this observation of continual transformation in Nature sprang an abundance of rich and varied religious beliefs.

What happened in Nature would also happen in human beings; therein lay the hope, the excitement, the meaning in human life. The life cycle of a plant, for example (intimately connected with the myth at hand) became a vivid paradigm of the fate of humanity at death. From a seed hidden under the earth, a plant germinates, breaks through to the upperworld in a sprout, thrives, and develops. Perhaps it blossoms, like Kore, the bud of her mother, bears fruit, becomes the Mother itself, falters, withers, begins to die. Its fruit falls, rots, begins to decompose but then the miracle occurs. The rot mixes with the earth, becomes compost, enriches and revitalizes the soil, and from this "fertile death" spring forth the newly germinating seeds, the life inherent in the fruit, released at death to manifest the power of the Crone who endlessly recycles death and starts the life process again. To see oneself as a part of Nature, to feel oneself as subject to her powers, to participate in the cycle of her endless transformation of life-into-death-into-life again, engendered in the ancients a vibrant spiritual vision of human destiny. So the human dead, like seeds, were "planted" in the earth and called "the Mother's people" (Demeteroi) or burned to hasten transformation; so too they "mixed with earth" so that they would also decompose and open to new life again. In Nature, everything recycled; nothing stayed the same. Change was the only constant, the signature of continuity. There was no linear process, no beginning and no end, no eternity of either life or death—transformation was the essence and the ground of spiritual belief. And Spirit stood within the natural process rather than outside of it or in opposition to it (compare, in contrast, the Christian doctrine of the Virgin Birth, an antinatural or supranatural event). Remnants of this vision remain; we still plant flowers on graves or use the Easter lily to represent the resurrection from the dead. To understand the myth of Demeter and Persephone, we need to apprehend the richness and fluidity of the pagan matrix from which it emerged.

Drawing from both the pagan vision, as we can reconstruct and reimagine it, and from Jungian psychology, we can explore this myth in depth by tuning our thinking to an awareness of cycles, paradoxes, or opposites, and the compensatory aspect of the unconscious (the latter is explained below).

Perceiving time and process in terms of cycles rather than linear development is especially relevant to an attempt, to paraphrase Carl Kerényi, "to expand our thinking to fit the phenomenon." A focus on cyclicity in Nature gives rise to the observation (which in turn became a religious formulation) that every ending brings forth a new beginning and that each phase of a process comes round again. An awareness of cycles is important to this myth in order to grasp the meaningfulness of Persephone's return from the dead and the nature of her powers of transformation. It is also vital in comprehending the ritualization that subsequently takes place within the myth itself: part of the myth's resolution is that Persephone must continue to leave

9

her mother each year and return to Hades for a period of several months, though after she has been returned from the dead the first time, this experience is no longer a rape but a ritual, a voluntary descent. An understanding of cycle is also important to approaching the meaning of the Mysteries and the need for their regular celebration.

Thinking in paradoxes or opposites is also vital to appreciating the fullness and complexity of this myth and understanding its meaning for our times. I believe that this myth marked and reflects a transition point in the collective unconscious (and possibly literal history as well) that held in tension two opposing accents and perspectives: a "matriarchal accent" that represented the psychological predominance of the transpersonal Feminine in the Old Religion of the Goddess and a "patriarchal accent" that reflected the psychological predominance of the transpersonal Masculine in the religion of the northern (Indo-European) invaders who infiltrated the goddess-worshipping southern Europeans in a series of conquests beginning around 3500 BCE. And while literal history depicts the gradual assimilation of the Old Religion to the New and radical devaluation of the Goddess and the Feminine in deference to the dominance of the archetypal Masculine that we live with still today, I think this myth hearkens back to a period in which this was not yet accomplished, when the two perspectives were held in literal and psychological tension. Thus the imagery and dynamics of this myth and its appearance in the modern psyche can be read from either of two opposing perspectives: they can be seen through a matriarchal accent in which the power of the transpersonal Feminine is emphasized and the Masculine is effaced or peripheral (or subject to the Feminine) or a patriarchal accent in which the transpersonal Masculine is beginning to gain power and ultimately triumphs over the Feminine, ushering in a whole new order. Which of these accents is the appropriate one in the interpreting of the myth's appearance in contemporary psychological material will depend on what the unconscious of any given individual is trying to fill out and compensate for in his or her conscious life.

Many earlier or later myths are more clearly weighted in one direction or the other, their matriarchal or patriarchal dominants at the transpersonal level more clear. (The Hero myth, for example, in which the Masculine rises and triumphs by surviving and overcoming a series of "ordeals," reflects the dominants of a patriarchal psychology, whereas the myth of the Year King portrays an older, matriarchal

10

perspective depicting a Feminine dominant to which the Masculine is subject and ultimately sacrificed for renewal.) The Demeter-Persephone myth is unique in that it holds these opposites in tension and does not unequivocally resolve the tension in favor of one side or the other. Thus it lends itself to extremely rich, many-sided, and even contradictory interpretations that may apply to a whole variety of psychological situations. Perceiving the myth as a whole, then, requires the entertainment of a "both/and" stretch of mind that can comprehend that contradiction and multiplicity may come closer to truth and wholeness than linear, logical thinking.

My contention is that both these accents through which the Demeter and Persephone myth may be read have some validity (including psychological validity) even though opposing; each is grounded in some (but not all) aspects of the myth itself and in what we know of the Mysteries. Depending on which lens one looks through when attempting to understand and interpret this myth, different aspects are emphasized and different elements are valenced positively or negatively (see the accompanying table).

Looking through the lens of a matriarchally accented point of view, one finds an emphasis on the Feminine and its powers of transformation. The central relationship in the myth, from this perspective, is between the two goddesses who embody a positive "matriarchal bond." This bond excludes the Masculine or assigns it to the periphery but is not necessarily hostile to it or in opposition. While the main rendition of the myth makes no mention of husband and little of father (though it was assumed in classical Greece, reflecting the patriarchal assimilation of the Goddess religion, that Zeus was Kore's father and Hades her uncle) and focuses instead almost exclusively on the positive bond between Mother and Daughter, Demeter has had positive alliances with masculine figures in the past and has even borne children by them. Yet even this is effaced, her other children are scarcely mentioned, and Mother and Daughter hold central stage. There is no hint of hostility; Demeter does not oppose the Masculine until her daughter is violated (or she is). In addition, there is no evidence in the myth that the goddesses are in any way at odds with each other or that separation is internally necessary. Thus Hades appears as particularly violating, rupturing a positive feminine bond. From this perspective, Hades is valenced as strongly negative (congruent with the terror and dread with which the ancient Greeks perceived this

11

THINKING PARADOXICALLY: TWO VIEWS OF THE MYTH

Emphases and Valences in the Myth and Mysteries	Matriarchal Accent	Patriarchal Accent
Transpersonal Feminine	Predominant, supreme, matrix of all	Relativitized, effaced, subordinate to Masculine
Transpersonal Masculine	Effaced or on periphery, no husband or father mentioned	Dominant, rising to dominance, appropriating Goddess's qualities and powers
Demeter	+, benevolent, preserving and reclaiming, becomes negative only when violated	−, binding, possessive, overreacting, opposes usurping Masculine
Hades	−, split off from upperworld, Feminine, and life; rapist; invades, splits, and ruptures feminine bond	+, releaser of ingrown Feminine, gains ground for patriarchy
Kore	Mother's daughter, resists Hades	Desirable maiden, has to be snatched forcibly from mother
Persephone	Reclaims Crone for Goddess, transforms Hades	Becomes wife of Hades and, with him, ushers in new age
Mother-Daughter bond	Matriarchal, reclaimed and preserved by both goddesses, excludes Masculine	Ingrown, broken, and relativized to husband-wife relationship
Birth of Son in Mysteries	Masculine transformed and reintegrated into Feminine, "Son of the Mother," serves the Goddess	Persephone becomes Mother of "wholly other," Mother-Daughter gives way to Mother-Son (and eventually to supreme Father-Son, mother only human)
Mythic resolution	Feminine triumphs in reclaiming of Daughter; Life and Death reconnected; Goddess gains ground as Queen of the Dead; Masculine reintegrated	Masculine triumphs; Hades' claim on Persephone is permanent though partial; Goddess becomes wife (Queen of the Dead); supremacy of matriarchy broken, makes way for coming of patriarchal supremacy
Historical resolution	Goddess religion overwhelmed by patriarchy; Feminine effaced, devalued, distorted, diabolized, lost, or underground	Patriarchy triumphs, transforms religion and culture to present day; dominates religion, politics, and culture in much of "civilized" world

underground god and the version of death he represented); he appears as the usurping Masculine that invades, splits, and attempts to permanently rupture the matriarchal bond.

Viewed through a matriarchal accent, the Goddess prevails in the mythic drama. As Mother, she effects the return of her Daughter from the dead, from the arms of the masculine invader, thus preserving (although only in part) the matriarchal unit. This return—the reunion of Mother and Daughter that the Greeks called the "heuresis"—is the center of the myth from a matriarchal perspective and holds the essence of its meaning. But it is not only in her Mother form that the Goddess prevails. As Daughter, she transforms the invader himself, birthing him anew in the child of the Mysteries, bending the Masculine back into her matrix and her service. In the process, she regains an ancient power seemingly lost to her under the initial impact of patriarchy; Kore's transformation into Persephone, Queen of the Dead, restores the powers of the Crone to the Mother and Daughter, reestablishing the integrity and supremacy of the ancient Triple Goddess.

Through effective protest, gestation, and transformation of the would-be usurper, the Feminine triumphs from this perspective, reuniting death with life as well as re-membering herself in the ancient fullness of her powers. And what began as patriarchal invasion becomes the prima materia of her capacity to recycle and transform. Much of the myth as we know it, as well as the essential meaning of the Mysteries as a triumph of life over death, supports this interpretive stance. But not all. There is also evidence for the patriarchal perspective, for a triumph of the usurping Masculine, and from this point of view, the central characters and events in the myth look quite different.

From a patriarchal perspective, what is central in this myth is the power of the rising Masculine that has already appropriated some of the Goddess's qualities and powers and successfully disrupts the matriarchal bond, ending its exclusivity forever. Here Demeter is valenced negatively, seen as binding, possessing, and overreacting to her daughter's marriage to Death. Her power to retrieve Persephone is only partial since, as Queen of the Dead, Persephone is never again her mother's daughter alone; she is also committed to Hades and must spend part of each year with him in his underworld as his consort.

Seen through this accent, Hades is valenced positively; he appears as the Releaser who frees the Daughter from an ingrown feminine sterility, awakens her to her sexuality, and deepens her to a world beyond her mother's and to a new role as consort and wife. And in the birth of the Mystery child, the Feminine gives birth to its "Other," ending the supremacy of Mother and Daughter and paving the way via Mother and Son for the eventual rise of the New Religion whose Father-Son core would overwhelm the Feminine as Deity and relativize it to this day. What is interesting, given the predominance of the patriarchal perspective historically (even in contemporary thinking), is that its grounding in the myth, though undeniable, is also limited. It appears in the attitudes of Zeus and Hades, not surprisingly, and is represented most fully in the viewpoint of the sun god Helios, who chastises Demeter for her "excessive grief" and urges her to reconcile herself to this marriage. Demeter's own view, as well as her daughter's unambivalent resistance to Hades, stands strongly in opposition to this perspective, as does the fact that the Mysteries were entered into through a sympathetic mimesis of Demeter's experiences. Yet the myth and the Mysteries, in an exquisite and provocative holding of a tension between opposites, never resolve fully in either direction alone.

While my personal belief is that the matriarchal perspective accounts for more of the myth's original meaning and is more in tune with the tenor of early Greek belief, history bore out the patriarchal perspective, underscoring and moving forward the orientation that is most familiar to our consciousness today: the de-emphasis and relativization of the transpersonal Feminine and the predominance of patriarchal thinking and values. The familiarity of the thinking and values inherent in the patriarchal viewpoint perhaps accounts for the fact that nearly all of the depth psychological commentaries on this myth to date have reflected the patriarchal accent, sometimes even skewing and distorting major aspects of the myth and the Mysteries to make their points.[11] So, for example, Demeter's behavior is repeatedly reduced to the human level and presented as pathological: neurotic,[12] depressive,[13] overpossessive,[14] narcissistic,[15] a midlife "folly,"[16] etc., while Kore-Persephone is seen as naive, innocent, and teasing,[17] lacking depth,[18] and needing to break away from her mother.[19] Remarkably, Hades' violent and unrelational behavior is consistently reframed positively and presented as what Kore needs to enable her

14

to separate from a "binding" mother. What the ancients named directly as kidnapping and rape is recast into "initiation."[20]

In the Homeric hymn and its variants there is little mythic evidence for any of this interpretation, save for the viewpoint of the sun god and the patriarchal gods Hades and Zeus. There is no suggestion at all of tension or discord between the two goddesses or of any internal necessity of separation; indeed since the goddesses both maintain their passion for and delight in each other while separate and never reconcile themselves to Hades' power, it is hard to adequately ground the patriarchal accent in the myth. For the most part such commentaries focus largely on Demeter, downplay or fail to understand the significance of the joyous reunion of mother and daughter, and do not address or make sense of the meaning of the Mysteries.

My own sense is that these interpretations see through a contemporary patriarchal filter that has informed and infused long-standing collective views of relationships between women, including and perhaps especially framing our views on the relationship of mother and daughter. This filter, which has dominated decades of formal and informal thinking about the psychology of women, depicts ongoing connection with the mother as essentially regressive for both sons and daughters, urges separation as the pinnacle of mature developmental process, and suggests that mothers and daughters have special problems in differentiation—in achieving separate identity on the daughter's side and letting go from the mother's side. Recent, more empirical research in the psychology of women is evolving a different view of women in relationship and of mothers and daughters. Drawn from extensive exploration of how women see themselves rather than beginning with theoretical formulations, this research has amplified and grounded Jung's intuition years ago that women are bound by the "Eros principle" and are essentially relational in their orientations and decision making. Even adolescent and adult daughters seek to maintain an ongoing dialogue and connection with their mothers rather than a differentiation that eschews common boundaries.[21] If the behavior of the goddesses in this myth is viewed in the light of this human behavior, Hades can be seen as representing a threat to feminine relatedness and the heuresis a triumph for it.

Nevertheless, a view that appears so frequently and persistently today, even if skewed, must have psychological validity for some people in our culture. By our time, the patriarchal view that valences

Hades as positive, separation of the two goddesses as desirable, and Demeter as pathological or preventative predominates. This was especially true when I first started working on this book back in the 1970s and remained true until fairly recently when poets, storytellers, feminist scholars, and even some Jungians have reconsidered the myth's meaning and recognized the positive power of its female protagonists.[22]

My own work, conceived originally to compensate the existing literature in the 1970s, remains unabashedly representative of the matriarchal accent. As such it is by no means intended to be the definitive view of the myth; rather it seeks to flesh out and write large a perspective more foreign to us and, at least to a great extent, more ancient as well. I offer this as a balancing factor vis-à-vis a collective consciousness still deeply permeated by the legacy of patriarchal thinking. Nevertheless, I both value and take personal delight in what Christine Downing has called a "polyphonic appreciation of the myth."[23] Ultimately, I believe we need to view the myth through many interpretive lights to adequately grasp its complexity and fullness and to dream it forward in such a way that it can be meaningful and instructive for human life today.

As I have demonstrated, embracing a mind-set that can think in cycles and appreciate paradox is vital to comprehending the Demeter-Persephone myth and dynamic. The third addition to our thinking necessary for approaching this myth is derived from Jung's theory of the compensatory nature of the unconscious, a cornerstone of his orientation to dreams. This approach to psychological interpretation of imagery emphasizes the importance of the starting point and consciousness of the person whose psychology is being explored. Being abducted away from the Mother as an archetypal motif has different meanings for a woman who has only recently made connection with a positive Mother within herself or in relationship, than it does for a woman who has been submerged in the Mother-world and needs to separate from it. Considering this myth in terms of a possible compensatory function is in looking at women who (reflecting the collective situation of many women in our culture) have grown up steeped in patriarchy; unlike Kore, they *begin* their lives in the realm of Hades and must live the myth backward, discovering their connections with the Mother and separating from a more familiar realm dominated by the patriarchal shadow of Hades. Only after finding the Mother and her strength can they effectively deal with patriarchy's shadow. (I will explore this at length in chapter 7.)

In summary, to comprehend this myth and the Mysteries that grew out of it we need to create in ourselves a multifaceted consciousness that can be open to the spiritual potency of Greek myth, empathically appreciate the fluidity and continuity within the pagan mind-set, and perceive cyclicity and paradox. To interpret this myth psychologically, we need to be familiar with several major concepts of Jungian psychology: (*a*) the concept of the collective unconscious that links imagery and meanings across time and cultures; (*b*) the symbolic nature of the archetype that always points beyond its contents and ultimately beyond psychology into the realm of the spirit; (*c*) the perception that the archetype can appear both intrapsychically and relationally; and (*d*) the concept of compensation, which directs us to look for what is being filled out in the modern consciousness in which the archetypes are appearing. Holding all of this as a backdrop, we can begin to approach the richness of the myth itself and the fullness and complexity of its three main characters.

Anne-Marie de Barolet, *The Rape of Kore*, 1983.

❦ 2 ❧

The Myth, Its Variants, and Its Mysteries

A myth is like an ecosystem. It is more than the sum of its parts, and no single event stands without the relatedness of all other parts of the story. It exists on all levels at once, material, spiritual, ecological, personal, and physical. The myth, when spoken or enacted, has meaning and potency only in the present. It takes shape according to who is telling it, when it is being told, who is hearing it, and the environment or season in which the performance takes place. No matter how carefully it is studied, analyzed, and understood, the very nature of myth undoes any fixed meaning or analysis. The myth is alive—more close to truth than fact—and must be approached like wilderness, on its own terms, to be experienced fully.

——Laura Simms,
storyteller, The Long Journey Home[1]

THE MOST COMPLETE and well-known source of the story of Demeter and Persephone comes from the first Homeric hymn to Demeter, composed around 650 BCE (for a ready reference point, the reader might consider that the book of Genesis in the Bible was written between 1000 and 500 BCE).[2] This was long after the northern invaders infiltrated the Greek mainland (which occurred around 2000 BCE,[3] relatively late as compared to other parts of southern Europe); by 500 BCE, Greece, according to one historian, would have been "thoroughly patriarchal."[4] While preserving and elaborating the most coherent form of the myth, the author of the Homeric hymn screened out many of its more archaic and most interesting elements. These are to be found in variants of the myth, which survive only in fragmentary form. In the following rendering of the mythic tale, I have used the Homeric hymn as a baseline (drawing from the translations of Charles Boer and Paul Friedrich in particular); the relevant variants appear in my commentary on each part of the Homeric story.

Saluting Demeter as the "awesome" goddess and describing her daughter as the Kore whom Zeus "gave away to be seized by violence" by Hades, the Homeric author begins his tale: *Kore was playing in a field one day, far from her mother, picking flowers with other maiden goddesses. Suddenly she came upon a flower never seen before—the narcissus—which Earth (the goddess Gaia) had grown as a favor to Hades and Zeus. The young woman was amazed and reached for the hundred-headed blossom in delight but as she did, the earth opened wide and up from its chasm leapt the Lord of the Underworld. He snatched the girl and carried her off in his chariot. Kore resisted and cried out, screaming for her father Zeus. But Zeus was far away receiving offerings. No one heard the maiden except Hecate in her cave, Helios the sun, and Kore's noble mother Demeter, who immediately put on mourning clothes and began to search for her daughter. As long as the girl could see earth and sky and sea, as long as she could hope to see her mother again and the other gods, she took heart, but Hades carried her away to his kingdom under the earth.*

Demeter was hailed as the awesome goddess, a title connoting religious awe and used almost exclusively for her, according to Friedrich.[5] The nature of Kore's abduction is immediately made explicit, for the Greek word for the young girl's "seizure by violence" means "kidnapped and raped."[6] In some versions of the myth, Kore cries out "A rape! A rape!" as she is being carried away to the underworld.[7] Further underscoring the nature of the abduction perhaps is the redoubling of Kore's virginity in the description of her playmates as other "maiden" goddesses, though virginity (*parthenos* in Greek) does not necessarily mean physical virginity; for the Greeks, the designation of virgin could also mean a woman who was one-in-herself, that is, complete within herself, rather than someone who was sexually chaste.[8] Many commentators, however, both ancient and contemporary, assume that Kore was a physical virgin and that her abduction by Hades was her introduction to sexuality.

What is also assumed (though ambiguous in the original sources) is Kore's age. While it is usually believed that she was at least an adolescent at the time of her abduction, one later version of the myth (as told in Ovid's *Metamorphoses*) depicts her to be so young that she cries as much over the loss of her flowers, which spill to the ground when Hades grabs her, as over being violently snatched.[9] In art as well, she is depicted variously, some images presenting her as a young woman, others as a child.

Zeus, Hades, and Earth collude to make the abduction possible. Hades, who was often driven by lust, desired Kore and wanted her as his wife. Zeus, knowing that Demeter would be furious, neither dissented or assented; he simply allowed the abduction to happen. In this version of the myth, Zeus is Kore's father and Hades, her uncle; this reflects the gradual assimilation of the Goddess and the Old Religion to patriarchy in actual historical events. In the Old Religion (like Demeter in this myth) the Goddess was husbandless, took as her lover whomever she wanted but was not bound to any male, and reigned supreme. As the New Religion of patriarchy ascended, the goddesses increasingly became "wives of—" or "consorts of—" or "daughters of—" the gods. Robert Graves adds, "[Kore's] abduction by Hades forms part of the myth in which the Hellenic trinity of gods forcibly marry the pre-Hellenic Triple goddess—Zeus, Hera; Zeus or Poseidon, Demeter; Hades, [Kore]. . . . It refers to male usurpation of the female agricultural mysteries in primitive times."[10] Part of the outrage of the abduction and rape in the myth lies in the fact that neither Demeter nor Kore knows initially through whom this event has taken place (i.e., Zeus); neither mother nor daughter were approached for permission or choice. Kore's betrayal by her patriarchal father is poignantly underscored in her ignorant appeals to him for help and his preoccupation with offerings while the abduction is taking place. Only connections with her mother and her mother's world afford her any hope; when they disappear from her sight, she is completely in the hands of the patriarchal gods.

The question of why Earth, the goddess Gaia, would collude with

Zeus and Hades is an interesting one. From a patriarchal perspective, the will of Zeus is supreme and Gaia, like the other gods and goddesses, is subject to and obeys it. From a matriarchal perspective, however, Gaia may collude for her own reasons, perhaps out of some awareness that this will enable the ancient Triple Goddess to be reconstituted, regaining both the underworld and her supremacy as Crone. In Ovid's version of the myth, even with its more patriarchal and anti-Demeterian tone, it is a goddess (Aphrodite) who sets the abduction in motion in order to extend her kingdom—an interesting parallel to the matriarchal emphasis here considered as one interpretation of the Homeric drama.

The seductiveness of the never-seen-before narcissus is central to the drama in this part of the myth and lends itself to rich psychological interpretations.[11] It has usually been seen as an "obvious male phallic symbol," as Friedrich puts it, yet this same author notes that it was otherwise the flower of the goddess, again suggesting an intriguing ambiguity.[12] Still another possibility of the flower's meaning is brought to light by an alternative version of the myth in which the flower Kore picks is not a narcissus but a poppy. Graves comments on the meaning of this particular flower by noting,

> An image of a goddess with a poppy-headdress was found in Crete, another goddess . . . holds poppies in her hand; and on the gold ring from the Acropolis treasures at Mycenae, a seated Demeter gives three poppy-heads to a standing [Kore]. Poppy-seeds were used as a condiment on bread and poppies are naturally associated with Demeter since they grow in cornfields but [Kore] picks or accepts poppies because of the soporific qualities and because of their scarlet colour which promises resurrection after death.[13]

Red was also the color that was sacred to the dead. Here we already have some hint of both the connections and differences between Demeter and Kore-Persephone; the poppy connects to the upperworld of Demeter where it grows in her cornfields but has consciousness-altering capacities that link it to the underworld and to Persephone as ruler of a world beyond life.

To continue the story: *No one would tell Demeter the truth, so for nine days she wandered, grieving for her daughter. On the tenth day she was joined by Hecate who had heard Kore's cries but did not see who bore her away.*

22

Together the goddesses went to Helios who knows and sees all, and he informed them that it was Zeus who gave Kore away to Hades, his own brother, to be his wife and that Hades had carried her off screaming. Then Helios chided Demeter for her distress, saying, "But goddess, stop your own great weeping. It does not fit you, this anger that's so vain and insatiate."[14] He went on to champion Hades' cause, claiming that the underworld god was not unworthy as a son-in-law, reminding Demeter that Hades was her own brother and had received an entire kingdom under the earth when the world was originally divided into three. But Demeter's grief and anger only deepened at these words and she became outraged at Zeus.

The presence of Hecate and her companioning of Demeter as she seeks to know what has become of her daughter is significant, even though it is not emphasized by Homer. Hecate was the goddess of ghosts, connected with night and the moon; in her full powers, she was the Death goddess and embodied the Crone aspect of the Triple Goddess. By the time of the Homeric hymns, she was no longer the potent goddess of Death but simply seen as a witch and valenced negatively, though still imaged in triple form and worshiped at the places where three roads crossed. Her minor role in the Homeric poem mirrors well the later fate of the Crone aspect of the goddess in patriarchy, which all but disappeared in subsequent religious life (the Virgin and Mother faces reappear in the Virgin Mary, for example, but the Crone disappears altogether in Christianity).[15] Nevertheless, the appearance of Hecate is significant, presaging perhaps the aspect of the Goddess recovered in the transformation of Kore to Persephone; she appears again at the end of the myth as Persephone's companion.

The perspective of Helios, also implied in Zeus's attitude and echoed later by Hades as well, appears to be, "Don't make waves, don't rock the boat, stop 'overreacting' and be *reconciled* to this." Although Kore was seized against her will and raped by the dreaded god of Death, Demeter is expected to see this as positive and acquiesce to it. As Friedrich comments, "This speech by Helios ironically underscores the theme of bitterness and injustice: the mother should *take heart* at her daughter's rape because the rapist is her brother and has great wealth and power."[16] Demeter's response to the patriarchal perspective with its claims of the supremacy of the "fathers" is ferocious and unambivalent: grief, rage, and outrage. She never buys into the patriarchal perspective, refuses to go on serving the system that has brought this about, and effectively protests and subverts it on both a human and transpersonal level. Never will she reconcile herself or her daughter to such a brutal and unrelational display of power!

Furious with Zeus, Demeter left the company of the gods altogether and went to live among mortals, disguising her beauty so that no one who saw her knew she was the goddess. "Looking like an old woman who was beyond child-bearing, beyond the gifts of Aphrodite," she went to the town of Eleusis and sat near the Virgin's Well where the people of the town came to draw water.[17] Soon the daughters of Keleos, the local king, came by and took pity on this sad old woman. They asked her where she was from and why she didn't approach the houses for friendship with others and for work as a housekeeper and children's nurse.

Demeter's decision to disguise herself as an old woman "beyond the gifts of Aphrodite" is both moving and highly significant. The Mother takes on the guise of the Crone, foreshadowing the return of this aspect to the Triple Goddess that takes place by the end of the myth. ("Old nurses in Greek myth," notes Graves, "nearly always stand for the goddess as Crone.")[18]

The goddess as Maiden is also represented here, mirrored in the young women who take pity on Demeter. The Maiden is also symbolized in an even more central way in the name of the community well near which Demeter sat. The story of the well is a particularly beautiful one. It was believed to be an entrance to the underworld and was known by many names. It was called the Virgin's Well and also the Well of the Beautiful Dances. Carl Kerényi mentions the existence of Greek myths within which virgins disappear while dancing around a well. It was also known as the Well of Flowers, "presumably," Kerényi contends, "because a flowering from the depths was thought to take place here."[19] (The abduction of Kore while picking flowers may also be relevant here.)

With Demeter's departure from the realm of the gods, the myth begins to deepen, already unfolding toward its mystery dimension. The town Demeter chooses to live in has intimate connections with the underworld realm which has claimed her daughter. Even the name, Eleusis, refers to the underworld but in a positive sense; it means "the place of happy arrival."[20] Here we have the first intimations that Demeter's journey is going to parallel her daughter's and that the underworld is more than an experience of stasis and death. These intimations are further unfolded in a variant of this part of the myth. According to an Orphic hymn to Demeter, in which she is addressed as "the ghostly mother" (further linking her with her underworld daughter), there were no kings in Eleusis; Demeter went instead to the house of a peasant named Dysaules. The son of Dysaules, a swineherd named Eubouleus, was tending his pigs in the same area in which the abduction of Kore took place. When the earth opened to afford Hades a passage to the upperworld so he could snatch the maiden, Eubouleus's pigs fell into the chasm. In this version of the myth, Demeter went with the swineherd to retrieve both his pigs and her daughter after he showed her the way.[21] Thus mother and daughter alike made journeys to the underworld, one voluntarily to retrieve what belonged to her, the other in terror and much against her will.

The pigs in the chasm are also of primary significance, reaching both back into the harvest festivals celebrated only by women in ancient Greece and dedicated to Demeter and forward into the practice of the Eleusinian mysteries. In the Thesmophoria, a primary harvest festival celebrated only by women, suckling pigs were thrown into chasms in the earth as a sacrifice to the fertility powers of the earth. The pig was considered a particularly fecund animal; hence its sympathetic connection with the Mother aspect of the Goddess and with the grain mother Demeter. Women also descended into these chasms during the Thesmophoria and brought up portions of the rotted flesh from previous sacrifices; these were mixed with the seed corn to be used for the next planting.

On a level of sympathetic magic, the intermixing of seed corn and the rotting flesh of the sacrificed piglets expressed a powerful motif that becomes even more profound in the myth of Kore's rape and the Eleusinian mysteries: the connection of death and fertility (a decidedly different vision than the one afforded by Hades' version of death as stasis and disembodiment). It is this theme of the connection between death and fertility that Demeter and her later human followers are initiated into. The presence of the pigs reappears in one of the known aspects of the celebration of the Mysteries. Initiates had to bring with them a suckling pig, wash it in the sea along with themselves in a ritual act of purification, and offer it as a sacrifice to the Eleusinian goddesses; here too was the intermixing of death and fertility, but fertility on a level beyond the Thesmophoria's literal view of enabling the harvest.[22] In the Mysteries human beings too became the seed corn who were mixed with death and sprouted anew.

These meanings stand behind the more prosaic Homeric story; at this point in the poet's version of the tale, Demeter responds to the pity of the young girls by telling them a most interesting "cover" story: *"Doso is my name," the goddess contends. "My mistress mother gave it to me. Just now I came from Crete over the wide back of the sea, not willingly, for pirates brought me away unwillingly, by force, under compulsion."*[23] *She goes on to say that she fled those "arrogant masters" rather than letting them hold her for ransom, and wandered until she came to this town, a town that is foreign to her.*

Although part of the disguise Demeter assumes to conceal her identity as the goddess, the story she tells about herself and her origins to the young women leads like an ever-descending spiral deeper into the meaning of the myth. The name "Doso" means "giver" and is an epithet for Earth; thus Demeter connects herself with the oldest and most basic of the goddesses.[24] Moreover, she identifies herself only through her connection to her mother, preserving and emphasizing again the integrity of the matriarchal unit. Underscoring this on a broader level is her claim to have come from Crete, for Crete was the last place to succumb to the patriarchal invaders and preserved the Goddess-centered Old Religion long after the rest of southern Europe went under.[25]

Demeter's tale at this point presents a remarkable parallel to what has just happened to her daughter. She too has been seized from her matriarchal origin against her will (note the repeated emphasis on her unwillingness) and by violence, but unlike Kore, she has escaped. And here too, variants of the Homeric version of the myth continue to establish parallels between the two goddesses' experiences. Thus in one variant, Demeter too is raped. While searching for her daughter, she is accosted by the third of the patriarchal brothers, Poseidon, god of the Sea. Fleeing him, she turns herself into a mare but Poseidon continues to pursue her, changing himself into a stallion. In that form, he ravishes her, begetting a mysterious daughter (whom no one may name) and a famous mythical horse. Enraged, Demeter turns into an ancient avenger of violence done to a mother, the Erinyes, but later bathes in a river and becomes tender and mild again.[26]

Over and over the myth and its variants reveal that what happens to the daughter happens also to the mother. This pattern of parallels suggests a profound empathic bond between the two goddesses, moving toward the more ancient vision of them as separate-yet-one. Moreover, it makes visible the fact that Demeter's journey is essentially an initiatory one. Step by step in the myth, she is being initiated into the meaning of her daughter's abduction. Step by step (though in a nonlinear progression, as we will see, a progression marked by back-and-forth shifting between humanlike ignorance and goddesslike understandings), the goddess begins to grasp the transformation taking place through her daughter and embodies and undergoes this transformation herself. Laying the ground for all of the "ignorant" humans who will follow her, Demeter is the first initiate—into her own mysteries and the mysteries of her daughter's transfiguration.

Continuing the story: *After telling her story, Demeter asked the young women to advise her as to where she might find employment, offering her services as a nurse and housekeeper. The daughters of Keleos replied that no one would turn her away, for she was obviously well-bred and looked like a goddess; in fact, their own mother might hire her, for there was a newborn son in their house, long awaited and much desired, who needed a nurse's care. Having said this, they ran to their house to discuss this with Metanira, their mother. Metanira quickly approved and told them to bring Demeter to her. "Like deer or like heifers in the season of Spring, who leap about in the meadow when they're glutted with food, so they, holding up the folds of their lovely garments, darted down the hollow path [to the well where Demeter sat waiting]. And their hair streamed out around their shoulders like crocus flowers."*[27]

By offering herself as a baby nurse, Demeter appears to be re-establishing her mothering role, but what she will bring to this child goes far beyond ordinary mothering, as we will see. Demeter's loss of her own child is made all the more poignant in this part of the myth by the poet's description of the daughters of Keleos, evoking the image of Kore and the field of flowers from which she was kidnapped.

The goddess veiled her face and allowed herself to be led back to the house of Keleos. When she crossed the threshold to enter the house, her head grazed the ceiling and the doorway was filled with light. Metanira was overwhelmed with awe but didn't recognize Demeter; she asked her to sit down. Demeter hesitated until the serving-maid Iambe provided a chair for her; then she sat and sank into depression, "wasting away with longing" for her lost daughter.[28] *But Iambe told jokes and clowned around, making the goddess laugh, and her cheerful nature soon returned. She also brought the goddess a barley drink when Demeter refused to drink wine, claiming it was unlawful for her to drink wine in these circumstances.*

The Homeric hymn does not reveal the content of Iambe's jests, but a variant of this part of the myth is more forthcoming. In the variant (part of which was previously mentioned in the tale of Eubouleus and his hapless pigs), Demeter has gone to the house of a peasant named Dysaules instead of the house of Keleos. The name of this peasant links him with Hades and the underworld, for its meaning is "he in whose house it is not good to live." Dysaules has a wife named Baubo, whose name means "belly." It is she who makes Demeter laugh; she does so by throwing herself on her back in what is described as an "obscene way" and lifting her skirts to reveal her "uncomely womb." There, dancing in her womb, is Demeter's own son Iakchos (the offspring of a joyous coupling between the goddess and a Titan, Iasion).[29]

I believe this scene with Baubo to be one of the several initiation points in this myth, moments when the curtain is drawn back on things as they appear on the surface and a deeper meaning is revealed; inevitably, this deeper meaning involves the transformation of what at first glance seems to be only violation and death. Baubo's gesture of throwing herself onto her back in an obscene way suggests a parody of being raped. Coupled with the appearance of Demeter's own child, alive and dancing in the womb, it seems to instruct Demeter to look deeper, there is more here than meets the eye. What appears to be rape and, by extension to Kore, a rape unto death, is instead the gestation of new life. Moreover, the new life is intimately connected to the goddess herself, belongs to her. This foreshadows what little we know of the Mystery goddess Persephone who, coming back pregnant by the lord of Death, brings forth a son, a male who no longer opposes the goddess like his father but issues forth from her underworld power. In so doing, the male aspect relinks with the Goddess and serves the life she embodies in all of its cycles.

The Mysteries begin with a cry to Iakchos, and a child representing him was chosen to lead each Mystery procession. So Baubo's display is a deepening point for Demeter, revealing the meaning of what has happened to her daughter (and is happening to her). And though Demeter appears to lose hold of this knowledge, to "fail to understand" throughout this myth, by the end she too has been initiated into the Mysteries that she herself inaugurates into being.

There is also a deeper meaning of Demeter's refusal of wine in the story. In variants of the myth and also in hidden meanings of the

28

names of some of the male characters, Hades has connections with the wine god Dionysos. While a drink made from barley (which was later used in the Mysteries) befits a goddess of grain, drinking wine was clearly impossible: both mother and daughter consistently refuse any food or drink linked with Hades. And while Dionysos in his earlier, matriarchal form, was a cereal god and god of beer (and so would obviously link with a grain goddess), by the time he became a god of the vine he was already evolving toward a more patriarchal religion. Though he retains his connection with women in his form as the wine god, in his link with Hades he opposes the goddess. Hence she refuses the drink that is sacred to him but would link her with her daughter's seducer.

Metanira then offered Demeter the position of nursemaid for her newborn son and the goddess accepted, saying he would not suffer in her care. She would nurse him well, she claimed, and knew of a remedy for teething and a spell against witchcraft. So she reared Demophoon, the baby, and he grew strong as a god without any feeding at all. But at night Demeter secretly held him in a fire to burn off his mortal parts and make him immortal.

One night, however, Metanira happened to see the goddess holding her baby in the fire. Immediately she began to wail and mourn, beating her thighs in terror. "My child, Demophoon," she cried out, "the stranger woman is hiding you in all that fire and she makes grief and bitter sorrow for me."[30]

Again there is a deeper-than-surface level of meaning. In her care of Demophoon, Demeter begins to recall and remanifest her powers as a goddess. On the surface, she appears to be merely an old woman, competent in resuming a mothering role with a child. But as goddess, she is no ordinary mother. From the beginning, her nurturing transcends the human level, surpassing ordinary human limits. The child thrives from the presence of the goddess alone, receives transcendent "food," participates in a more-than-human realm. Where this is leading becomes even more clear in the secret, nightly ritual. Drawing up her full transformative powers, Demeter subjects the child to what, in a human realm, would be certain death; understandably his human mother perceives it exactly this way and responds accordingly. But here again is an initiation point, as the next part of the myth will clearly convey. For the goddess intends not a killing of the child, but a *transformation*, precisely the drawing out of a new form of life from the death experience. Conveyed first by Baubo in her parody of the death-rape, this message is now embodied by Demeter herself.

Metanira, however, reacts as any mother of a much-loved child would—with grief, terror, and protest. The stranger is killing her child, or so it certainly seems. It is interesting that Metanira also becomes a grieving mother, who, like Demeter, thinks that the fate of her child at the hands of a stranger in a secret, hidden place will be certain death. But notice Demeter's surprising response to the mother's display of grief:

Demeter grew furious, lifted the child out of the fire, and threw him on the ground, denouncing Metanira for her foolishness. "Stupid people," she raged, "brainless, you don't even know when fate is bringing you something good or something bad."[31] Revealing herself now as the goddess Demeter, she told the terror-stricken Metanira that she would have made her son immortal, saved him from death, but now this is impossible. Throwing away her disguise, she instructed Metanira and her husband the king of Eleusis to have the people build her a temple immediately; here she would inaugurate her Mysteries.

Demeter's fury and denouncement of Metanira's reactions as stupid and ignorant are remarkable since she has been reacting in exactly the same way to Kore's abduction by the Death god. But here a different aspect of Demeter manifests, essentially conveying that the human perspective on death—human grief and terror—is ignorant. Human beings do not understand that what looks like certain death is, in the hands of the goddess, transformation and new life. Metanira represents the human perspective that cannot get beyond itself, can't give credence to or recognize the Divine when the latter is disguised. She sees Demeter as if she were another human being, a killer at that. But Demophoon is not being harmed! Demeter takes him beyond the human realm from the beginning; she feeds him nothing but herself, her care, and he thrives like a god. He becomes precocious, growing "ahead of his time." From a human perspective, Demeter is starving him, refusing the usual, logical nourishment that human life needs—and on top of that, burning him to death. But he thrives, lives beyond human capacity, and is not harmed by the fire. When Metanira interrupts Demeter's ritual, Demophoon has already been held in the fire many times and rather than being hurt or killed, he is thriving; he is becoming the Goddess's.

Yet it is also Metanira's interference that forces Demeter to reveal herself as the transformative, death-defying goddess, something that even she appears to lose contact with periodically throughout this myth. Faced with Metanira's ignorance of her, she reveals herself in her true form. Demophoon is now lost to her and remains human, but his loss is humanity's gain, for it seems that his mother's reactions, her grief and protest at what seems like certain death, become a sort of human paradigm that calls forth divine revelation. Like Judas's betrayal in the Christ story, Metanira's interference is needed to set in motion a deeper revelation and fulfillment of the divine dimension within the myth. Moreover, it makes clear the need for the Mysteries, the need for the human realm to be "initiated" out of its ignorance by the Great Goddess herself; thus it is at this point in the myth that Demeter takes steps to institute her greatest gift.

Keleos quickly set in motion an order to fulfill Demeter's request and soon the townspeople had built her a temple to which she retired, only to sink again into grief over her own lost child. But now she devised a terrible punishment; she withdrew her gift of grain from the land. The seed would not germinate, and gods and mortals were threatened alike: humanity was in danger of starving and the gods received no offerings since there was no longer a harvest. Zeus took note of this and sent many other gods and goddesses, one after the other, to appease the wrath of Demeter. They offered her wonderful gifts, exhorted her to restore the grain, but she would have none of it; growing ever more angry, she vowed that she would never set foot on Olympus again until she saw her daughter's beautiful face.

From the linear, rational perspective that usually defines our visions of progression or development within a story, this part of the myth makes no sense. Demeter has already manifested her power to transform the death experience, as well as having earlier received the revelation from Baubo that what appears to be death-rape is actually new life. That she now falls again into depression and grief—the perspective she has just denounced as ignorant and a misunderstanding of fate—seems inexplicable. From a human perspective, we would say she seems split within herself, for it is as if she continually loses hold of what she knows and of her own deeper power to transfigure and transform. The myth proceeds in a nonlinear way, rhythmically, laying out an irrational path of development. The goddess keeps shifting, gaining knowledge and losing it, embodying power and not knowing what her power is, transforming the death experience and falling back into depression and grief around it. She shifts back and forth, embodies and suffers the pain of the ignorance she has denounced while moving deeper and deeper into the transformative power that that pain will draw forth.

This vacillation is profoundly meaningful and is itself a gift from the Goddess. Clearly possessing the power to transform life out of death, the power she has always had as the Death goddess, she nevertheless *bends low* to us, takes on the human perspective on death—the grief and terror and rage and depression we humans feel when faced with what seems like the certain and final end of the life that we love. It is as if she goes before us, takes on our dumbness and our pain, becomes initiated herself, setting forth the model and the pattern that human beings would follow for the next fifteen hundred years. She gives us the Mysteries that will "hold the whole world together" and instill in every initiate a hope in the face of death. She goes first, shows us the way, takes us through the pain and grief and rage and human ignorance that can ultimately be transformative and lead toward participation in her power.

There is another meaning as well, one that mirrors a historical-psychological reality that is still extreme in its influence and still profoundly relevant to our lives today. For this myth also mirrors the need for the death-dealing forces inherent in patriarchy to be resisted and transformed, for the patriarchal version of death and the power-hunger it feeds to be stood up to and stopped. This part of the myth especially addresses the need to refuse the whole system, refuse to support it until its values and methods are reintegrated with the service of life and an older and more organic life cycle. Demeter accomplished this on a mythic-religious level, but human history embodied the opposite path, moving further and further into the clutches of patriarchy. It remains for us to this day to recognize and repeat the path that Demeter laid out for us before the Hades forces have swallowed not only the Greeks and ourselves but the entire planet, the earth goddess Gaia who is herself now at risk of death or permanent poisoning.

At this point in the myth, Demeter takes action. Mildness and tenderness, the usual attributes of this basically benevolent goddess, give way to rage and grief written large in an act of protest; as one of my colleagues once put it succinctly, her position is: "Nobody eats!"[32] Nor do the gods receive their due, the first fruits of the harvest, for there is no harvest and will be none until Kore is released. Just as it was unlawful for Demeter to drink of the vine that is sacred to her daughter's seducer, so is it unthinkable that her gifts go on serving the religion of Zeus, through whom all this has come about. Demeter takes on the entire system here and flatly refuses to serve it.

Hearing that Demeter had withdrawn her gift of grain, Zeus relented, sending Hermes to retrieve the maiden from the underworld and to lead her into the light again. Hermes found her pining away with longing for her mother in the house of Hades. He explained the enormity of Demeter's vengeance to Hades and relayed the command of Zeus that her daughter was to be returned. Hades did not disobey but spoke to his reluctant wife of what would be hers when she was with him; echoing Helios, he asserted that he was not an unworthy spouse for her and that while she was with him, she would reign over his kingdom as Persephone, Queen of the Dead, and share in his honors. Then, when she leapt up with joy to begin the long trip back to her mother, he secretly slipped her a pomegranate seed. Unwittingly, she ate it, thus ensuring her return to the underworld.

In Graves's version of the myth, the messages from Zeus to both Hades and Demeter are particularly strong. To Hades, Zeus says, "If you do not restore [Kore], we are all undone!"—a powerful reflection of the impact of Demeter's protest. To Demeter, Zeus adds, "You may have your daughter again, on the single condition that she has not yet tasted the food of the dead."[33]

Anyone who ate the food of the dead was committed to stay in the underworld. The Greeks believed that food was communion, a participation with the gods. In the usual renderings of the myth, Persephone has starved herself throughout her stay with Hades and persistently cried for her mother; these are her only available means of protest and resistance.[34] Like Demeter, Persephone remains unreconciled to Hades' power. In some variants of the myth, however, she eats the seeds in secret out of Hades' garden, driven by her hunger, and Hades' gardener observes this and reports it to the god.[35] Yet never does she do this by choice; she too was unambivalent. (The patriarchal view is not supported here.)

The "seeds of death" that consummate the marriage of Kore and Hades are part of a complex and powerful symbol. The pomegranate's many seeds make it an obvious symbol of fertility that was used both in marriage rites and at funerals in Greece, thus linking the two and underscoring again the motif of fertile death. The pomegranate also reveals twin mythological themes of vital import to ancient Greeks and found still among some Greeks in rural areas today: marriage as death and death as marriage. The color of the pomegranate also links it with the poppy, which some have suggested was the flower that Kore picked: red, the blood color, was also sacred to the dead. Another link with the realm of the dead was the belief among the ancients that souls nibbled at the pomegranate seeds laid on their graves, just as they felt themselves to be nearly human again when given offerings of blood. The pomegranate was also sacred to Dionysos.[36]

Although many scholars suggest that the pomegranate connects with the shedding of hymeneal blood, the symbolic death of the virgin, there are other darker links between this fruit and literal death. Thus in another Greek myth the virgin Side took her life on the grave of her mother because her father wished to seduce her; from her blood, the earth caused the pomegranate to grow.[37] Here the pomegranate springs forth as the poignant, mute testament of resistance to incest and a return to maternal origins. But other myths connect this fruit with pregnancy and new life; in one the goddess Nana (a name for the Great Mother of Asia Minor) was "got with child" by the fruit of the pomegranate tree and bore a divine son—as does Persephone once she becomes the Mystery goddess.

It seems that at this point in the myth Kore becomes Persephone. Her name makes the nature of her transformation clear, for "Persephone" means "she who brings destruction," that is, the goddess of Death. Yet while this looks like Hades has triumphed by claiming a wife, the goddess Persephone has an earlier origin. "Persephone," Graves contends, "is the title of the Goddess as Nymph when she sacrificed the sacred king and replaced him with his son who would impregnate her and thus ensure the fertility of the land."[38] Eating the pomegranate, she is also the goddess of Hell, according to Graves, devouring the lover-son while her upperworld side grieves for his death.[39] Thus Persephone's eating of the pomegranate seeds does not just consummate the marriage and triumph of Hades but hearkens back to an earlier, matriarchal origin involving the sacrifice and essential transformation of the Masculine.

To return to the tale: *Hades harnessed his horses to his chariot and returned Hermes and Persephone to the world above. When Demeter saw Persephone, she "darted forward like a maenad down a mountain shadowy with forest."[40] Persephone, seeing her mother, leapt off the chariot and ran into her arms. Suddenly Demeter became frightened and asked anxiously if Persephone had eaten anything in the underworld. ". . . If you have partaken [of any food in the underworld]," the goddess told her daughter, "you will go back again to the secret places of the earth and dwell there a third part of the seasons of the year and two parts among men and the other gods. When the earth blooms with sweet-smelling spring flowers of all kinds, then up from the misty darkness you will come again, a wonder to gods and to all mortal men."⁴¹* Then Persephone told her mother the whole story of the unwilling abduction and her sojourn in the kingdom of death, concluding with an account of how Hades "by force, against my will" made her eat the pomegranate seed. But Zeus and Demeter agreed to the arrangements the goddess had foretold in her anxious inquiring: for two-thirds of the year, Persephone would be with her mother in the upperworld. The remaining third, she would spend with Hades in his kingdom under the earth.

It is interesting that Demeter is described as "dart[ing] forward like a maenad" when she sees her daughter. The maenads were women ecstatically possessed by the god Dionysos. This provocative link of the goddess with the god she so staunchly stood against when refusing the wine earlier in the myth perhaps foreshadows a softening of the opposition between the two worlds the mother and the Death god represent and the beginnings of their reconciliation.

The softening of opposition is evident as well in the new willingness of both Zeus and Demeter to reach an agreement regarding the consequences of Persephone's consumption of the pomegranate. Both god and goddess compromise: Zeus allows the commitment of Persephone to the underworld to be partial and cyclical instead of total and static, and Demeter acquiesces to a less than complete return of her daughter to her origins. Rape becomes ritual at this point; what began as an involuntary descent by seizure becomes now an annual, voluntary descent. Like Hermes, Persephone becomes a psychopomp—one who is capable of living in two worlds and becomes the bridge between them. Hades too takes on a softer stance; one scholar reports that in an ancient sculpture depicting the later ritual descent of Persephone at the start of winter, Hades is seen looking on empathically as mother and daughter say goodbye to each other for another season; the god is no longer the enemy of either of the goddesses. All this takes place once the Mysteries have been inaugurated and Demeter's insistence on her daughter's return to the light has been met.

The seasonal aspects of Persephone's subsequent descents and returns have often been commented on, but this connection of the myth with the cyclicity of Nature is far more than an explanation of how the seasons came about. It expressed the fluidity of vision so beautiful and profound in pagan religion that could recognize in Nature and her vicissitudes the presence and drama of the goddess and draw from it to assuage the human hunger for participation and meaning, inspiration and hope. To "feel into" the season of winter: to take into one's self the barrenness, the dormancy, the separation from and seeming cessation of life; to experience it all as if it were the loss of the Kore child, vibrant and cherished; to draw it even deeper into one's own life and experience the bitterness, the grieving, the raging over all of the places where life spirals downward and appears to be lost: this is the start of initiation. But to follow Kore-Persephone on this path, to see her in Nature, is also to experience return. For at the darkest point of winter, the solstice, the light returns and life begins to stir again, breaking forth from its hiddenness under the earth, reemerging in the miracle, the utterly dependable sequel to death: the season of spring. Persephone returns, and with her the dead are reborn, blossoming forth like flowers and grain: the initiation is complete, the vision fulfilled—only to begin and repeat the whole cycle again.

Even Demeter seems to grasp this now, for though she is anxious that her daughter may have eaten in the underworld and thus be committed to return there, the richness and fullness of her words go beyond her despair. "When the earth blooms with sweet-smelling spring flowers of all kinds, then up from the misty darkness you will come again, a wonder to gods and to all mortal men."[42] It is as if Persephone is now the narcissus, the never-before plant of wonder that opens the path to another world and to her transformation of it. Faced with the fullness of her daughter's journey and the joy of her return, possessed of the knowledge of her own initiation experience, Demeter is reconciled at last; she agrees to the compromise that reconnects her world with Zeus and celebrates reunion with her daughter.

It has always moved me and is, I think, of great psychological significance that Demeter receives her daughter fully and with joy despite her transformation from Kore to Persephone. Once her daughter has been returned, Demeter embraces who she has become and stops her mourning; she wants her daughter, not an image of what she once was. Persephone will never be her mother's little girl again nor the maiden picking flowers in her innocence; she has been marked by her underworld experience and returns transformed, committed now to realize her power in two realms. Far from the rigid, regressive mother she is often depicted as being, Demeter wants only her daughter's life to be returned to the land of the living, not a restoration of an original matriarchal "Eden." She accepts what has changed and rejoices in her daughter's return.

The goddesses spent the day embracing and cheering each other's hearts. Friedrich translates the fullness of this most poignantly in a single line: "The spirit stopped its grieving."[43] *Hecate joined the reunion and from then on preceded and followed Persephone. Then Demeter restored the grain, and the fields grew fat with crops. She also began the teaching of her Mysteries, initiating first the sons of Eleusis, Triptolemus, Eumolpus, and Keleos, teaching them her rites whose secrecy is impossible to transgress. For all who take part in the Mysteries, their fate is different at death from that of the uninitiated. And to those they love, the goddesses send Plutous, child of prosperity, who brings wealth to humankind. Thus ends the Homeric hymn to Demeter.*

The reunion of the two goddesses is the high point of the myth: the triumph of Demeter's unshakable protest and the most public display of her deep and transformative power. Persephone's power to transform is not yet seen; it will be revealed only in (what we know of) the height of the Mysteries she later inhabits and jointly with her mother transmits to human beings.

At this point in the myth a detail is given such short shrift in Homer's telling that it is possible to bypass its significance. The tripleness of the Goddess is restored: Hecate becomes the companion of Persephone, preceding and following her. The ancient Death goddess, the Crone and her darkness, are restored to their proper place; like winter, which both precedes and follows the seasons of spring and of harvest, the Crone is relinked with the Maiden. The cycle is restored: the Maiden who germinates from the Crone's fertile death grows into the fruitfulness of the Mother and dies back into the Dark One, only to rise from her ever anew.

It is also at this juncture in the myth that Demeter restores her first gift to the gods and humanity, the gift of the grain, and more fully comes forth with her second, the gift of the Mysteries and initiation. Her first initiates are the king of Eleusis and his sons. Triptolemus is particularly significant, a figure of rich and fluid symbolism whose contact with the Goddess embodies the first full picture of the kind of transformation that takes place in the Masculine through this myth and Mysteries (and, by extension, to men who offer themselves to her for initiation).

The first hint of masculine transformation through the Goddess appeared only briefly, though significantly, when Demeter holds Demophoon in the fire, an act that transforms what should be certain death. This was already connected with the later Triptolemus, for the name Demophoon means "slayer of the people" and is a variant of the name Triptolemus.[44] Known as the "thrice-fold warrior" before his initiation, Triptolemus becomes the "thrice-fold ploughman." He thus bears the mark of Demeter's civilizing influence, which not only saved humans from having to forage like beasts for their food but also saved them from the savagery of war.

Demeter initiated Triptolemus and also gave him seed corn, a plough, and her serpent-drawn chariot so he could travel all over the world and fulfill the two missions she commanded: to disseminate her art of agriculture and to bring religious hope to those beyond Eleusis. Bearing her seeds, the aggressor-turned-planter is a vivid representation, echoed later in the son Persephone brings forth in the Mysteries, of the death-dealing Masculine no longer at odds with the Goddess and life but relinked in her cycle and bent back to her service. This is one of the meanings of the Mysteries for men and has profound implications for masculine attempts to confront and transform the destructive aspects of patriarchal power. While not the only way of accomplishing this and undoubtedly not the chosen path of many men who struggle with patriarchal destructiveness, the Mysteries nevertheless provide the profound possibility of a path of initiation through and beyond a patriarchal version of death. For some men, even in contemporary times, it may still be the path of the Self, despite the traditional psychological bias that sees reconnection with the Mother as only regressive.

Triptolemus is also Plutous, the "wealth" of the Goddess, from whom Hades' euphemistic title of "Pluto" is borrowed. While Pluto as a title of Hades reflects the arrogant appropriation of the Goddess's attributes enacted historically by the patriarchal invaders of southern Europe millennia ago, the Plutous connected with Triptolemus is in his original form: the son of Demeter and the Titan Iasion who is generally depicted as a little boy with a basket of grain. He represents the richness and blessings of the goddesses which, like Triptolemus, are sent forth to all who meet with their favor.

The myth of Demeter and Persephone is the public face of the initiation experience. It is mainly Demeter's story, a poignant portrayal of her passage from humanlike ignorance and grief in the face of what looks like certain death into gradual understanding and re-embodiment of her ancient goddess power to transfigure and transform the death experience, reclaiming it to life. It is the path her human initiates will subsequently follow, a path that culminates in a vision of her power. But her daughter's power is still unknown at this point to humankind; beyond Kore's cries to her mother and only partially successful attempts to resist the food of Hades, her own capacity for transformation is unseen in the myth, hidden instead in the secret places of the Mysteries. In part, she remains there forever, eternally closed to the uninitiated who are barred from knowing her secrets—and yet the feeling heart, the fluid eye that lends itself to vision and to dream, perhaps can see the power of Persephone glimmering through the very fragments of the Mysteries that have come down to us. It is not up to us to pry the Mysteries open, to rip them from their sacred hiddenness and arrogantly claim a "right to know"; that would only seek to violate her once again. Perhaps if we approach these fragments that remain with reverence and acceptance of their limitations, we can—like archaeologists dreaming the pot from the tiniest shards—imaginally receive a vision of the whole. Perhaps the daughter, like her mother, will lend herself to human ignorance and teach us what we seek to know.

The Eleusinian mysteries began sometime in the middle of the second millennium before the Christian era and continued to be celebrated at least once a year until 396 CE when a false priest claimed access to them and corrupted the rites.[45] In nearly fifteen hundred years, virtually no one betrayed their innermost secrets; what little we know comes to us via literary or historical allusions or from Christian denouncements of pagan practices. Thus the information available to us remains fragmented or distorted at best; nevertheless, we can ascertain some of the power and meaning of these holy rites.

The Mysteries were considered to be so vital to both Greece and the world at large that in 364 CE one Roman official—himself a worshiper of the gods and an Eleusinian initiate—pleaded their case before a Catholic emperor who sought to abolish them. Without the Mysteries, this Roman claimed, *bios*—life itself—would become *abiotos*, unlivable. To the individual, participation in the Mysteries provided life without fear in the face of death. Most likely originating in Crete (giving further meaning to Demeter's cover story of being pirated away from her Cretan origins), the Mysteries were open to all, including foreigners; the only requirements besides the ritual preparations and sacrificial animals were that the aspiring initiate spoke or understood the Greek language and had not murdered anyone.

The priests in charge of these rites were descendents of two Eleusinian families: the Eumolpidai, who claimed a mythical ancestor, Eumolpus (one of the sons of Keleos in the myth), and the Kerykes, whose mythical ancestor was a son of Hermes. From the Eumolpidai family line was chosen the Hierophant or high priest, from the Kerykes family came the second priest, the Dadouchos or torch bearer. Interestingly, there were also priestesses who served at the rites, but little is known of their origins or participation.

Preparations for the Mysteries at Eleusis included participation in what came to be known as the "Lesser Mysteries" held at a small sanctuary just outside of Athens. Originally not connected with the events at Eleusis, these rites were declared the first level of Eleusinian initiation around 450 BCE and were dedicated to Persephone and other abducted virgins, to Demeter, and to the god Dionysos (a major Dionysian festival celebrating the god's marriage took place in the same month). The Lesser Mysteries were essentially rites of purification. Some said they were invented so that the hero Heracles, who had killed many times, could be purified of his sins and be eligible for initiation into the "Greater Mysteries" of the two goddesses. Men and women who passed through these lesser rites had to wait for another year and a half before they were eligible for the Mysteries at Eleusis.

The Eleusinian mysteries took place during a nine-day span, beginning annually on the sixteenth day of Boedromion (around September 28 on our calendar) with the call, "Initiates into the sea!" Heeding the cry, all those previously prepared for initiation marched down to the sea near Athens where they washed both themselves and the sacrificial pigs they carried with them in a final rite of purification. In the two days that followed, sacrifices were made to Demeter and a procession in honor of the physician god Asklepious took place in the streets, which the initiates did not attend. A libation to Dionysos was offered during this procession—a wine offering—but, like Demeter who had refused wine in the house of Keleos, the initiates also refused it, shutting themselves away in their houses until the procession was over. At this time the barley drink (the *kykeon*) that Iambe offered to Demeter and that in turn would be offered to the initiates was prepared.

The actual Mysteries began on the fourth day of the celebration with a procession of initiates along the Sacred Road from Athens to the temple grounds at Eleusis, a distance of twelve miles. Along the way, various aspects of the myth were reenacted, culminating in the most secret events that took place at night in the innermost room of the temple. From the very start of the procession, all events were kept secret. What we do know is that each initiate, man and woman alike, entered into the Mysteries via a sympathetic mimesis of Demeter's experiences. The way into the Mysteries was the emotional and literal path of Demeter, and all who aspired to fulfill the requirements of these rites took on themselves the experiences of the sorrowing mother: her grief and rage and failure to understand, the Mystery points of the myth and their revelations of deeper meaning, the recognition of Demeter's power to transform the death experience into new life, and her gradual understanding and grasp of her daughter's fate.

To this end, various events and characters from the myth were encountered along the way from Athens to Eleusis. Shouts of "Iakchos!" were heard, and a statue of the young son of Demeter was borne along with the procession. It was said that Iakchos and Hecate led the initiates into the Mysteries, Iakchos the men and Hecate the women. This singular differentiation of the initiates by gender has rich implications. In the myth, Iakchos appears in the womb of Baubo, a harbinger of the deeper meaning behind the rape of Kore and the transformation to come. In the Mystery context, he represents the fullness of the transformed Masculine; here he is an alter ego of Dionysos, not as a wine god but as "Dionysios at the breast," the son-of-the-Mother, relinked with the Feminine as source.[46] Kerényi suggests that the Eleusinian Iakchos who leads the Mystery procession also represents another aspect of Dionysos: his capacity to lead into the underworld and return. For Dionysos also made the underworld journey to retrieve his mother Semele whom Zeus had killed when the sky god revealed himself as her lover in a dazzle of lightning; Hades allowed Dionysos to bring back his mother in exchange for the gift of the myrtle plant, boughs of which were also carried in the Eleusinian procession.

These connections suggest that for male initiates, it was the son-of-the-Mother who could lead into the Mystery experience and the ransoming of life back from the death encounter. Still linked with his matriarchal origins, Iakchos/Dionysos foreshadowed the transformation of Hades in the height of the Mysteries through the birth of his luminous son. Perhaps for the male initiates at Eleusis, the journey toward hope in the face of death included not only an identification with the sorrowing mother in the loss of her daughter but also with the fate of the son, the luminous Masculine returned from its split-off, static, death-dealing state—the godhead of Hades—and reborn through the Feminine into reconnection not only with her but with the service of life.

For women, however, what leads toward initiation and the knowledge of hope after death is different, for it is Hecate who leads the women at Eleusis. Women were not only to experience the wrenching division of mother and daughter, the ravishing of life by the patriarchal death force, but also to follow this path through the Crone, the Death power that Demeter reclaims and Persephone becomes. For women, what led to the Mysteries was the Crone "before and after," the goddess of Life linked again to her powers of death and the death-into-life recycling she embodies as her essential transformative power.

Having fasted, having drunk the *kykeon*, having encountered the revelatory message of Baubo/Iambe (interestingly, the woman representing Baubo appears on a bridge on the Sacred Way, further intimating the importance of Baubo's jests as a transition point in the myth), the initiates proceeded closer and closer to the culminating vision of Death's transformation. Once they reached Eleusis it was night, and now the torch-bearing Dadouchos, the second high priest, led them onto the dance grounds and into the temple area. Then a boy celebrant, a child representing Demophoon, took over. Known as "the boy of the hearth," this child was an innocent who, unlike the adults, required no purification; he was chosen by lot from among the most distinguished families of Athens and initiated at the expense of the state. Kerényi writes, ". . . it was he who now precisely enacted the prescribed sacred actions on behalf of the entire festive community, so moving the Goddess to grant the great vision of which the mystai (initiates) were to partake in the Telestrion (the great temple)."[47]

Only a little is known about what took place inside the Telestrion; the most secret part of the Mysteries took place at this time. We do know that within the innermost room of the temple, a roaring fire was lit. Then the Hierophant sounded a gong, said to resemble the thunder that was believed to have come from the realm of the dead. The sounding of the gong was a summoning of Persephone, and some believe that an actual epiphany of the goddess took place at this time. Whatever happened at this point, the high priest then proclaimed in a loud voice, "The Mistress has given birth to a holy boy! Brimo has brought forth Brimos!" Kerényi vividly captures the meaning of this holiest of moments when he writes, "Brimo is primarily a designation for the queen of the dead, for Demeter, Persephone, and Hecate in their quality of the underworld. . . . She then gave birth in fire; the goddess of death gave birth! And now it was claimed in the loud, chanting voice of the Hierophant—that the queen of the dead herself had given birth in fire to a mighty son."[48] Recalling the earlier transformative fire in the myth vis-à-vis which Demeter first displays her transformative powers, Kerényi continues: "A birth in death was possible! And it was possible also for human beings if they had faith in the Goddesses; that is the message which Demeter herself proclaimed at Eleusis, when she laid Demophoon in the fire to make him immortal."[49]

Ravaged by the dark god, "contaminated" by his food, having taken in his seeds, Persephone comes back from the underworld pregnant by Death, but from this pregnancy comes not horror, not ghost life, not death but a reintegration of death into life. The return of the goddess from the underworld reunites not just mother and daughter; Persephone, because of her encounter with death, reunites both her mother and herself with their most ancient form, the Crone. Persephone becomes Brimo, ancient goddess of Death, and remanifests the triple form and triple powers of the prepatriarchal Goddess: Maiden-Mother-Crone. The split-off god of the patriarchal version of death is reborn in her womb as a variant of her: Brimos, son-of-the-Mother—the Masculine no longer stuck in death but recycled in it through her gestational, life-giving powers. This born-anew god is multiformed but all forms are in the service of Life. We see him now as Iakchos, son-of-the-Mother who revealed the transcending of rape and death and co-leads the Mystery procession; as Triptolemus, the warrior-turned-ploughman who spreads Eleusinian hope and her seeds; as Plutous, the riches of the goddesses sent as a blessing to those whom they love; as a now kindly husband of Persephone, co-equal with her in the underworld but no longer opposed to the upperworld she also belongs to. Echoes of Dionysos surround him: the older form of Dio-

43

nysos, a cereal god, the son of the cereal Mother, his ties to her still overt and still honored. The patriarchal power that rapes and kills life and seeks to fixate it in death or the limbo state of ghosts has been recycled through the Feminine power it sought to rob and is bent back into her service.

At this moment in the Mysteries, amid profound silence, the Hierophant displayed an ear of newly mowed grain. So too graves were sowed with wheat to purify them and return their dead to the living. Embodied as plant, the gift of her mother to humans and gods alike, the Kore sprout has been harvested and from the harvest comes not death, not finality, but the seed corn for the ongoing cycle of life. And from that seed, hidden in the ground again, buried like the dead, the new sprouts—the *koraia*, as they were called by the Greeks—break forth into life once again. Fertile death was the power of Persephone and what she brought back to the living.

This theme was met again on the last day of the Mysteries, the day called the Plemochoai, "the pourings of plenty." On this day, two vessels with unstable, circular bottoms were filled with liquid and overturned, one toward the East and one toward the West. This probably took place in the Ploutonian, a small cave on the temple grounds at Eleusis, which was said to be an entrance to the underworld. As the vessels were overturned, the priest looked first skyward and cried "*Hye!*" and then earthward with the cry, "*Kye!*" *Hye* meant "flow!" while *kye* was a command to "conceive!" Thus the Mysteries ended with an appeal to both heaven and earth, the realm of the Olympians and the realm of the chthonic world below, to unite and make fertile, like the goddess in whom the worlds met who now moved forever between them, the goddess whose human followers could now follow her path and find for themselves the reunion of Life and Death.

The temple at Eleusis stands in ruins. The tourists who tread the dance ground now no longer know the sacred movements. For over sixteen hundred years, Eleusis has been silent; the myth and the Mysteries once thought to hold the entire world together have long disappeared from conscious apperception and reverence. Yet Spirit doesn't die; suppressed, oppressed, it merely changes forms, hides in the nooks and crannies of the new religion that replaces it, surfaces in images and rituals whose origins have been lost to the consciousness of the people who still go through the motions in the present, appears unrecognized in dreams and visions, life events and histories within the unsuspecting psyches of people far from knowledge or awareness of their ancient meanings. Bits and pieces of the old imagery remain outwardly in Greece, threading through the funeral customs, the grave-side lamentations sung by grieving women, the folk beliefs and legends still held by rural people in contemporary Greece. But the contextual meaning and cohesiveness of these images is lost, overshadowed by the Christian vision of death and resurrection that replaced them.

A cohesive version of the myth of Demeter and Persephone survived in Greece at least as late as 1860 when it was told to a visiting scholar by an old Albanian priest.[50] As happened with many pagan deities and practices that were assimilated into Christianity in its effort to present itself as more palatable to the people it sought to convert, the goddess Demeter was reduced, yet preserved by the Church, in a masculine saint figure: Saint Demetrius, patron of agriculture. But in Lefsina (the modern name for the village of Eleusis), the peasants rebelled at the change in gender and, unrecognized and unsanctioned by the Church in Rome, constructed a female saint, Saint Demetra, around whom the myth was still woven but with significant changes.

According to the Albanian priest, Saint Demetra was a kind old woman who had an exceptionally beautiful daughter and who fed the poor with the meager means at her disposal. On Christmas night, while Demetra was in church, her house was broken into and her daughter seized by an evil Turkish magician who carried her away to the mountains of Epirus. When Demetra returned and saw what had happened, she was beside herself and turned to her neighbors for help and information. But no one would tell her anything, out of fear of the Turks. Weeping and lamenting, she made a poignant appeal to Nature. "She turned her enquiries to the tree that grew before her house, but the tree could tell her nothing. She asked the sun but the sun could give her no help; she asked the moon and the stars but from them too she learnt nothing."[51]

Finally she asked the old stork on the roof, who replied, "Long time now we have lived side by side; thou art as old as I. Listen. Thou hast always been good to me, thou hast never disturbed my nest, and once thou didst help me to drive away the bird of prey that would have carried off my nestlings. In recompense I will tell thee what I know of the fate of thy daughter; she was carried off by a Turk mounted on a black horse, who took her towards the West. Come, I will set out with thee and we will search for her together."[52]

It was winter. The old woman was freezing and feeble. Doors were shut in her face when she tried to find out if people had seen her daughter; people laughed at her or didn't answer at all. "For men love not misery," the old priest explained.

Finally Demetra and the stork came to Eleusis. Overwhelmed with cold and exhaustion, the old woman threw herself down by the roadside. At this point, the wife of the mayor of the village happened by, took pity on Demetra and brought her home to her husband. Both were kind to the old woman and tried to console her; she in turn blessed their fields with fertility and an abundance of crops.

Seeing that Demetra couldn't possibly continue her search for her daughter, the mayor's strong and handsome son offered to go in her place, asking only for the daughter's hand in return. This was granted and the young man set off with the faithful stork as his companion. After walking for many days, he saw a light in the forest and hurried toward it. There he found forty dragons guarding a caldron boiling on a fire. With one hand, he lifted the caldron, which all of the dragons together could not lift, and lighted his torch. The dragons, astounded at his strength, prevailed on him to capture a maiden they had been trying to get to—Demetra's daughter—who had been shut up in a tower by the magician.

The dragons took the young man to the tower. Driving nails into the sides of the tower to make steps, he climbed up, inviting the dragons to follow; as each dragon reached the top, he successively killed them. Alone with the stork, the young man now encountered Demetra's daughter and immediately fell in love with her.

Then the magician appeared and attacked the young man. The Turk was a shape changer, by turns appearing as lion, serpent, bird of prey, and fire, trying to exhaust the young hero, but at each turn the young man held his own. This struggle continued for three days; the magician was weakened. Finally, regaining his strength momentarily, he killed the young man in a final attack and cut his body into quarters, hanging one piece on each side of the tower. "Then, elated by his victory," the old priest reported, "he did violence to Demetra's daughter, whose chastity he had hitherto respected."[53]

Now the stork entered the drama more actively. With the help of a magical herb, she revived the young man, reuniting the pieces of his dismembered body. Thus reconstituted, he threw himself on the magician again, this time with greater fury, seeking to punish him for his further crime of ravishing the young woman. Again, the hero was about to be killed; in a last desperate moment, he invoked the help of the Panagia (the Virgin Mary in Greek Christianity), vowing to become a monk if he was successful in overcoming the Turk. His prayers were heard and he overcame the magician. Again the stork appeared, plucking out the eyes of the Turk and pulling out of his head the one white hair on which his life depended. The magician immediately died.

Spring graced the land and the young man returned Demetra's daughter to her waiting mother and went off to the monastery. Demetra went off with her daughter. No one knows where they live, but the fields of Lefsina have been fertile ever since.

This astonishing tale, still extant nearly fifteen hundred years after the Mysteries disappeared in Greece, is on the one hand a testament to the vitality of the ancient religion, preserving even now some of its power; on the other hand, it is a telling reflection of the distortions of the Goddess under the influence of patriarchy and Christianity. All the old characters are here: Kore, Demeter, Hades, Keleos, and Metanira, their son Triptolemus, and Hecate the Crone, but disguised, distorted, effaced, and shifted in extremely significant ways.

Kore is barely more than a glyph. Unnamed, unempowered, untransforming, she is little more than an object of masculine desire, a "damsel in distress," simply in need of rescue; her goddess capacity is entirely obliterated. The essence of the old myth and the Mysteries is gone: Kore never becomes Persephone.

Demeter has suffered a similar fate; she too has been stripped of transformative power. Old, feeble, mocked, and rejected, she mirrors both poignantly and well the fate of the Goddess under the influence of patriarchy and the Christian religion. What remains of her pagan character are her agricultural powers and her basically benevolent nature. Her mourning, too, remains, but it has been stripped of its potency. No longer does her grief turn to rage and the power to ransom her daughter from death, nor does it open for gods or for humans an initiatory path. The Goddess as saint cannot even make the journey anymore; a hero must do it for her. Demeter, too, does not make the transformation to Crone or embody the Crone's essential power.[54]

Hades, however, remains empowered. A master of magic, he now claims the shape-shifting capacity more often attributed to his ancient brothers Poseidon and Zeus in the older tales.[55] As a Turk, this Hades is even more clearly linked with foreign invasions than was his pagan counterpart. But aside from these echoes, so very much is lost. The context from which he emerges, his link with the kingdom of Death, is missing. The tensions between worlds, the essential encounter between patriarchal Masculine and matriarchal Feminine, between two visions of death and two awesome powers, are gone. The struggle now is between men: a Christianized hero and a presumably barbarian foreigner. The death-dealing Masculine opposes what earlier was its transformation (i.e., the Hades figure here opposes the modern Triptolemus) and endeavors to kill it off. Hades too does not transform in this tale.

The presence of the dragons in this story seems superfluous. Perhaps they represent a split-off chthonic world of earthbound instinct so inimical to the Christian sense of spirit—the world of carnal flesh and animal desire that in the Christian mind is ever to be overcome and slain so that the higher life of spirit may emerge. Saint George slays a dragon as well, Saint Patrick drives out the snakes; such images abound. The lower beast of Nature and the body must be transcended if spiritual achievement is to be attained. This type of transcendence is also mirrored later in this modern tale when the Triptolemus figure must sacrifice his own desire for Demetra's daughter and vow eternal chastity as a monk in order to achieve the rescue. Though still retaining the pagan stamp of empowerment through the Feminine (here appearing as the Panagia), he achieves his goal through a decidedly unpagan denial of the body. He slays the dragons of desire within himself as well as those outer beasts that lusted after Kore. Having thus become the opposite of Hades, he goes on to overpower the rapist Turk.

At first glance, this appears to be a kind of hero's tale. The power of the Goddess is effaced, and Triptolemus emerges as the only one possessed of the gifts, strength, and courage needed to make the journey that the mother can no longer undertake. The archetypal ingredients of the hero myth are here: superhuman powers, dragons to be slain, obstacles and challenges to be met, the compelling need to rescue the maiden from the clutches of an evil magician who has imprisoned her. But the outcome doesn't follow prototypic lines. The hero doesn't "get the girl" and like his ancient predecessor (albeit in diluted form), he still must turn to and serve a higher power—the trans-personal Feminine (here carried by the Virgin Mary)—before he can achieve his goal, sacrificing his personal claims to Kore in the process.

The nearly hidden powers of the hero's humble helper animal, the stork, also give this tale a decidedly older, matriarchal cast. Though seemingly in a secondary role as companion and aide to the hero, the stork is the true possessor of the powers that determine the outcome of this story. She alone maintains the truest touchpoint with the an-cient myth, for she retains the powers of the Crone.

Reduced to animal form, she is nonetheless clearly a double of Demeter. "Long time . . . we have lived side by side; thou art as old as I": her words establish their parallel, but so does her variation on the Doso story. As with Demetra, she is not threatened by the bird of prey; her nestlings are. She bonds with Demetra as mother and prom-ises her aid, as once Demetra aided her. But this is potent aid!—the power to bring back life from death and the power to kill. The stork alone in this modern tale embodies the old secret, the transformation from Mother to Crone. It is she who re-members the hero, bringing his life back from death so that he may subdue the magician again. But the hero alone cannot overcome the magician; in the end it is the stork who depotentiates the Hades power and finally takes the magician's life. Though deprived of her once-profound meaning, her link with the world-saving Mysteries, in the end it is still the Crone who is stronger than Hades, even in the nineteenth century.

By our own century, however, the Crone and her powers of death and rebirth appear to have faded completely. Some of her form re-mains; in parts of rural Greece today, women still grieve extensively when someone dies, hoping to influence the fact of death, in uncon-scious imitation of the mythic Demeter. But grief, though prolonged and intense, is no longer initiatory; it ends now in bitterness and a brutal confrontation with the absoluteness of death. Grief then ceases and the mourners submit to the doctrine of the Church—redemption and resurrection no longer through Mother and Daughter but through the dying and rising Son of the Father. Yet even here, in a thoroughly Christian, contemporary approach to death, the imprint of the myth and its Mysteries is still visible. Even the figure of Hades is retained, remarkably unchanged in some ways, standing alongside the higher figure of the Christian god.

In 1979, the anthropologist Loring Danforth set out to study the beliefs, customs, and rituals surrounding death in a rural village in modern-day Greece, a village he called Potamia.[56] While Danforth did not concern himself with pagan origins, his findings provide yet another mirror of the persistence of some of the ancient symbols, images, and emotional experience connected with the myth of Demeter and Persephone. Remnants of the ancient myth were visible in funeral practices, but the most vivid echoes of the past were discovered in the emotional experience of feminine grief and in the images inherent in the funeral lamentations sung by and, in some instances, composed by grieving women.

Danforth found that death is a major communal event in Potamia, especially for women. The most powerful reflection of Demeter in this contemporary village is the centrality, longevity, and intensity of grief borne by the women. Men are required to mourn only in brief and abbreviated ways, usually at funerals and memorial services, while women grieve intensely for a period of at least five years (the time between burial and exhumation of the body). Extensive, often daily acts of tending the dead and immersion in the death experience are the responsibility of women. These include meticulous care of the grave, empathic companioning through daily vigils, and the singing of elaborate funeral laments. The usual rituals of everyday life in the family and neighborhood are no longer maintained or are sharply attenuated by women who are grieving: holidays are not celebrated; even the wedding of one's child may not be attended. Family life is disrupted by the vigils at the grave, and the bright colors of everyday dress are replaced for years by the somber colors of death—black, brown, blue, reflecting successive stages of mourning.

Although the women most directly involved with the deceased—mothers and daughters, sisters and wives—maintain the grave, the expression of grief is communal. Women grieve with each other, keep vigil together, attend other funerals in the village, and sing laments together for their own and each other's dead. Maintaining an ongoing "conversation" with the dead, as Danforth puts it, becomes the central focus of each bereaved woman's life and the new definition of her social responsibilities. As it was for Demeter, grief becomes the touchstone of feminine existence and upperworld life is disrupted or even stopped altogether.

When Danforth raised the questions of why the women mourn so intensely and so long for the dead, the answer was always the same:

"the pain [*ponos* in Greek] pulls me". The word *ponos* refers to pain, grief, suffering, or sorrow. A related emotion, *kamoudhia*, which means anguish, yearning, or pained longing, was also given as motivation for the maintenance of vigilance and grief. Without these emotions, the women would not spend so much time at the graveside. *Ponos* and *kamoudhia* are essentially relational; they express an empathic companioning of the death experience and at the same time carry the denial of death's finality and hope for the loved one's return.[57]

The recognition of *ponos* as a religious emotion is vividly evidenced in the words of the following lament:

How can a ribbon rot? How can an amulet get covered with cobwebs?
How can a precious carnation from Venice wither and die?
My child, where can I put the ponos I feel for you?
If I toss it by the roadside, those who pass by will take it.
If I throw it in a tree, the little birds will take it.
I will place it in my heart so that it will take root there,
so that it will cause me ponos as I walk, so that it will kill me as I stand.
I will go to a goldsmith to have it gold-plated.
I will have it made into a golden cross, into a silver amulet,
so that I can worship the cross and kiss the amulet.[58]

Danforth comments on this lament, "Here the bereaved mother expresses the view that she must not allow the ponos she feels at the death of her child to dissipate. She must nourish her ponos, her grief, her sorrow, as long as possible. She must cherish these emotions dearly because it is through them alone that she is able to keep alive the memory of her child."[59]

But this concept of *ponos* expresses far more than keeping a memory alive. Life, death, and religious transformation of death into resurrection are the qualities of *ponos*, all brought about by the mother's devotion. *Ponos* is living; like a plant, it takes root in and grows from the mother's heart. *Ponos* can kill, enabling the mother, like Demeter, to empathically follow the child's path into death. But *ponos* is also death's transformation. It does not "rot," "get covered with cobwebs," or "wither and die"; through the mother's reverence and tendance, it is made into the permanence of gold and then transposed to an even higher level, a more fluid religious vision of death-that-becomes-resurrection. Life, death, and resurrection—the path of the

Mother's mourning—shine through their Christian clothes in the grief still held intensely and exclusively by rural Greek women. But the ancient Matrix that gave this grief its meaning and its effectiveness is no longer consciously known; the imitation of Demeter is no longer recognized as the initiatory path into death's Mysteries. The image of the Mother is lost to modern consciousness, even by those who unwittingly repeat her intensity as ritual and passionate lament.

Remarkably, this is not the case with Hades. Unlike Demeter, his image and power remain, still vividly etched overtly in the Greek consciousness of death. He is named quite directly as Charos (or Haros), more rarely as Hades, and his personification of death is still as Snatcher of the living. It is around his figure as it is richly depicted in folk song and image that the motifs and personages of the ancient myth still appear.

Hades' image as Haros is itself an amalgam of his ancient counterparts. Sometimes he is depicted as a white-haired old man with harsh features, sometimes as a lusty Triptolemus-like warrior with black or golden hair. Whatever his form, Haros still carries off people whose time has come and holds them in the underworld, which is itself still called Hades. It is said of a man in his death throes, "he is wrestling with [C]haros."[60] In Christianized form, Haros is seen as an angel or archangel or a servant or messenger of God whose duties are sometimes repellent to him; in this form he is sometimes compassionate. But in a more pagan form, which still survives, he is without kindness or mercy; he is black, bitter, hateful, merciless, and independent of God.[61]

> Sometimes he is enlarging his palace and he takes the young and the strong to be its pillars; sometimes he is repairing the tent in which he dwells and uses the stout arms of heroes for tent pegs and the tresses of bright-haired maidens for the ropes; sometimes he is laying out a garden and he gathers children from the earth to be the flowers of it and young men to be its tall slim cypresses; more rarely he is a vintager and tramples men in his vat that their blood may be his red wine or again, he carries a sickle and reaps a human harvest.[62]

Echoes of Triptolemus as planter and Dionysos as wine god reverberate in these images of Haros.

Faded versions of Demeter, Persephone, and Brimos also thread through the mythology of Haros. He lives with his mother "who entreats him sometimes, when he is setting out to the chase, to spare mothers with young children and not to part lovers newly wed."[63] He has a wife named Charissa (note the patriarchal shift here; the modern Persephone's name, Charissa, is merely a variant of Charos, whereas in earlier times the Masculine as Brimos was a variant of her in her death form Brimo). Like the Kore figure in the legend of Saint Demetra, Charissa has no distinct character of her own. Haros also has a son who keeps a second set of keys to the underworld and for whose wedding feasts Haros slays children and brides instead of lambs.[64] No longer euphemized, his horror as Death lord is now graphically imaged in this contemporary mythology.

Many aspects of the ancient myth are still visible in funeral laments and in folksongs referring to death. Thus in one folksong, Haros is depicted as a pirate and elements of the Doso story are suggested. The mourner calls out to the deceased:

In what boat will thou be
and at what haven wilt thou land
that thy mother may come and ransom thee again?[65]

Still another reiterates the vision of the death experience as a kidnapping:

In the green and golden meadows
they kidnapped Eleni. They stole her away from us.
"Eleni, you didn't cry out so that we could rescue you."
"How could I cry out? How could I answer your call?
My mouth was gagged. There was a kerchief around my neck
and that vicious Haros was raining blows on me."[66]

Funeral laments in particular, sung over and over by the women in mourning, reflect the more ancient motifs and images of the experience of death. Death is still seen as a marriage; many songs are sung at both funerals and weddings. In rural Greece, a bride leaves her home with her parents to live with her new husband in his father's house. These patriarchal arrangements are occasions for mourning, the grief felt most keenly by mother and daughter.

The analogy between marriage and death is especially vivid when the deceased is unmarried. Then the funeral becomes the person's wedding; he or she is buried in wedding attire. A man at death is said to take the earth as his bride, recalling perhaps the collusion of Gaia in the death experience, while a woman takes Haros or Hades as her husband or the marriage takes place in the underworld.

When a young woman's death is referred to as a marriage, "the husband is portrayed as an unknown and feared stranger who has snatched the young bride away from her home."[67] The figure of Death as a stranger intersects with another motif: the connection of death with foreign or distant lands or with living a life in exile. The link of Hades with the earliest foreign invaders, the northern patriarchal peoples who invaded Greece and other parts of the Mediterranean and southern Europe millennia ago, appears to persist in the Turkish magician image in the legend of Saint Demetra as well as in this contemporary assumption that Death as Snatcher has a foreign origin.

Even closer to the ancient pagan formulation of death is the tendency, still vivid and poignant, to juxtapose the life and fate of human beings with the life and fate of plants.

For the world is a tree and we are its fruit
and Haros, who is the vintager, gathers its fruit.[68]

Here Haros appears as the harvester, assuming the powers of the Crone. But he is also the planter, the Demetrian son, and death is a "being planted" by Haros:

Haros decided to plant a garden.
He turned over the earth and tilled the soil in order to plant trees.
He planted young women as lemon trees and young men as cypresses.
He planted little children as roses all around and he posted old men as
    a garden fence.[69]

Having thoroughly assimilated the powers of the ancient Triple Goddess, this modern Hades is both sower and reaper, transforming the dead into seedlings and picking them as fruit.

Like plants that become food to nourish life, the dead also become food to nourish the earth, picking up another ancient theme. Death retains its fertility and promotes the lives of those who feed off it. First and foremost of its benefactors is the earth itself:

> Young men should not rejoice;
> they should not strut with pride.
> Only the earth should rejoice;
> only the earth should strut with pride,
> the earth, which eats young men and rejoices,
> which eats young women and is proud.
> The earth which eats tender bodies
> and muscular shoulders.
> It eats children who have mothers
> and brothers who have sisters.
> It separates married couples,
> even those who are very much in love.[70]

Here the death dealer is Gaia, the earth, recalling her savagery as Death goddess, as well as her collusion with Hades and Zeus in the abduction of Kore. But Haros is identified with this goddess as well, for sometimes it is he who eats the bodies of the dead. Danforth unwittingly captures the ancient meaning precisely when he comments on these contemporary images: "If the body is eaten by the earth, then it nourishes the earth and gives life to the world of nature. Being eaten, therefore, not only involves destruction and death, it involves the giving of nourishment and life to that which consumes. If that which dies is really eaten, then from death there emerges life."[71]

Finally, the following lines appear in a contemporary lament, which could have been written for Kore herself:

> My little ear of wheat, husked and reaped before your time,
> reaped before your time by the reapers of Haros.[72]

In unconscious memory of the deeper meaning of this essential image, the mourners at rural Greek funerals are given *koliva* to eat, a sweet made with boiled wheat; *koliva* is said, even now, to signify the resurrection of the dead.[73]

Like a lodestar, still present but with its meanings nearly obscured by centuries of patriarchal and Christian influence, the ancient imagery remains; it glimmers through the grief of rural Greek women, the mythology of Haros, the themes and metaphors within the laments, even in a few elements of an otherwise Christian funeral rite. But ultimately, the path to initiation has been lost to modern consciousness, no longer lighted by the goddess who once inspired it with her own lavish mourning.

The excess of grief now ends in a brutal confrontation with the ineluctability of death: the exhumation of the body of the deceased. After the five-year period of feminine mourning is over, the bones of the deceased are dug up, ritually greeted, grieved over, and then relinquished to their final de-individualization: placement in the village ossuary among hundreds of other bones, no longer distinct from each other or mourned as beloved.[74] *Ponos* and *kamoudhia* lead not to vision and return but to the stark fact of death's triumph. At this point, the Christian belief in resurrection through the Son appears to take over, oddly disjunctive with the pagan echoes that once unfolded a different meaning of mourning.[75]

The real dancing ground for this myth and its dynamics and meanings is now the modern psyche. It is in this arena, far beyond the confines of ancient or even contemporary Greece, that the forces of Hades are still to be found. It is in this arena that the Goddess still manifests, trying to balance, both individually and collectively, a patriarchal power so dark and so large, so inflated with unchecked power, that the planet itself, the earth that enables our lives as a species, is threatened with permanent rupture and death.

The abuse of power that Hades represents, the lust for conquest that is not concerned for the life it disrupts, the relationships it violates: this is the core of patriarchy's shadow. The dishonoring and eventual annihilation from consciousness of the feminine Deity and all that she represented; the false claiming of her powers by a renegade masculine invader; the dominance of a split-off masculine vision that defines itself by its independence from female, body, and nature; and the imposition of this independence as the normative model for identity in both men and women: all this is the legacy of patriarchy's triumph so many thousands of years ago and the underside of the Zeus expansiveness we know so well.

The patriarchal perspective has long held sway over our consciousness, both individually and as a culture, and it is to this that the ancient myth attempts to speak—no longer through the vessel of official religion and known initiation rites but through our visions, our dreams, our struggles in relationship, through the unconscious that ever seeks to compensate one-sidedness and initiate us into becoming and being whole. Sometimes fully, sometimes partly; sometimes in old clothes, sometimes in new; sometimes progressing along its ancient path, sometimes appearing to reverse and begin in the underworld: the dynamics of this myth and the figures of its main characters continue to appear with their urgent messages of hope beyond despair, life after ravaging and the threat of death.

To heed this message now, to welcome it from our own urgent needs to address and rebalance the patriarchal shadow in our lives, we need to tread a different path from the ancients, a path to an inner dance ground where the old and healing forces still appear. Using the tools of depth psychology, infused with the "protoplasmic fullness" of our knowledge of the ancient myth and pagan mind-set, we will meet again the themes of rupture and separation, mourning and rage, the ancient power of the Crone to recycle fertile death, and the transformation of even the would-be annihilator now in our own psyches, in our own time. We begin the journey to the world of the psyche with a deeper look at each of the three main characters—Demeter, Kore-Persephone, and Hades—to learn their more extended mythology and how they appear now in the dynamics between people or in the inner world of the individual, struggling, modern soul.

Käthe Kollwitz, *Seed for the Planting Shall Not Be Ground Up!*, 1942.

∾ 3 ∾

"Seed for the Planting Shall Not Be Ground Up!":

The Goddess Demeter

So perhaps the first significant lesson in my life was that it takes one human being who really cares to make a difference between life and death.

—Elisabeth Kübler-Ross,
Death: The Final Stage of Growth[1]

Käthe Kollwitz's antiwar lithograph entitled *Seed for the Planting Shall Not Be Ground Up!* moved me deeply long before I knew of the goddess Demeter. The ferocious, almost feral determination on the mother's face to protect her children from the threat of death, echoed in the emphatic lines that define her sheltering arms and body, convey succinctly the power of the archetypal Mother. Her fierceness, contrasted with the wide-eyed innocence, fear, and even playfulness of the children she enfolds, provides a powerful vision of maternal protectiveness toward the young life, the "seed" she seeks to preserve. Kollwitz's mother is implacable and unambivalent; as for Demeter, nothing will persuade her to give her children over willingly to the forces of death. Her fierceness is, in the artist's own words, "not a longed-for wish, but a demand, a command!"[2] Like Demeter, this mother stands forcefully for life. Kollwitz's drawing was a passionate antiwar statement, engendered by the searing pain of losing her son and her grandson to two world wars. But such a maternal response to the threat of death does not only appear in the context of antiwar sentiment. Recently I came across an autobiographical reflection by the renowned advocate of humane treatment for the dying, Elisabeth Kübler-Ross. Musing upon events in her childhood that might have contributed to her choice of career as an adult, she tells the following tale of her origin:

> The first impresssion both my parents had of me was of great dismay. I was barely two pounds, bald, and so tiny that I was clearly a disappointment. Little did anyone expect that this was just the beginning of more shocks; another two pound sister was born fifteen minutes later, followed by a six pound girl who finally met all the expectations of new parents. It is hard to say if my precarious introduction to life was the first "instigator" to going into this field. After all, I was not expected to live and if it had not been for the determination of my mother, I might not have survived. She strongly believed that such little infants could only survive if they received a great deal of tender loving care, frequent breast feedings, and the warmth and comfort that only home could give them—not the hospital.
>
> She cared for the three of us personally, nursed us every three hours day and night, and it is said that she never slept in her bed for the first nine months. All three of us—needless to say—made it. So perhaps the first significant lesson in my life was that it takes one human being who really cares to make a difference between life and death.[3]

Kübler-Ross's mother believed in life, tended it, and poured herself into its preservation. Remarkably, like Kore-Persephone, Kübler-Ross took her mother's fierce value for life into her own journey into the world of death, completing the cycle of life and death intertwined, just as Persephone eventually completed her mother and reunited the fierceness for life with the transformative nature of death in the realm of the Goddess.

Both the mother of Kollwitz's drawing and the determined mother of Kübler-Ross exemplify one of the faces of the goddess Demeter. They mirror in human form her passionate standing for life, especially the seed life full of potential that is not to be cut down by premature death. But there is more to Demeter than the fierce stance she takes on behalf of her daughter.

In her fullness, Demeter was the Triple Goddess of old: Maiden, Mother, and Crone. By Homeric times, this tripleness was differentiated into three separate but interlinked goddesses: Kore as the Maiden, Demeter as Mother, and Hecate as Crone. Originally, however, these three were aspects of one wholeness, and even the later myth retains some of this three-persons-in-one-goddess quality.

In a very real way, this myth and its variants are the tale of the great goddess Demeter: the initial loss of her Maiden aspect via the patriarchal splitting of the Feminine, her gradual initiation into understanding her own Mysteries, and the subsequent restoration not only of a transformed Maiden but also of the Crone. This view, seen psychologically, has profound implications for visioning the wounding and reparation of the feminine Self in its relationship to and transcendence of the destructive aspects of patriarchy. I will discuss this further in chapter 6.

At the same time, the later differentiation of Demeter into three persons allows an expanded interpretation of the myth from perspectives other than the mother's (one can, for example, look at the myth as experienced through Kore-Persephone, linked to but also separate from the experience of Demeter). This symbolic flexibility allows for more in-depth treatment of any one of her aspects and also invites application of the myth to relational situations.

Robert Graves sees the three-but-one vision symbolized on an agricultural level as well: Kore as the green corn, Persephone as the ripe ear, and Hecate as the harvested corn but with Demeter as her general title.[4] Demeter thus can be seen as goddess of the whole myth as well as the spiritual-psychological-agricultural process it depicts.

Her tripleness is further suggested in the variations of her attributes, as reflected in the many ways she was named. Her Maiden aspect, for example, is suggested in one of her titles, Demeter Chloe, goddess of sprout life and greening, lady of verdure. The origins of this name, according to the classicist Louis Richard Farnell, suggest an even more essential form of Demeter. Farnell notes that there was a pre-anthropomorphic version of this vision of the goddess in which the natural object, the sprout or greenness of Nature, embodied the Deity; the Deity was not yet separated out in personal form.[5] So Demeter once was verdure itself, rather than goddess of verdure. This depiction of her as essence rather than person was perhaps echoed in another vision of Demeter: she was also seen as the life force in plants. From a psychological perspective, these portrayals of Demeter suggest that we can experience her as a force or vitality as well as a personified being through whom we can picture an aspect of ourselves or with whom we can enter into a relationship.

Demeter as Maiden is seen most obviously in Kore—her daughter before the rape. Seen as an aspect of Demeter's wholeness, Kore represents what Starhawk calls the "younger self"—that part of ourselves that embodies the child in us at any age, close to direct and naive experience of life, to preverbal fullness and perception, playfulness and spontaneity. Kore is the springtime in both a woman's life and in this aspect of the Goddess: the time of beginnings, of potential ripe for development, of womanhood nascent and budding. To lose contact with this aspect of oneself or to have it damaged or taken away is a loss at the deepest level of a woman's being, often resulting in profound depression and stagnation.

Demeter is most often described as a mild and tender goddess, basically embodying and representing the radiant, positive aspect of the Great Mother. She becomes negative only to those who uphold the patriarchal order, never to her daughter and only when dishonored or after Kore or she herself is raped. Although her image derives from a matriarchal stratum of the collective psyche, she is not antimasculine. Nor is she antisexual, though in contemporary psychological commentary, she has often been presented this way, seen as a kind of "super virgin." The mythic evidence for this perspective is derived only from a late tale of Demeter and her daughter, found in Ovid's *Metamorphoses* (written around 8 CE); there, Aphrodite expresses concern that Demeter intends to keep her daughter a literal virgin, much like Artemis or Athene.[6] But earlier tales about Demeter do not support this picture of her, for she herself had male lovers (and her priestesses taught the "secrets of the marriage bed").[7] Some myths speak of a coupling with Zeus (probably reflecting the historical assimilation of the mother goddess to the sky god of the patriarchal invaders); this resulted in a son Iakchos and her daughter Kore-Persephone. But she also had a Titan lover named Iasion and this relationship was described as a joyous, lusty one out of which was born the child of plenty, Plutous.

The emphasis, I think, is on *choosing* a lover instead of being overpowered and raped. Demeter is positive toward the Masculine and toward sex when she chooses her lover. (And despite the repeated commentaries that see Hades as a positive lover for Persephone, no authentic version of the myth that I have seen shows Kore as willing to go with him or wanting this relationship.)

At the same time, the Masculine as god or mortal is in the background in the Demeter myths, effaced instead of prominent. But Demeter is never defined by her connection with a male—whether as wife, lover, or mother (even though she has two sons and both are mentioned in her mythology: Plutous appears in the Homeric hymn to Demeter as bringing blessings to those whom the goddesses love; Iakchos appears beneath Baubo's skirts and leads the Mystery procession).

Demeter also transforms certain aspects of the Masculine in the myth, particularly the male as warrior in the figure of Triptolemus (see plate 1). But her primary relationship is with the archetypal Feminine and her daughter.

In the myths and fragments still available to us, it is her mother face that is most evident and emphasized. This mothering is twofold; she is the mother of the grain and the mother of a daughter. As Mother, Demeter was differentiated out of an older vision of the Mother Goddess, the Earth Mother Gaia.[8] Although rooted in Gaia and related to all fruitfulness, Demeter was also more refined and specific than the earlier image. As goddess of agriculture, she was related especially to the fruitfulness of the cultivated field and the harvest. Her Roman name, Ceres, is the basis of our word "cereal" (see plate 2), and all cereal products (such as bread) and cereal spirits (e.g., the earliest form of Dionysos as beer god) were connected with her. Although intimately concerned with plant life and its fruits, she was less a goddess of raw nature than of what could be consciously planted and deliberately grown, tended, and harvested, both for food and for spiritual offerings.

Demeter's special gifts to humanity were the gifts of grain and the art of agriculture (the power and numinosity of such gifts were recently driven home to me when I discovered that even in modern Greece, only 10 percent of the land is arable). With reference to these gifts, it was said that Demeter was the "bringer of civilization" to the Greeks. She brought to human life not only the bounty of Nature, the fruitfulness of Nature as Mother, but also a generous instruction so that Nature could be partially contained and controlled, civilized for the benefit of humankind. She is not the Mother in some natural, generic sense (e.g, not "natural abundance"); rather she is the one who teaches mortals how to plant for themselves.

Demeter teaches human beings a new kind of relationship to Nature, that is, a partnership in which people can participate in Nature by sowing the seeds and tending and harvesting the plants. Thus people can learn to feed themselves as well as be fed by her and in so doing, discover a different relationship to the Mother as well as to natural life. In spite of the way she has often been seen in psychological commentary, Demeter does not stand primarily for the binding aspect of the elementary Mother (in Erich Neumann's terms) who holds everything fast; in her very image, she embodies transformation.[9]

Humanly embodied, this aspect of Demeter is reflected in the mother who teaches beyond dependence, who encourages self-sufficiency by supporting the child's extension into the world and teaching the child how to feed itself. She is the fullness of the mother, developed beyond unconscious self-serving into the mother who not only nourishes and punishes by withholding nourishment but who also teaches the child how to transform the seed life (e.g., a talent, an interest, the beginning of a relationship, the first stage of a project) into self-nourishment. (She may be especially manifest as the positive mother of adolescence who teaches skills that will take the child away from her into the broader world and who encourages independence.)

Within us, Demeter as mother of the grain is a feminine principle—an energy or being—that brings the bounty of Nature to us and teaches us how to tame it into life we can grow for ourselves (psychologically, for example, it might be the Demeter in us that can recognize in newly felt rage the seeds of a genuine but undeveloped self-assertion and stand behind the psychological work needed to be done to civilize and channel its rawness into an ego quality that will add to the growth of a fuller and more expressive personality). Demeter teaches us how to work with what is given but also how to go beyond it, to develop and refine and weed it so that the most nourishing life is what is protected. As such, she is the opposite of self-destructiveness; we might indeed see her as self-constructive. Demeter in this aspect is the goddess of the conscious and intentional planting, nurturing, and harvesting of our lives. A Demeterian ego would be characterized by the recognition of what is inherent or "in one's nature" and the capacity to consciously cultivate it.

This participation with Nature, however, does not mean dominion (as in the Adam and Eve story) or conquering or overpowering Nature; it means "learning from and working with." Control in this process is at best only partial; cultivated life is still subject to blight, insects, and the vicissitudes of the weather. So too within ourselves, our ego life is neither the center nor the whole of the fuller personality and is subject to attack from unconscious complexes, emotions, woundings from others, and the vicissitudes of both the inner and outer environments. Our best intentions; our most passionately held determinations; our most careful tendings of our projects, relationships, or inner lives sometimes go awry, disrupted by unexpected storms or droughts. And all of us suffer sometimes from the loss of a harvest.

Death and blight in this picture are inevitable; they too are part of the Demeterian domain of the cultivated field. Taken in her fullness, Demeter stands for life and its development and process, but this process includes death as part of its cycle, a death that does not stand apart from life like Hades but is integral to its cycle and rhythm. Because the Crone face of Demeter is effaced in the myths of her that are most familiar to us, this relationship with natural death is not apparent until the end of the myth, when the full meaning of its process and drama has been revealed.

Demeter is also the mother of a daughter (see plate 3). This face of the goddess is perhaps closest to a human dimension; it invites us to view her not just impersonally as the mother of the grain but also through a personal love relationship. As mother of a daughter, Demeter is characterized by passionate love: a positive bond and a capacity for profound empathy with her daughter; rage, depression, and refusal to accept or or be reconciled to the sudden loss of her daughter; and active, effective protest that leads ultimately to transformation and return of her daughter from the claim of death. Some psychological life themes or dream motifs connected with this aspect of Demeter include positive mother-daughter bonds and their disruption by a masculine figure (or animus); kidnapping and rape motifs; severe depression over aging or damage to the inner (or outer) child; and hunger and starvation as punitive or sacrificial acts.[10] These themes and motifs may be played out between people or appear in an inner psychological process.

When Demeter is experienced as qualities that are either found in or attributed to another woman with whom we have a relationship, that woman will appear to be not only a positive mother figure but a source and matrix for our developing feminine selves. Demeter is experienced as passionate, protective, and possessive in a positive sense. She is embodied in another as the intention to nourish whatever is sprout life—beginnings—to maturity. The Demeter aspect of a woman is unambivalently for life; she may fear separation and death, disembodiment and abstraction, and all other psychological experiences connected with "descent." She may see all of these as an end and fail to consider that they might be part of a transformative process, one stage only in a larger process of growth and change. But the myth suggests that such failure to comprehend is a forgetting rather than a not knowing: the Demeter woman has within herself, at least unconsciously, the knowledge that life can be brought back from death, that life and death are interconnected, but she has become separated from that knowing—and from her own power to bring back that reconnection.

What is also striking about Demeter as the mother of a daughter is that she is never impersonal in her relationship to her daughter; her passion is for her *particular* child who is *not* replaceable (unlike the daughters of the biblical Job, for example, who when wiped out by God in Job's test of faith are simply replaced by other daughters—as if that makes everything right again. I have often wondered why Job seemed to accept this and stopped his grieving). This passion for the particularity and irreplaceability of the individual child appears commonly in positive maternal dynamics, as it did in the determination of Kubler-Ross's mother to save all three of her daughters.

I vividly remember some of my own early experiences of this level of passion. This sense of irreplaceability was ferocious in me when I was carrying my first child and threatened with the possibility of an early miscarriage. It was only during the miscarriage threat that I learned that a particular form of severe retardation in our extended family history might be hereditary. At first I was filled with terror and inadequacy—I knew that early miscarriages sometimes indicated a defective fetus. What if this were the case with the fetus I was carrying? What if the baby was born severely retarded? Would I, who knew next to nothing about babies to begin with, be able to cope with, love, and adequately care for such a child? At first I was only afraid. But then my fears gave way to a passionate feeling of wanting this particular child, this baby I was carrying, the one I felt moving around inside of me. In spite of my fears, I wanted this particular child no matter what. My feeling was fierce and irrational—it went beyond what I knew of my own limitations or the stress it would mean to bear and raise a severely limited child. My feeling just *was*, particular and fierce, and it didn't abate when my son was born normal; it surrounds my experience of mothering.

I feel it now, like Kollwitz, when I think of this same child, now grown, being inducted into a government-waged war. Here too, I am fierce and irrational and unambivalent. This child cannot be replaced! This particular child with his particular history and habits, his maddening and endearing qualities; this child whose feet I remember pressing against me in the womb, whose first day of kindergarten is vividly etched forever in my mind; this child who turned the entire house into a road-map system, who *thanked* his stepmother for caring for him when he was sick; this child who glued himself to the phone for late-night talks as a teenager, who reveled in his first experience of "college" at a New York City art institute the summer before his senior year of high school and triumphantly reported that navigating the subway system was "a piece of cake"—this child whom I have watched grow into a fine and sensitive young man is a totally unique combination which will never exist again in the same form and can never be replaced. And when I think of supporting a dictum to send him off to war to kill or be killed, I become irrational, outraged, possessive. There is no reasoning with this: my feeling is as ferocious as the forces that want to claim him, that expect me to agree and be reconciled. Instead, I become Demeter, grieving, raging, and issuing a battle cry of my own: *never* will you have my son!

This kind of passion for the value of life has roots in my personal history; on this level, I suspect it is an inner compensation to the indifference with which the potential death of a loved one was treated in my childhood (my parents often suggested that my grandmother might die at any moment—which filled me with terror and a terrible sense of responsibility—then went off to work and left me alone with her as if this was nothing to be concerned about). At the same time, the depth, intensity, and irrationality of my adult passion around my children when I think their lives are potentially threatened suggest an archetypal grounding. This passion feels at times beyond my ego control and can possess me. Not only does it feel bigger than me, it also opens me out into a greater and more communal vision, becoming in my antiwar sentiments a passion for the lives of all young men and women, a passion and even a compulsion to preserve life itself.

Jung suggested that every archetype has a "foot" in instinct and a "head" in Spirit—that is, every archetypal force extends us downward into our "animal" natures and upward into our most sublime visions of what is beyond and greater than human, Divinity.[11] In my own example of Demeterian passion outlined above, the foot of the archetypal dimension of this passion would lie in the basic instinct of any maternal animal to protect and preserve the life of her young and thereby ensure the continuity of the species. The head of my passion would most likely be found in a god-image or god-story; in this case, I see it most vividly in Demeter's refusal to relinquish her child to the splitting-off forces of death.

As literal mother, I am not always objective enough to differentiate my passionate feelings and consider the archetypal context to which they belong, nor (as my children might tell you) can I always meet the challenge to modulate such feeling through my ego and tame it into less possessed proportions so that it is more tuned to and easier to bear in relationship. But as therapist, where my training has made it possible more often to observe as well as participate, I can sometimes manage this challenge and then I get a glimpse, at least at moments, of the way a whole mythological story may embrace and infuse the dynamics of therapist and client. Here too I have come to know Demeter in myself or at least to catch glimpses of her and her meaning as she comes through me in response to another.

I clearly remember the first time I experienced this level of passion with a client. It was relatively early in my practice, and I was listening to a young woman describe a childhood of unspeakable emotional and physical abuse at the hands of her father. The more I heard about this man, the more my feelings were roused, feelings of rage so intense and so deep that I felt myself nearly undone by them. "Therapeutic distance" (as I conceived of it then) went out the window early with this woman; I was incensed at this man, incensed at the damage he had done to his daughter, and even more incensed that he continued to titillate and harass her from time to time in her adulthood. I struggled to modulate my rage, to consider the father's story as I had been taught then to do, to adapt my feelings to what my client was able to take in, but something deep had come into play. Whether or not I tried to be objective, even as objective as my client who could take her father's mental illness better into account than I, I could not contain my rage. And though I sensed that something bigger was present in my rage, that now there was a third factor present in the therapy in addition to the client and myself (i.e., I felt the presence of the archetype as it often comes through to me), I was nonetheless upset and chagrined. Since this level of rage came up almost immediately after the therapy began, which was especially unusual for me, I was even more unnerved.

But then I began to be aware of the impact of my rage upon my client, of the fact that a first-time bond was being forged because of my anger. At first my rage frightened her and I struggled to pace it with where she was and what she could take in, but increasingly she began to let me have it and to take in the fierce protectiveness and outrage at violence that it mirrored. Eventually she was able to tell me that for the very first time in her life she felt safe—she, who was as terrified of negative feeling and anger as I was conditioned to be from my own childhood history, learned that rage could be fiercely maternal, nurturant, guarding, in the service of life and in opposition to what would threaten or kill off young and vital growing. Later, as I became better grounded in the process of this particular therapy, I was able to differentiate the layers of my reaction from a more conventional clinical perspective, to discern transference, countertransference, and projective identification (the client's unconscious evocation of feelings in the therapist that are actually part of the client but unacceptable to her ego and thus still unconscious), but the archetypal dimension continued to be present and predominant. In the particulars of this woman's story, in the nature of our bond as it grew deeply between us, from unconscious material, and even in the way we worked, the myth of Demeter and Persephone began to unfold and I came to recognize it. I learned a great deal from this process about the healing impact of Demeterian rage and what it is like to feel, not only personally but archetypally, the preciousness of the daughter and the outrage at violence done to her.

Men and women alike need this feeling experience in our culture. This passion, this particularization, stands diametrically opposed to the leveling-down effect so prominent in patriarchy, the reduction to numbers and abstractions (aptly reflected in the military expression "body count"), the depersonalization of life that we encounter daily via the patriarchal collective. We all need to experience what it means to be the recipient of such particularized care and protection. Many of us did not experience this aspect of the archetype coming through our personal mothers; it is left to the Goddess or to other human beings (or sometimes, even animals) to convey and mediate this sense of being passionately valued for who we are, of being individually irreplaceable.[12] Ultimately, the experience of this kind of love from another can be internalized and become the ground-note not only of a healthy self-love but of a passionate drive to individuate—to actualize as fully as possible one's own, authentic, individual self.

To experience this aspect of Demeter in one's own mother or a mothering figure is not simply to feel cherished as unique and irreplaceable. In full form, this kind of motherly concern will not only care for the hurts and damage done to the child, but will passionately oppose them and actively protest (this is not the mother—or therapist—who blames her child or client for rape or incest experiences, for example). It means experiencing a mother who will fight tooth and nail to undo lasting damage to the child's life or separations from its source of nourishment and well-being, a mother who will do whatever it takes to oppose what symbolically or literally is raping the child. I think as I write of Dr. Elizabeth Morgan, a Washington, D.C., plastic surgeon, who was sent to prison several years ago for refusing to disclose the whereabouts of her six-year-old daughter, Hilary, after the child conveyed that she had repeatedly been molested by her father. When a judge refused to believe Morgan's evidence on this matter or to allow the child's own testimony, which had instigated the mother's claims, and instead ordered unsupervised visits with the child's father to continue, this mother put her daughter into hiding to protect her. Because of her defiance of the authorities, Elizabeth Morgan was initially sentenced to prison indefinitely.[13]

This refusal to serve the authorities that fail to protect the seed life from unnatural harm and danger (like Zeus, who allows his brother Hades to abduct and rape Persephone) is the essence of Demeterian behavior. Ultimately, it reflects her power to hold accountable and transform even the distortion of "father-right" reflected in both the myth and in this real-life contemporary drama. And the anger that underlies such determination to resist this "authority" is part of another side of Demeter, the aspect that is most effaced in the Homeric

70

hymn but that the Greeks recognized nevertheless in the names they gave her as Crone: Demeter Chthonia, Demeter Erinys, Demeter the Black.

Demeter Chthonia is a Crone aspect not connected with the Goddess's anger; she is simply the underworld form of Demeter (just as Zeus Chthonious referred to the underworld Zeus, or Hades). Like Persephone, she is sovereign over the realm of the dead, and the dead are called by her name, "Demeteroi" or "Demeter's people." A summer festival in honor of Chthonia involved the sacrifice of a full-grown cow that offered itself voluntarily to the Goddess.[14] Three old women immolated the cow and no one else, particularly men, was allowed to witness the burning. The age of the women priestesses for this rite and the exclusion of men suggest a prepatriarchal origin to this ritual and to the aspect of the Goddess it honored.

By the time of the Homeric hymns, however, the Crone aspect of Demeter appears to have been largely effaced, appearing (as noted in chapter 2) only in Demeter's disguise as an old woman when she goes to Eleusis. The Crone appears again in Demeter's magical ritual of holding the child Demophoon in the fire to make him immortal. The chthonic Demeter no longer rules the underworld as Home; her place has been usurped, apparently, by the patriarchal underside of Zeus. In a very real way, both in Demeter's transformation and "coming to know" through her own initiation (reclaiming and manifesting her transformative powers over death) and in her daughter's transformation from Kore to Persephone, the myth of Demeter and Persephone involves the reintegration of this essential third person of the Goddess. But before this takes place, it is foreshadowed in her lapses into rage and punitive action.

Demeter is not essentially an angry or punitive goddess. She becomes so only when what is sacred to her is dishonored or when her daughter or she is violated. The most vivid tale of Demeter's capacity to punish appearing outside of the Persephone myth is recounted in Ovid's *Metamorphoses* in the story of Erysichthon. Erysichthon was an arrogant man who refused to make offerings to any of the gods and regarded them with scorn. One day he determined to cut down a mighty oak tree that stood in a grove that was sacred to Demeter. When his servants hesitated to carry out his orders to cut down the tree, Erysichthon swore that even if the tree were the goddess herself, he would chop it down. When one of his men tried to stop him, he

71

became so enraged that he swung his ax at him and cut off the man's head. Then he turned on the tree and struck the first blow. Blood gushed forth from the tree. The nymph who lived in the tree warned him with her dying words that he would be punished for what he was about to do, but he continued chopping until the tree could be pulled down and the nymph was dead.

All of her sister nymphs begged Demeter to punish this defilement of her grove. She, the essentially nourishing goddess, decided to curse this man with perpetual hunger. Summoning a mountain spirit to go and meet with the spirit of Hunger (she could not go because she and Hunger are inimical to each other), the goddess implored her to seek out Hunger's barren land and "bid [her] bury herself in the wicked stomach of this impious wretch; tell her to fight and overcome my powers of nourishment and to let no amount of food defeat her."[15]

Hunger, a skeletal, hideous creature (reminiscent of one form of the Indian Death goddess Kali who appears as a skeletal hag), received the goddess's orders and though always opposed to Demeter's activities, carried them out, insinuating herself into Erysichthon's body as he slept. He awoke overwhelmed with hunger and immediately ordered a great feast, but from then on, no matter how much he ate, he grew only more ravenous. Soon he had eaten his parents out of house and home, exhausting their wealth, and turned to selling his young daughter into slavery in exchange for more food. Finally, growing ever more desperate, he began to devour himself.[16]

This gruesome story reveals quite a different side to Demeter, who is most often described as gentle and benevolent. The motifs of hunger and death by starvation as punishments in the story of Erysichthon are echoed in the Persephone myth. When leaving Olympus has no effect and her grief, rage, and attempts to find her daughter are met with refusal and attempts to placate her, Demeter becomes directly punitive; she withdraws her gift of grain. But she is not only punitive or throwing a petulant fit. Demeter refuses to support a system that expects her to provide her gifts while simultaneously raping what is bonded and sacred to her— her daughter. Zeus and his brothers' expectations of Demeter are remarkable and typically patriarchal. She is supposed not only to go on providing what she has always provided, the food that supports the Olympian system and the mortals who live under it, but she is also not supposed to notice or protest her daughter's rape. She is supposed to collude and even be glad this has happened, believe the euphemisms, and go on feeding. But her answer, her rage, is a resounding refusal of these outrageous expectations: she refuses to support without being supported, to honor what deprives and violates her.

She stands against the gods and is willing to deprive in return: to withdraw, to starve out, even to kill. She is willing to kill even the innocent, if necessary. All her tender, nurturant, mothering powers are withdrawn. She will feed no one, will turn the cold eye of death on everyone, rather than go on nurturing and giving when there has been such profound violation. She stands for the eye that can see through the patriarchal tricks that pretend riches when there is really rape and greed. She is the ear that can hear and then cut through euphemistic doublespeak and refuse to buy it. And she makes her being, ultimately, a single, powerful statement: no one eats, no one gets fed by me, no one receives my generous, civilizing gifts until what belongs to me, what is precious and sacred and part of my very being, is returned. She claims what is her own no matter what the price will be for others.

Yet—she is not quite this singular, this ferocious. Even grieving and raging, she tends the newborn Demophoon, nurses him with her own transcendent milk, the ambrosia of the gods—as if she cannot quite give up or deny altogether her gifts, her nurturance.

Ravenous hunger is her antithesis, but when she herself has been denied, when she is hungry for the sight of, the touch of, the being of her daughter, she will embrace even her antithesis to reclaim what belongs to her. If this is "mother-right," it is a far cry from its patriarchal equivalent—the lust of Hades—for it claims life, not death; seeks to nurture, not to desubstantiate; attempts to undo only what tries to stand outside the order of her world and its rhythms. Demeter is generous, but she is not self-sacrificing. She gives out of a fullness of herself and withdraws and even attacks if that fullness is violated. She is not "unconditional." As rape fighter, Demeter is a moral response that refuses to collude or adapt, refuses to go on as usual and give in to the cutting down, and ultimately refuses to extend her gifts unless she is respected and honored—and complete in herself. The implications of this kind of power for women and others in our culture who oppose patriarchal lust in any of its various forms of power over others are profound; so too in the smaller arenas of the family and of psychotherapy.

Demeter is punitive when her grove is defiled and fierce on behalf of her daughter, but she becomes even fiercer when the act of rape is redoubled and she herself is raped. When she is ravished by the third of the patriarchal brothers, the sea god Poseidon, while she is searching for her daughter, she becomes even more terrible and primitive, shedding her essential maternity and tapping into a more ancient manifestation of the Goddess as deity of vengeance and death.[17] (Or perhaps we could say that maternity itself transforms and becomes a window into the ability of the deeper powers of the Death goddess to take in violation and transform it into rebirth.)

When raped by Poseidon, Demeter was called by two names: Demeter Melaina (i.e., Demeter the Black) and Demeter Erinys. Demeter Melaina is a simple epithet; the blackness refers to the color of the mourning clothes she wears to represent the loss of her daughter to the Lord of Death. Demeter Erinys is a more complex and more powerful vision, personifying her feeling response to this latest of outrages.

Erinyes is an early Greek word for the state of "being in a rage," but *erinyes* is not only an emotional experience; it is also a being or beings. [18] Conceptualized variously by the Greeks at different times in their history, the Erinyes were feminine creatures who lived in the underworld and from there sought vengeance. One vision of the Erinyes pictured them as human ghosts, but not all ghosts were Erinyes; the Erinyes were those ghosts who were angry because their lives as human beings had ended in being murdered. Relentlessly these spirits would hound the still-living murderer, thereby inducing in the murderer the same state of panic and terror that they had experienced at the moment of being killed. This relentless pursuit could drive the murderer into madness or illness.[19]

At other times, the Erinyes were held to be avenging spirits who put forth a blood curse in response to crimes within a family, particularly matricide or dishonor to a mother. Jane Harrison, in her discussion of these spirits in her book *Prolegomena to a Study of Greek Religion*, describes them as "goddesses of Cursing" or "personified Curses that attend the shedding of kindred blood."[20]

All of this gives us deeper insight into the nature and meaning of rape in the Demeter myth, particularly when the mother herself is raped. The experience of rape is equivalent to death in this context (as it is also in the more obvious imagery of Demeter's daughter being taken by the Lord of Death); more specifically, it is equivalent to being murdered. The vehicle of unchecked patriarchal lust and assertion of unrelational power over the Feminine, it is also a gross dishonor to the mother, against the natural order (which patriarchy repeatedly seeks to overcome and transcend in its peculiar vision of Spirit as something apart from and against Nature), and evokes from the most primordial layer of the Feminine it violates—the Crone—the darkest revenge: the blood curse.

Further elaboration of the nature of this blood curse makes even more visible its link with the Crone and her power; it also sheds light on the Crone in the background of Demeterian punishment. The curse that's called forth from this deep and most primitive layer of the Goddess involves an issue of feminine blood, a blood that can terrorize and kill. In the story of Orestes in Greek literature, for example, the Erinyes relentlessly pursue him after he has killed Clytemnestra, his mother; at one point, these avengers threaten "to let fall a drop of their own hearts' blood which would bring barrenness upon the soil, blight upon the crops, and destroy all the offspring of Athens."[21] (So too Demeter expresses her ongoing rage by withdrawing her gifts from the land, making everything barren, and threatening death by starvation.)

Commenting on this blood curse in the Orestes story, Graves suggests that "hearts' blood" in this context may be a euphemism for menstrual blood, which we know from other sources was also considered to be a lethal blood that could kill a man by turning him to stone.[22] Feminine blood that can petrify and kill is not only menstrual blood, however. In the Medusa legends, it issues forth from Medusa's head; a drop from the left side was said to be able to raise the dead while a drop from the right side could kill.[23] Here the fullness of the Crone's power is displayed, her capacity to bring about rebirth from the death experience as well as her capacity to kill.

The curse of the Crone who uses her blood to avenge the rape of her younger self is a theme emerging from the deepest layer of the archetypal Feminine. While I was researching the mythological background behind the image of Demeter Erinys, a local storyteller brought to my attention a similar configuration in an Eskimo ghost story whose graphic and gruesome simplicity helped me further understand this archetypal dynamic. In the Alaskan tale, several boys in early puberty leave their parents' homes to live together in a special igloo; here, under the tutelage of the men in the village, they will be instructed in the skills and knowledge needed to initiate them into manhood. This works well as long as the men are in the village and can oversee their activities, but when the adults are away for a long time hunting, a boy described as a "very bad fellow" assumes the leadership. Under his influence, the band of boys catch and abuse a little girl who afterward runs screaming to her grandmother with whom she lives (the storyteller assumed the abuse was sexual abuse). Only a younger boy who lives with the others because his parents are dead does not participate.

The grandmother is enraged when she hears what has happened to her granddaughter and determines to take action against these young men. She paints her face in a hideous manner, but when she asks the little girl if that will scare the boys, the child says no; it will only make them laugh. Then the grandmother rubs ashes and soot on her hair and her face; still the child insists this is not enough to scare the boys. After similar further futile attempts to make herself an object of terror, the old woman finally goes off in a corner, strips off her clothes, and slashes her body in various places. Dripping with blood, still covered with soot, she crawls on her hands and knees toward her grandchild. The child gives a scream of terror and agrees that now the old woman will frighten the boys who have abused her.

Just after twilight, the grandmother approaches the igloo where the boys are singing and dancing. The younger one who has not participated in the girl's abuse sees her coming and tries to warn the others that some terrible ghostly creature is approaching, but the older boys only tease him for being afraid of the dark. Looking again, the young boy comes face to face with the old woman, whose demeanor is so grotesque that he does not recognize her as a human being. Terror-struck, he bites one of his fingers until it begins to swell and sticks it in a hole high above the floor, thereby suspending himself away from the others just as the "terrible, bloody thing" creeps into the igloo.

At the sight of what appears to be a blood-covered ghost, the older boys are stricken dumb and nearly senseless. The ghost crawls around on the floor, circling the room again and again. Mesmerized and completely unable to resist, the boys fall on their knees one by one behind the old woman and follow her out the door over the tundra and up the side of the mountain. Only the youngest, still stuck in the hole in the wall above them, is able to resist; only he remains alive to tell the tale to the men when they return from the hunt.

Following the trail, the men come upon the boys' bodies, all of them frozen; they have been led to their deaths by the bloody old grandmother. They are never buried; each turns to stone and there they lie still on the side of the mountain.[24]

In this tale, the abuse of the young girl (the Kore figure) is attributed to an aberration in the development of young masculinity that is just beginning to solidify its identity; the abuse is presented here as a consequence of young masculinity gone awry when not held in check by its more mature mentors rather than fully developed patriarchal power-over. The tenor of the original narrative implies that the adult men also see the abuse as wrong, since it is presented as a failure of the mentoring system, though they characterize it in the story by the softer word "mischief." As in the myth of Demeter, the Crone's response bears no euphemistic softening; she sees the abuse as an outrage and responds with ferocious punishment. Like her Greek counterpart, she is also unambivalent. Unlike Demeter, who is a fuller and more richly etched mythological figure (embodying many qualities of the Goddess, including the more fertile aspects of the Crone), the grandmother in this Eskimo tale is more singularly drawn. She embodies in essence one side of the Crone: she judges, punishes, petrifies, and—ultimately—kills.

It is important to remember that this kind of judgment and ferocity of response comes from a primitive, profound archetypal level. It is not civilized or tamed; it appears to a reflective, well-developed consciousness the way the blood-covered grandmother appears to the boy who has not taken part in the abuse: as something grotesque and inhuman. When anything from this raw, archetypal layer invades and infuses our human consciousness, it is feared as a frightening "possession"—and it can be exactly that unless it is met by a well-developed ego that can take a conscious stand toward it.

When such raw content as the Crone's murderousness appears in our dreams or at the core of an intense emotional state, it is imperative that it be met by a strong human ego that is differentiated enough to recognize that this is something bigger than ordinary emotion, something whose presence is to be carefully considered. It then requires human courage, courage not to just get rid of it or to literally act it out but to receive this content from the deep unconscious and attempt to discern its meaning.

Part of the Crone's power is to see clearly through euphemism, to judge, to protest, and if necessary, to kill. In Demeterian form, this is done on behalf of the seed life that has been violated, whether within Demeter or within the person of her daughter. But focused rage that protests and kills is not the full range or meaning of the power of the Crone. She also has the power to transform the death experience whether she herself has brought it about or whether it has come about through the death-rape perpetrated by the patriarchal abuser.

The grandmother in the Eskimo folktale exemplifies only the first half of the Crone's power: to avenge what has been violated by killing. It is only in Demeter and even more in her daughter Persephone that we see the fullness of the Crone become manifest, moving through and past the death experience, recycling and transforming it into rebirth (as we will see below in the full story of Demeter's rape by Poseidon). Even the most terrible side of Demeter, the rage-filled Demeter Erinys, brings about a rebirth of what has been violated, i.e, gives birth to the seed life again, for out of the death-rape experience the Goddess Avenger gives birth to a daughter. The Mother-turned-Crone becomes also the Crone-become-Mother; through her, the Maiden ravished by Death becomes the Maiden reborn.

Carl Kerényi, discussing Demeter Erinys in his provocative essay on the Kore, points out this rebirth of the Maiden through the Crone and gives several mythological examples. [25] In the story of Nemesis (another Kore figure originally, according to Kerényi), the goddess is pursued by Zeus, shape-shifts into various animals to try to avoid him, and at last is raped as a goose by the god in swan form. Overcome by his violence, she becomes Nemesis, "the eternal avenger," but out of this rape comes a new Kore, a daughter named Helen.

There is a similar outcome in the story of Poseidon's rape of Demeter. In this story too, the goddess attempts to elude her pursuer by changing into various animals until she is finally caught in the shape of a mare by Poseidon posing as stallion. Her form as Avenger—Demeter Melaina/Erinys—was pictured as having the head of a horse with snakes and other animals growing out of it. But precisely in this form, she is also creative; she bore a horse-son named Areion and a Kore called Despoina, the "Mistress" or "she who is not to be named"—a ritual name of Persephone.

Here the entire Persephone drama takes place in the mother. Keré-nyi writes, "The goddess becomes a mother, rages and grieves over the Kore who was ravished *in her own being,* the Kore she immediately recovers, and in whom she gives birth to *herself* again. The idea of the original Mother-Daughter goddess [and, we might add, also the Crone], at root a single entity, is at the same time the idea of *rebirth.*"[26] Again a link between Demeter Erinys and the killer Medusa appears in the snakey coif they share, but even Medusa in one of her stories emerges as killer-turned-rebirther. Like Demeter, Medusa was also the bride of Poseidon and gave birth to a horse named Pegasus and a son, Chrysaor, whose name is also a name of Demeter. To seal her connection with this particular symbolic complex, in some tales Medusa's murderer Perseus was linked with or identified as Hades.

These variant tales of rape-marriage-murder stand outside the drama of Eleusis yet condense it succinctly. In their essence, as Keré-nyi again puts it, "the primordial god and goddess undergo endless transformations before they come together; the maiden dies, and in her place there appears an angry goddess, a mother, who bears the Primordial Maiden—*herself*—again in her daughter."[27] At Eleusis, the mother and daughter are separated out from each other—yet in variants, the mother empathically goes through the same trauma as her daughter. In these variant tales, the mother goes through it all; the entire myth is her own experience, for she carries her daughter within her. But even at Eleusis, it is her experience that is critical, for it is through the mother's experience that the initiates move into the Mysteries.

Clarity that sees past euphemism to the truth of patriarchal usurpation and abuse of the seed life; a refusal to adapt or collude with the patriarchal death god or his brothers; the attempt to bring about justice through determined protest and confrontation and stop the misuse of power; murderous rage when justice is thwarted; a willingness to kill—and the capacity to bring forth new life out of the death experience: these are the powers and fullness of Demeter as Mother and Crone. To tap into this aspect of the Goddess, to find her as rape fighter, is an extremely profound, powerful, and complex experience. For anyone who has suffered from or empathized with those who have suffered the ravages stemming from the abuse of patriarchy's power (whether in the most personal realm as in childhood abuse, rape, battering, or other forms of personal abuse or in the more collective realm of arrogant, unrelational claims to power over other peoples, animals, or even the earth itself), this archetypal pattern—the goddess Demeter—offers a veritable road map for transformation and healing.

To draw from her energies, take on her values for life, submit to her care, hold her as an image of Higher Power, and commit one's life to an *imitatio Dei* is to set forth on a lifelong path, the Mystery path into hope beyond the death experience. As spiritual imperative, the path of Demeter is as compelling today as it was to the ancients— perhaps even more so, since we have lived even longer with the ravages of the shadow of patriarchy and succumbed even more deeply to its dissembling and its power. In our time, this path can also form the archetypal backdrop for some experiences of deep therapeutic process, particularly relevant to those who are trying to get past experiences of patriarchal abuse (either personal or cultural). If the therapy allows for and understands a spiritual dimension, recognizes the mythic level when the archetype appears, and has reverence for the transpersonal power embodied by the archetype, then both therapist and client may be able to see their work together, the psychic field that they share, and their various responses to the client's experience of suffering as windows into a deeper and older story—a story that still opens into a path of renewal.

Demeter's story and the path it still opens offer directives that are as sound psychologically as they are spiritually. These directives can guide the therapeutic process of recovery. Psychologically, they include the following imperative tasks:

1. To see past euphemistic disguises and rationalizations (e.g., "She asked to be raped; I only gave her what she wanted"; these men were killed by "friendly fire") to the reality of power abuse and to place the responsibility where it belongs, that is, to get past denial.

2. To empathize with the life that has been cut down and ravaged, the younger self, the vital spirit. This means not colluding with the abuser by blaming the victim or abusing oneself. (This pathwork is also and perhaps especially applicable to internalized abuse dynamics—the introjected abuser [the abuser within] must also be seen through and dealt with as much as the abuser out there. This is part of the self-constructiveness of the goddess Demeter who never blames or turns against what has been ravaged in either herself or her daughter.)

3. To uncover and learn to value even the most frightening dimen-

sions of one's rage—not to literally act out its murderousness but to find symbolic forms of killing off what continues to ravage or rape; this may be done by withholding one's gifts and attention that had previously served the abusive system or person, by holding accountable and confronting (including, in our times, mass protest and legal actions against individuals and institutions), or by total withdrawal and self-protection.

4. To bear the depression and hopelessness that inevitably accompany experiences of being overpowered and violated and seek to transform them into the powers to name and confront or withdraw.

5. And, finally, to gestate the experience instead of attempting to magically undo it or deny its effects, that is, to take it in when doing so cannot be avoided but in the taking in, to draw to it creative life energies so that out of this experience and its suffering come renewal and rebirth.

All of these endeavors are psycho/spiritual tasks. All of them are profoundly grounded in the goddess Demeter: her passion for life and her powers to stand against and transform what threatens the life she holds so dear. The final task in this list of imperatives—the difficult task of gestative transformation—also belongs to her daughter, the Mystery goddess to whom we now turn.

Suzanne Benton, *Persephone*, 1985.

ꙮ 4 ꙮ

Gestative Transformation:

The Goddess Kore-Persephone

And I am her daughter, I
in whom seeds of death are planted
and will sprout.

—RIVER MALCOLM, *"Persephone"*[1]

IN HIS PROVOCATIVE ESSAY on the archetype of the primordial Maiden,
Carl Kerényi asserts that in the figures of the classical Greek gods
and goddesses, psychic forces are balanced in equal strength on a bor-
derline: the figure of Zeus, for example, balances might and right;
Dionysos, life and death; Apollo, the darkness of death with the
brightness of clarity.[2] Viewed through this lens as a balance of forces,
the goddess Kore-Persephone is "not . . . above all feminine connections with mother or husband but . . . she embodies these connections
as two forms of being, each carried to extremes and balanced against
each other. One of the forms (daughter with mother) appears as life,
the other (young girl with husband) as death."[3] In other words, Kore-
Persephone is Life's daughter and Death's bride, and these are the
forces she balances. Yet life and death are not the only poles she represents; given the differing religious origins of her mother and her husband, she also carries woman-in-matriarchy and woman-in-patriarchy
(and the darkest side of the latter, not its brilliance but its death-
dealing shadow).

Kore-Persephone is a dual image expressed both as progression from child to Queen of the Dead and as back-and-forth rhythm from upper- to underworld or even perhaps as simultaneity, living in both worlds. As progression, she is a movement from one state to another, beginning as Kore in life and becoming Persephone in death. But at the myth's end and beyond it, when rape is transformed into ritual, this goddess becomes a psychopomp, moving back and forth between two worlds or, as some authors have suggested, residing in both simultaneously.[4] Never only her husband's wife, by the end of the myth she is also no longer exclusively her mother's daughter. Rich and deep, she carries within herself and unites not only two worlds but two visions of the transpersonal Feminine—Maiden and death goddess—revealing their hidden connection and embodying their transformation dynamic.

She begins as the Maiden (see plate 4). Her name at this point, Kore, reveals little about her. It is virtually a generic name, meaning young girl or maiden (even in modern Greek, there are reflections of this; *koritse* means girl, while one word for daughter is still *kore*). Many goddesses were Kores or had Kore sides: Artemis, Athena, Hera. Kore's name alone does not distinguish Demeter's daughter. What makes her different from other maiden goddesses in ancient Greece, as Chris Downing points out, is that her relationship with her mother is prominent, whereas the mothers of other goddesses are effaced or barely mentioned, if at all.[5] Kore is also different from the other maiden goddesses because she is abducted. She alone undergoes a death experience that profoundly transforms her.

The Homeric hymn to Demeter tells us little more about the nature of Demeter's Kore, yet her behavior in this version of the myth provides insight into both her attitudes and her loyalties. In the beginning of the myth, she is out in a field, picking flowers with other maiden goddesses. The Homeric hymn gives no indication of her age, but she is most often assumed to be an adolescent or young girl (in Ovid's version of this myth, written considerably later than the Homeric hymn, she is presented as a very young child; in Greek art, she is depicted variously, ranging from young child to a woman nearly indistinguishable from her mother; an example of the latter can be found in plate 5). The hymn also does not specifically name Kore's companions, referring to them only as "the daughters of Oceanus." In variants, she is said to have been with Athena and Artemis. The presence of these goddesses, neither of whom were known to have taken male lovers, reinforces another frequent assumption about Demeter's daughter: that she was not only Maiden or Virgin as "one-in-herself" but also a physical virgin. (This assumption is made explicitly in later, historically more patriarchal versions of the myth but is not implied in Homer.) Thus by association with Athena and Artemis, both physically virgin, Persephone's experience with Hades also becomes her first sexual experience.

One component of Kore's behavior in the Homeric version of the myth is particularly important because it is consistently overridden in the patriarchally accented interpretations of this myth: Kore resists the abduction. She struggles, screams, and calls for help. Moreover, she continues to resist in the underworld, never accepting or inviting Hades' desires in any way. All ideas of Kore choosing or desiring the connection with Hades hinge on interpretation of the narcissus as phallic (in Ovid's version of the myth, the specific flower is never named; still other sources have suggested the flower may have been a poppy, sacred to her mother). [6] She does reach for the narcissus, the flower grown as a trick but also sacred to her mother, with joy and desire, but she consistently resists Hades and refuses to reconcile to him. Even after she is returned to the upperworld as Persephone and her downgoing to Hades becomes ritualized, she was said to prefer the company of Hecate to that of her husband. But while she is still in the underworld, she languishes, mourns for her mother, and refuses to eat, knowing the latter would commit her to Hades. Though more passive than her feisty, ferocious mother, she is unambivalent in her attitude; her loyalties and intentions are consistent.

Eating the pomegranate seeds is the pivotal, most fateful moment in Kore's experience, for it is this single act that commits her to Hades. Here too, it is not her chosen desire for Hades that propels her to take in his seed; she has maintained her fast in the underworld, taking in nothing voluntarily. She eats the pomegranate seeds either because she finally succumbs to hunger or because she is tricked into it. Thus, "consummation" is out of desperation or via trickery; Hades pretends to willingly let her return with Hermes to her mother, while plotting to force a commitment to him.

Forcing her to swallow his seeds is another violation of Kore as well as an attempt to sabotage her mother's power. From a patriarchal perspective, it is the moment of Hades' triumph over both goddesses and the pivotal point in the myth; here Kore, the child of Life, becomes Persephone, the bride of Death (see plate 6). But it is also a fateful moment for Hades. From a matriarchal perspective, this is also the point at which Hades submits his seeds, the "fruit" of his deadly kingdom, to the transformative powers of the goddess. Kore becomes Persephone, but in so becoming, she also reawakens to her ancient powers, not only paralleling but also deepening the journey of her upperworld mother.

The transformation to Persephone not only extends Kore forward into Hades' wife and queen of his kingdom but also extends her backward into a more ancient form of the Triple Goddess, into a prepatriarchal aspect that was never the victim of Death but its ruler and transformer. Hades' death power is made fertile through Persephone; she gestates its trauma. As Brimo, the raging one, the goddess of the high Mysteries to follow, Persephone also transforms and extends Hades. She transforms him out of his isolation and split-offness into the Mystery child who reconnects him to life while also bending him back to the son-of-the-Mother who serves life and the Feminine instead of opposing them. Like the goddess who becomes a bridge between worlds, the pomegranate is the perfect mediating symbol here. Although it was sacred to the goddess and, with its many seeds, an obvious symbol of her fertility, its blood-red color connected it to both life and death. In ritual use, it was the fruit that was present at both marriage and funeral celebrations.

The Maiden becomes Persephone, Queen of the Dead, yet even after this turning point, her attitude and loyalties are clear; she eagerly returns to her upperworld mother and the reunion is one of intense mutual joy (see plate 7). Further, we learn from fragments of myth outside the Homeric hymn that even committed to Hades as his wife, Persephone continued to stand against rape and violation. Though Hades no longer raped Persephone, whose annual return to the underworld became a voluntary, ritual event, he occasionally still fell into lust. Twice he went after the nymphs Leuce and Minthe. Both times Persephone intervened, protecting the nymphs by changing one into a tree, another into a plant.[7] Never again would her husband's lust result in forceful violation. Persephone has a power that Kore did not: she can prevent the rape from ever happening again and plant the innocent firmly in her mother's realm of vegetation.

Kore abducted appears to be a victim. She cannot prevent her own rape. She cannot get out of the underworld through her own power; it is her mother whose ragings and protests effect the return. She is not the active side of the Demeter-Persephone archetype. Yet her strengths are significant. She has tremendous staying power and keeps herself unambivalently focused on what is calling to her from above, the world she has come from and belongs to. She keeps the faith until help can arrive and steadfastly resists reconciling herself to Hades and his kingdom. She is true to herself and to what and whom she loves.

The mythic drama depicts at length how Kore *behaves*, thus lending some insight into how she reacts to abduction and what she is loyal to, but it doesn't really tell us much about who she *is*. To learn more about the nature and meaning of this goddess in herself, as her mother's daughter, and as archetypal presence in our own lives, we must look beyond the myth of her abduction. Only then can we understand who and what are being raped when she is carried away by Death and why Demeter is so distraught; only then can we also come to recognize and understand what it means when this archetypal drama reenacts itself in feminine and masculine psychology today.

Demeter's Kore is the Spring goddess, the Maiden, the young green wheat, but most essentially of all, she is her mother's daughter. As daughter, her meaning to her mother can be seen both relationally and intrapsychically; she is both outer daughter and inner aspect. As outer daughter, she is a separate goddess, the Divine Child of the archetypal Mother. As inner daughter, she is a part of Demeter, her younger self Chloe, the springtime of Demeter's own being. This dual meaning is important, for what happens to Kore can thus be seen as either happening to a significant other or happening to a part of oneself.

In his essay on the Divine Child archetype, Jung asserts that the Child is linked with both past and future, thus with girlhood and ongoingness for a mother. [8] In Demeter's case, Kore is also linked with greenness, verdancy, the surging of plant life in the spring. Connecting Demeter with her past, Kore extends her mother back into her own history, to (but also beyond) her younger self into her impersonal, pre-anthropomorphic form: the life force in plants. But through her trauma and transformation, Kore also extends Demeter forward (and, paradoxically, also backward again, retrieving a more ancient form of the Death goddess as well) into Melaina, the mourning one; Erinys the avenger; Persephone the transformer; Brimo the angry birth-giver; moving her past the death experience into a reintegration of the rag-

87

ing, death-defying, maiden-birthing Crone. Kore is Demeter's past, her vitality, and her future; small wonder the Mother is inconsolable when this is violated, split off from her, and appears irretrievably lost.

When this archetype makes its annunciation in human psychology, it can appear in many forms. Jung, reacting to the Freudian tendency of his time to reduce all images to personal psychology alone, was adamant in asserting that the Divine Child was not a memory of one's own personal childhood but rather "represents the preconscious, childhood aspect of the collective psyche."[9]

My own experience in working with feminine psychology, both my own and other women's, suggests more versatility and fluidity around the appearance of this archetype than Jung delineates. The Daughter as Divine Child can appear in a woman's psyche in many different ways: (a) pieces of girlhood memories or a vision of her girlhood self can become infused with Divine Child qualities, particularly the quality of vitality; (b) a woman's actual daughter may embody or carry through projection aspects of the Child; or (c) the "magical child" appears sometimes as an inner child in dreams, fantasy, or creative work but may also intermingle with these other forms. An aura of numinosity—the earmark of the archetype—often surrounds these experiences of the Child and she is felt to be special, enhancing, revitalizing, healing, and bigger than life. Her appearance has a strong emotional impact on the conscious self and is felt to extend it beyond its usual limits or render it more whole. As in pagan spirituality, however, these experiences are fluid; levels and content intersect and overlap; spiritual and mundane (literal, embodied) merge together, reflecting a spirit *in* matter that infuses ordinary life rather than being abstracted from or above it.

A recent dream of my own reflects some of this mixture of levels as well as the rich complexity within which the Divine Child may appear in the psyche. In the dream, I came upon a baby girl who had been abandoned by her mother. The baby's name was Anna. She was lying wrapped in wet bedclothes and needed changing. As I picked her up, I felt instinctively that she also needed to be burped, so I burped her. The baby was dark haired and dark eyed. She didn't make a sound, not even the smallest cry. It was clear in the dream that I was now to care for her and be her mother.

On the surface, this was a rather ordinary, personal-level dream; much of its content was well-known to me from past experience and inner work. The mother-abandoned daughter, the child who doesn't make a sound even in distress or physical discomfort, were well-known to me both as inner correlates and literal realities connected with my personal history. The dark-haired, dark-eyed baby girl was a signficant but familiar dream image that has come up for years and is deeply meaningful to me. In the midst of a painful divorce many years ago, I had begun to dream about having a third child. Unlike my actual children, both of whom are mixtures of their father's blond hair and blue eyes and my own dark ones, this child in my inner world looked only like me. I took her to be my inner child, the child who would be born of myself and my own inner work instead of my marriage. She also resembled the child I had been, my actual child self, who in the ensuing years would have to be refound, newly mothered by me. The third child also connected with an image that had come up in a drawing long before my divorce: the image of a baby connected with a ship's wheel, which I had associated with the lines of the old poem, "I am the master of my fate, I am the captain of my soul"[10] —an ego capacity that was also connected with Destiny or Fate.

What moved this current dream most clearly into the archetypal realm was my immediate, strongest, and most gripping association to the name Anna. I had no particular personal associations to this name, though it seemed to me to be somehow the most *basic* female name. Most vivid, however, was my memory of having seen, some months before the dream, a book whose title, *The Grandmother of Time*, referred to an ancient Roman goddess, Anna Perenna.[11] I didn't read the book then, nor did I seek out any further information about this goddess, but I was captivated by her name, and it stayed with me. Anna Perenna: the sound of it took me over and was extremely beautiful. I said it over and over to myself, like a mantra, its music going into my body, my being. This was my strongest and most immediate association to the name of this dream baby.

At this point, I looked up this Roman goddess to see if she somehow connected to the meaning of my dream; what I discovered moved the dream to a whole other level, and was incredibly relevant to the issues I was struggling with at the time. Anna Perenna was a Roman goddess, mother of the Aeons. She "stood at the change of the years, a two-headed Goddess of Time with two faces . . . looking forward and backward from her heavenly gate among the stars, where one celestial cycle merged into the next. So she stood for both Alpha and Omega, beginning and end. Under the name of Carmenta, she invented all the letters in between."[12] Like Nut in Egypt, she is the goddess of the entire life cycle, but she is also the goddess of cycle itself, of the changing of cycles, and of time. She appeared in various cultures, not only Rome. As Mother, she was goddess of wealth, treasure, and bounty. As Grandmother, she was the life-destroying Crone yet also connected with the Caldron of Regeneration.[13]

The goddess who looks backward and forward, holding past and future in balance, overvaluing neither nor splitting them from each other, holding the entire life cycle; the Grandmother Crone who accepts and is herself the instrument of decay and destruction yet also knows and brings about from destruction a regeneration of life—these images stood behind my dream daughter Anna, touching profoundly and incisively into the deepest issues I was struggling with at the time. I finally got the message.

All year I had been wrestling with the psychological impact of what appeared to be a significant, age-related physical disability that I was led to believe would be chronic, progressive, and significantly limiting for the rest of my life (it has since remitted or was misdiagnosed to begin with). This threw me into a classic "midlife crisis" with its focus on aging, limitations, time running out, and nostalgia for a younger and less limited body and self. What made all this particularly frustrating was that this was a time of life, in my late forties, that I had especially looked forward to; I had a basically positive image of aging in women, having observed again and again in both clients and friends that the forties and fifties in a woman's life often bring new energy and rejuvenation. Yet here I was, suddenly faced with pain, considerable physical limitation, and a body whose afflictions I could neither control nor make well.

I learned to care for myself, I sought alternative treatments, I tried to sense the deeper meaning of this new presence in my life, but mostly I was angry. I felt prematurely old, far older than my years; I felt like my grandmother, and for the first time began to have memories of her and had to begin to deal with the extent of her negative psychology and its effect on my childhood. I was totally focused on the past and felt cut down in the present and future.

As I was becoming physically well again, I began having dream after dream of new babies—babies rescued from death, orphan babies brought back from the wilderness, babies who came with knowledge of the "other side," all of them remarkably healthy, vital, and often connected with real children I knew who were particularly resilient even in the worst of adversities. The Anna dream, however, with its focus on time, on transpersonal cycle, on holding the past and the future together and grasping that death and regeneration are also inextricably linked through the Goddess, touched me the deepest. The recognition that this baby I was now to care for, who was now my daughter, was also the Grandmother of Time, filled me with awe and with recognition.

What also struck me was that the care she needed was so mundane and ordinary—warmth, dryness, being helped to release what she had inadvertently swallowed along with her food that might cause her internal pain—tasks that every mother knows how to do. (I thought of the kind of care given to the images of the Goddess in ancient times by her temple priestesses: the washing, clothing, and bejeweling of her statues, the endearing ceremonies in which the goddess of one temple was carried to the temple of another so they could "visit"—all the sensate, literal, mundane yet magical care that I had learned was part of "idolatry" yet is so very much a part of basic feminine responsibilities and care everywhere.) I could do this, I thought; I didn't have to slay dragons, climb mountains, perform impossible tasks to be close to this Goddess, who could hold my midlife with far more meaning than I had been able to do myself. I just had to welcome, care for, and mother the new and previously abandoned life, the Kore daughter who is simultaneously the Grandmother (uniting the opposites), the dark-haired, dark-eyed child who is both the literal child of my past, my girlhood, and the inner child born from my adulthood into the present and future.

Kore is not only the Divine Child; she is also the Maiden appearing as adolescent or even young adult. As such, she is Kore Protogonos, the "first-born," the "self-originating," as Kerényi puts it, rising out of the maternal ocean like Anadyomene or Aphrodite.[14] She is one-in-herself, the Virgin, eternally renewable through water and the gestative power of the Feminine. In this aspect, she appears in human psychology as a profound image of self-containedness or even the fullness of the Self for women. She also manifests in birth and rebirth imagery connected with a woman's inner or outer daughter.

This birth-and-rebirth theme appears easily in projection to a woman's actual daughter. Even more than a son, a woman's daughter takes her back to her own beginnings, her own girlhood, and beyond, to an archetypal Girl through whom the mother feels revitalized, reseeded, born again.[15] Thus a contemporary poet writes in a poem to her infant daughter:

> And through you
> I am born as I lie down
> in the seedbox of my own beginnings,
> Opening the wild part of me,
> Once lost once lost
> As I was breathing
> in the vines of childhood.[16]

One's own girlhood self may also carry some of the qualities of Kore, including the possibility of rebirth; in this case, however, there is also a sense of inevitable loss and the necessity of mourning, moving us closer to the experience of Demeter's Kore. For girlhood cannot literally be prolonged or reborn; here our culture in particular with its secular "cult of the maiden" that insists only one phase of womanhood is valuable (and measures this by the patriarchal yardstick of "attractiveness to men") vastly underestimates, literalizes, and splits the archetypal Maiden and her links with the equally valuable Mother and Crone.

Women caught in this secular distortion of the Maiden may project all their vitality to the young woman they were in the past and feel compelled to do almost anything, even undergo repeated surgeries to alter their aging bodies, striving to recapture the appearance of still being young and beautiful. None of us is totally immune to this. What we all fail to grasp is that the Maiden and her meaning are bigger than literal age and richer than cultural stereotype. Though the literal girl that we were must inevitably disappear and die on a body level and needs to be meaningfully mourned as we move through our Mother and Crone years, she is met again on other levels—as we call back the qualities and vitality of our true younger selves and integrate them into our larger adult personalities, as we struggle to realize the Self's goal of growing into Woman as Virgin, the one who belongs-to-herself.

I have worked with many women who needed to let the Kore of literal girlhood die in order to reseed their aging selves. Nowhere was this more vivid than in the therapeutic process that emerged in a woman I worked with years ago whom I'll call Emma. Emma came to me via her feminist daughter after having been seen and sent away by a male therapist in the local mental health system who told her therapy was irrelevant for her because she was "too old to change." I was enraged at his statement, not only because of its prejudice and insensitivity but also because there was such life in this woman underneath the depletion, depression, and psychosomatic maladies she presented as her symptoms. Moreover, with even the slightest bit of positive attention and care, this woman opened wide as a flower—to herself, to the therapy, and to me.

Emma was in her early sixties when she first came to me and was colossally "stuck," her considerable vitality and passion buried under a sludge of unexpressed feelings that took their revenge in the form of various physical ailments that came and went and defied diagnosis and treatment. She had been told by several doctors that her symptoms were psychosomatic and, as a former nurse, she herself had some sense that that might be true; thus she had come into therapy. We spent a great deal of time in our work excavating her true but hidden feelings: her resentment of her adult children's efforts to keep her in a "mothering" role with her grandchildren when she felt at last that she could have some freedom, her rage at her eighty-year-old mother's control of her, her grief over a particularly hard adulthood that had been characterized by abandonments from men, abject poverty, and the struggle to raise her five children alone. Together we mourned and raged, and the life underneath began to stir. Courageously, she began to express her feelings to her family; particularly when she could show the "teeth" of the Crone and express her rage, her psychosomatic symptoms dramatically ceased.

One day, however, the level of our sessions shifted as she brought up the other part of her life, before the hardships and the poverty—the girl she had been. She had to tell me about "May," she said. May was her middle name, the name she had been known by as a girl and young woman, and May was *wonderful*. Pretty, lively, mischievous, and full of fun, May was a flirt and the life of the party, the center of attention surrounded by ardent young suitors. Emma's voice changed as she talked about May, filled with humor, warmth, almost reverence. For weeks, our sessions were filled with the stories of her springtime self, the young woman May. Then came the inevitable sadness. She came in one day, talking of how she had looked in the mirror; in tears, she told me that she didn't see May anymore—only "an overweight old woman." May, on a literal level, was gone. Emma mourned her deeply and thoroughly, only gradually relinquishing her to a cherished memory of part of her past. But as Emma mourned and became more expressive and more actively involved in her life in the present, an archetypal theme became visible, this time in *process* instead of primarily in image: the Crone gave birth.

As our work went on, all the vitality that had once been experienced in May reemerged in the budding psyche of the older woman. Her physical symptoms disappeared or became more manageable, an intense intellectual curiosity reasserted itself, her passion for life reemerged and blossomed. She stood up to her mother's control; the older woman, unconscious of her hold over her daughter and baffled by her new assertiveness, simply backed off. Emma's "teeth" were effective. She pushed past her guilt over not wanting to be the stereotypic "grandma" and let her children know she had other things in her life that she wanted to pursue. She joined a women's spiritual group at her church. She began to talk about taking a course in archaeology, which had always intrigued her. She learned how to manage her finances and became increasingly self-sufficient and independent (her mother had handled her finances before, which Emma had passively allowed yet resented). Warmth, humor, and a passionate intensity returned to this now revitalized woman, and many of our later sessions were punctuated with her passionate cry, "I want to *live* before I die!" At the end of our work, when I was preparing to move my young children and myself to another state, Emma brought me a care package for our journey: a plastic box filled with a bar of soap, a swatch of safety pins, a box of Band-Aids, a couple of new pencils—and a mustache.

Emma's girlhood self May was a lot like Demeter Chloe; she carried the verdancy, the vitality, the surging upward of the life force in the springtime of personal history. And like the grain mother's Kore, this maidenhood too had to die and be mourned to bring about her connection with the qualities of the Crone. Here Hades was less the patriarchal god (except as it came through the ageism of the first psychotherapist) than aging itself, Chronos with his sickle, inevitably cutting down youth and the body. There was no unnatural violation here (though age can be seen this way by those raging against it), no kidnapping before one's time, no cutting down in the midst of spring as there is with Demeter's Kore. But the focus on loss and the mourning over lost maidenhood bring us closer to the daughter of Demeter.

The Kore that belongs to Demeter carries all of the qualities of the springtime phase of the goddess and of ourselves: the youth, vibrance, budding, and flowering of feminine being. Moreover, she is holy and suprahuman: she carries the image of self-possessed, self-originating Virgin womanhood, the female Self before the going under to patriarchal power and influence. She is the Mother-held Daughter, the original "woman-identified-woman," the Feminine who comes with her own relationship to a feminine matrix. It is *this* that Hades rips into and violates, and, moreover, he cuts her down in her springtime, prematurely, out of season—*this* is what distinguishes Demeter's Kore. She is ripped away from her matrix, lost to the upperworld of life and mother-love, and undergoes a profound death experience from which she emerges as transformer and transformed. The experience of violation, of going under against one's will, of disappearance, estrangement, and loss; the transformation of the vital child of Spring to the eerie, powerful, ghostly Persephone: this is the story of *Demeter's* Kore and the earmarks of her appearance in the human psyche.

Thus, if a woman finds Kore through her daughter and it is Demeter's Kore who is coming through, she may experience not only the delight and enhancement of the springtime child but also strange anxieties or nightmares in which the daughter is kidnapped, raped, lost, or subject to death. If this Kore is found in one's own girlhood, there may be intense loss and mourning over qualities from which one was cut off too young, a girlhood cut short by incest, abuse, or even the general fate of growing up in a patriarchal culture with its controlling and constricting images of femaleness. Intrapsychically, this archetype may appear in intense depression and self-estrangement, the experience of one's youthful vitality gone "out of season," and the sense of disappearing to oneself and to others, disappearing out of life itself. To experience this myth in any of its forms is to experience terrible loss of vitality and meaning, intense depression and mourning, terrifying disappearance and desubstantiation and, eventually, if the process is gone through in its entirety, transformation and revitalization.

Demeter's Kore becomes Persephone. To learn what this means and who it is that the Kore becomes, we must first turn to the vehicle of this transformation: the death-marriage.

In classical Greece, already well-entrenched in patriarchy, it was the custom for a young girl, usually an adolescent, to be promised in marriage by her father to a man considerably older than herself.[17] As is common in patriarchy, the power resided in the male members of the family and was defined by them; the marriage contract was essentially arranged by men. Once the marriage had taken place, the young girl moved away from the home of her family of origin and went to live with her husband's family. This type of translocation is still the custom in some parts of rural Greece; the bride and her new husband go to live in the house of the husband's father. In both periods, classical and modern, this departure was seen as wrenching and negative, the separation felt particularly keenly between mothers and daughters.[18]

We do not know when these father-dominated marital arrangements began. Although images and stories of divine personages and sociopolitical arrangements among human beings do not necessarily coincide in a culture, my own speculation is that perhaps these marital customs were inaugurated some time after the patriarchal invaders of Greece forcibly "married" their foreign gods to the indigenous, prepatriarchal Greek goddesses as part of their appropriation of power. At any rate, the myth of Kore's abduction takes what was apparently a familiar image of marriage among the Greeks at that time and unfolds it into a powerful metaphor for the experience of death. Zeus, the patriarchal sky god, assumes the role of Kore's father and sole parental power and gives Kore away to his underworld brother; mother and daughter not only have no say about this, but do not even know about it until Kore is snatched and raped. From the mother and daughter's point of view, the ensuing separation is devastating, ripping apart their bond; from the perspective of the Old Religion of the Goddess, it is outrageous and a gross dishonoring of the Feminine. Nevertheless, Kore is carried away to her husband's home, far away from her mother's world and with the intention that she never return. But the home she is taken to is the kingdom of Death.

Thus the trauma of death takes on the face of familiar, human experience. The agent of death is like an unwelcome bridegroom coming to claim his unwilling bride. The wrenching separation is like a mother's pain when her daughter marries and goes off to live in her in-laws' house. There is also a euphemistic softening of death inherent in the employment of the marriage metaphor as a death equivalent, for human marriages and literal geographic separations contain within them the possibility of return, whereas, from a strictly concrete, factual perspective, death does not.[19] Yet it is precisely this fact of death and the limitations of a human perspective that can only see literal loss that are transcended in the Mysteries; transposed to a divine level, the return is indeed possible (and extended to human beings through divine dispensation in the Mysteries). Even the rape-marriage becomes meaningful, not as the vehicle of the intended eternal estrangement and static death, but as the basis of a Mystery event through which the Goddess transforms, reunites herself with her own Death aspect, and integrates even the forces of Hades with the Feminine world he opposes. This inner reunion becomes then a paradigm for the more limited human being to witness and participate in through the Goddess and thus gain relief from the terror of literal death; the initiate gains the knowledge and trust that through the Goddess's power, there is always reunion and return.

In Greece, there is still a remnant of the ancient, mythic linking of marriage and death. Loring Danforth reports that in some rural areas, funeral and marriage images, customs, and music reproduce or profoundly overlap ancient themes. Death is still imaged as a marriage to Hades (or his modern counterpart, Haros) or to the devouring Mother Earth. The unmarried dead are buried in their wedding regalia or wrapped in the linens of their unused dowries. Marriage is still seen as estrangement and mourned, especially by mothers and daughters. And it is women, in unconscious imitation of a goddess they no longer know, who grieve longest and most intensely for the loved ones lost to death.[20] No longer revered or remembered, these mythic connections live on in the concrete customs and rituals surrounding these two eternally ongoing rites of passage: marriage and death.

Modern Greece is predominantly patriarchal in its values and social arrangements; the remnants of its prepatriarchal matrix are glimpsed only in folk customs and beliefs whose origins are often unrecognized and unknown to the people who perpetuate them. The collective mind-set of our own culture (or at least of its dominant majority of Eurocentric origins) is even more uniformly steeped in patriarchal thinking and valences. Mother and daughter separation is emphasized, even seen as a dire and difficult psychological imperative (as nearly every contemporary book on the mother-daughter relationship until recently has reiterated).[21] This imperative is congruent with a

97

culture that emphasizes heterosexual relationships as a developmental goal and de-emphasizes the primacy and value of women's relationships with each other. (Which of us was ever told in growing up that relationships with other women as mothers, daughters, sisters, friends, or lovers would ever be as central, important, or deep as our relationships with men?) It follows then that the separation aspect of marriage is seen as a natural, desired development, and that the new life represented by the marriage should be celebrated rather than mourned. The rites of marriage and the rites of death are kept sharply apart and seen as opposing; the only mourning Mother appearing among the images of our various spiritual traditions is the Mother of a Son.

Thus when the myth of Kore abducted by Death appears to us, it is most likely to manifest not through cultural imagery or customs that are collectively known and familiar, but in the hidden recesses of the individual psyche with its taproot deep in the transcultural collective unconscious. Fantasy, dreams, creative imagination, or the shadow side of patriarchally sanctioned institutions, relationships, or values are the arenas in which this myth manifests in contemporary times.

The theme of the death-marriage may still play itself out in an actual human marriage, but it is far more likely to reflect the conscious/unconscious relationship between the husband and wife than to appear in the rituals surrounding the literal wedding. A woman may marry a seemingly magnanimous, expansive, Zeus-like man, for example, whose hidden agenda is a Hades-like, unrelational, power-over dominance. As the marriage goes on, the woman may feel herself to be increasingly going under, desubstantiated, and self-estranged; she may even feel like she is dying as an independent self. Since it is rare in our culture that a woman's mother has carried a positive feminine potency in her daughter's experience of her and since the daughter's connection with her mother is not culturally seen as a primary, ongoing resource, it is unlikely that the daughter's "longing for reunion" will take the form of longing for her mother; rather she herself may become the mourning mother, grieving for a former state of self-intactness, the Virgin's state of one-in-herself, that she feels she has lost. Or—as I will elaborate at more length in chapter 7—the woman may never have felt this intactness, may have had no sense of an inner matrix at all, and the longing for this as yet totally unknown experience of self-cohesion may arise out of the more familiar experience of being married but insubstantial in the world of the Fathers. The Demeter-Persephone myth adds to this experience of dying and inchoate longing for re-membering the understanding that these painful experiences are part of a much fuller process that can be moved through and found meaningful as part of an uncovering of a powerful female Self. Thus the death-marriage is potentially a "prima materia" for a work of profound transformation whose implications reach beyond the individual and into the collective.

The death-marriage is the outer vehicle of the transformation in which Kore becomes Persephone. This transformation—from innocent young girl snatched from her playmates to formidable Goddess of Death—is the most dramatic aspect of the myth, even more dramatic than the rape. To begin to grasp what this transformation means, both mythically and psychologically, we need to look more closely at the figure of Persephone and her powers.

Persephone appears as both Queen of Death and, more hiddenly, as Brimo, the Mystery goddess. As Queen of Death, she embodies death's powers as well as the awesomeness and dread surrounding death as perceived by human consciousness. Viewed from a patriarchal perspective, Persephone is the bride of Hades and becomes his feminine counterpart, though rather than his cruelty, she brings to the death experience the qualities of graciousness and mercy.[22] But from a matriarchal perspective, Persephone is the underworld side of her mother, Demeter Chthonia, soon to manifest in her Mystery form as the essence of pagan spirituality: the Goddess of Regeneration. In this form, she transcends the limits of Hades, the fixity of patriarchal death as either heaven or hell, and the drama of the myth itself. The myth, with its focus on terror, loss, and provisional return falls apart like a shell, revealing what has gone under but never died: the endless recycling of birth-death-rebirth held by the Mother and Daughter of Life.

But first Persephone appears as the Queen of Death. The variants of her name in this form—Persephone, Persephatta, Proserpina—connote a being who is fearsome, awful, and brings destruction.[23] She possesses deadly powers to terrify, petrify with fright, turn to stone; here, like Demeter Erinys, she is linked with the Gorgon/Medusa (see plate 8). This link was foreshadowed in the earliest moments of the myth of her abduction in variants that name Athena and Artemis as two of her playmates in the field of flowers. Both Athena and Artemis are Gorgon-linked; Artemis appears in archaic monuments in Medusa form and Athena carries Medusa's head on her shield. Persephone shares access to the head of Medusa and can send it up from the underworld to warn or to petrify whoever approaches. The slaying of Medusa, the rape of Persephone, and the harvesting of the grain with a sickle are all mythologically equivalent.[24] In this form, Persephone is she who is cut down, dishonored, defiled, and comes back demonic—but also fruitful.

". . . [T]hrough the figure of Persephone, the stately Queen of Hades, we glimpse the Gorgon," Kerényi asserts. The Gorgon represents the most horrific aspect of death: the aspect of nonbeing that is also the essence of Persephone as Queen of the Dead. "It is not, of course, *pure* nonbeing," he elaborates, "rather [it is] the sort of nonbeing from which the living shrink as from something *with a negative sign*; a monstrosity that has usurped the place of the unimaginably beautiful, the nocturnal aspect of what by day is the most desirable of all things."[25] This monstrosity, this destructiveness, this horror is what the lovely young Maiden changes into when Kore becomes Persephone; it is a dramatic, horrifying, shocking moment in the myth, almost too much to picture and take in.

A recent, popular adventure movie, *Raiders of the Lost Ark*, contained an image of such a transition from beautiful young girl to death figure; readers who have seen this movie may recall this image when trying to imagine the transformation from Kore to Persephone. Late in the film, the sacred Ark of the Covenant has been appropriated by the Nazis and opened by the greedy archaeologist who has assisted them. Mysterious forces begin to stir when he opens the Ark, the atmosphere becomes charged and electrified, and out of the Ark rise powerful protective and destructive spirits. One of these spirits is especially striking. It appears to the leader of the Nazi expedition as a beautiful, alluring, young woman. "Beautiful!" the Nazi cries out, moving toward her. But just at that point, the image changes to a horrifying female death's-head, a visual parallel to the Kore-Persephone transformation; in this form, the spirit from the Ark destroys the Nazi.

But the movement from Kore to Persephone in the myth is not simply a transfiguration; it is the image aspect of a process that has profound psychological implications. Kore begins as a victim of death, as helpless and terrified as her human counterparts. Involuntarily, she undergoes the death experience; she is snatched out of life and the natural world of embodiment and goes under to a world in which that which was once alive and thriving becomes insubstantial and ghostly. She is powerless to refuse or stop this process; the Maiden is savaged by death and undergoes the experience of its worst metaphors— kidnapping, rape, violation, estrangement, and desubstantiation. But—she is not permanently undone.

Aboveground, her mother undergoes a parallel process of defile- ment and loss but still within her own world, she is able to become more powerful than her daughter below. Though she too is raped against her will (by Poseidon), and tries to resist it, she is also so profoundly empathic with her daughter's experience that she takes on the death experience as well and suffers it with her. What comes from Demeter's empathy—grief, persistence in seeking and naming the truth, and rage—coalesces into effective protest through which her daughter's return is brought about. Thus Persephone, coupled with her mother's active power, is able to return from the land of the dead; at this point, she is no longer a helpless victim of the death experience but becomes its survivor. Further, she has also become Queen of the Dead, ruling over what once overwhelmed her: this suggests that she has mastered the death experience and thereafter is able to ritually and cyclically descend into death's depths and return without damage. Finally, as Brimo the birth-giving Mystery goddess, Persephone undergoes a further transformation in which survivor be- comes creator.

This sequence from victim to survivor to creator presents an an- cient mythological paradigm of recovery from trauma and the threat of annihilation that is remarkably parallel to the healing process de- scribed by modern psychologists with regard to both individual expe- rience of trauma (violence, abuse, incest, the stress of war) and collective experiences of death equivalents (genocide or the threat of genocide, nuclear attack, natural disasters).[26]

The path of Demeter-Persephone, which gives meaning to intense and effective grief and rage, cuts through denial and euphemism, con- fronts the truth, and eventually masters the going under and return to life with greater power, offers sound and therapeutically accurate, ageless guidance through the death experience. (This will be further elaborated in the more clinically focused chapters that follow.) For the ancient Greeks, this path offered relief from the terrors of literal death and assurance of its perpetual reconnection to life. For us, it also applies to assaults on the psyche and soul. In addition, it recovers the power and beauty of a Deity who has been virtually lost to our knowledge and history and delivers a strong and poignant message about her; like us, she too has gone under to the shadow side of patriarchal power. She too has been dishonored, defiled, raped, kidnapped, and estranged. Our suffering is known to her; she has suffered it both involuntarily as Daughter and willingly taken it on as Mother. She has passed through the dismemberment of Self in the death experience. But she is able to transform the death experience through her own power. By recovering her to our consciousness and our lives, we too can participate in her essential transformation and recycle our deadly experiences into rebirth and new life. We need to learn again what it means in the realm of the Goddess to be "killed" and how we can use such experiences, even those that occur vastly against our intentions and will, to transform and regenerate not only ourselves but even the forces of death.

For this, we need to move on to the Mystery goddess. Persephone is not only the Queen of the Dead, she is also the Regenerator of Life. Persephone gestates Death; this is her most profound power, and it generates and undergirds the central event in the Eleusinian mysteries as we know them. As Kore, the goddess is forced to take in the experience of death. She swallows the seeds; her marriage is consummated. As Kore-becoming-Persephone, she passes through desubstantiation and ghost life, finally mastering and ruling over the death experience as Persephone. Through her mother's qualities of grief, rage, and effective protest and her own loyalty to her mother even while she is in the underworld, she is ransomed back to life. At this point, she becomes a psychopomp, able to move back and forth between two worlds; the rape out of life is replaced by voluntary and cyclical descent to the kingdom of death, representing knowledge more ancient than that represented by Hades—that life and death are connected through her and recycle into each other.

Persephone is Queen of the Dead, but the underworld cannot contain her, nor is this her final form or mastery of death her ultimate power. It is only as Brimo, the ancient one, the raging Crone, that Persephone reveals the fullness and potency of her powers: she can *bear* rape and death into *fruitfulness*. The seemingly helpless Maiden is not overwhelmed or killed; she takes in the death experience, even against her will, and gestates it in her womb, the ancient and forever Caldron of Regeneration. And in this magical caldron, death is transformed and reborn as fresh new life deriving from and bonded forever with the Goddess. Significantly, this does not happen in the underworld. Myth tells us that Persephone bore no children to Hades, yet we know that within the Mysteries, as Brimo, she brings forth a son.

I think this means that nothing is fruitful in the kingdom of Hades, where death means fixity and all is insubstantial and split off from life. It is only when Persephone has been reclaimed to the land of the living and after she "goes under" so deep that she, with her mother, recovers her most ancient powers and form, that a new level opens, neither upperworld nor underworld but transcending both—the level of Mystery. Here she transcends the lust and the triumph of Hades; here, like the comical Baubo, she reveals her transformative womb and the child dancing in it; here she extends her powers to re-create life out of death to all who seek her in despair and suffer what she has suffered.

The seeds of death are forcibly implanted in Persephone; perhaps, starved for nourishment, she even takes them in herself. But once inside, they do not vanquish her, they merely quicken and grow. She has the capacity to make this happen; she meets the forces of death with the oldest power she has, the Womb of the Goddess which for thousands of years before Hades was perceived as Creatrix of Life. In this womb, nothing is ever static and death has no final power: "She changes everything she touches, and everything she touches, changes."[27]

Change is the essence of the Old Religion; transformation and cycle are its constants. If Hades represents the shadow side of patriarchal power that dishonors and buries the Feminine, then we can learn much from the goddess Demeter-Persephone and her capacity to confront and transform—"If you must take the rapist in, do not give in and die. Rage and mourn for lost innocence. Cut through denial and euphemism and hold accountable the people and institutions responsible for violation and abuse. Refuse to serve their authority, to reconcile to their seduction. Hold fast to the values of life. If you must take the seeds of death into yourself, if they become implanted and threaten your very soul, go as deep as you can until you find not only survival but my power to create from the death place itself"—this is the message of the Goddess. It is a call to activism, to reconnection

103

with the buried and devalued Feminine, to clear-sighted courage and creative response to the death experience. This in no way condones the experience of rape in any of its forms in our culture. Persephone's message is after the fact. It conveys: *if* you are forced to go through this, *if* you cannot avoid it, there is nonetheless hope for creative, triumphant survival. The forces of Hades-like power are never the end of the story and never the ultimate meaning.

The poet Judy Grahn, in a poem about the Goddess Grahn calls "She Who," pictures the movement from patriarchal defilement to gestative transformation. In the beginning of the poem, there is only Hades dishonoring, spewing forth in a form we all know:

The enemies of She Who call her various names

a whore, a whore,
a fishwife a cunt a harlot a harlot a pussy
a doxie a tail a fishwife a whore a hole a slit
a cunt a bitch a slut a slit a hole a whore a hole
a vixen/ a piece of ass/ a dame-filly-mare
dove-cow-pig-chick-cat-kitten-bird
dog-dish/ a dumb blonde

you black bitch - you white bitch - you brown bitch - you yellow
bitch - you fat bitch - you stupid bitch - you stinking bitch
you little bitch - you old bitch - a cheap bitch - a high class
bitch - a 2 bit whore - a 2 dollar whore, a ten dollar
whore - a million dollar mistress

a hole a slut a cunt a slit a cut
a slash a hole a slit a piece
of shit, a piece of shit, a piece of shit

She Who bears it
bear down, breathe
bear down, bear down, breathe
bear down, bear down, bear down, breathe

She Who lies down in the darkness and bears it
She Who lies down in the lightness and bears it
the labor of She Who carries and bears is the first labor

all over the world
the waters are breaking everywhere
everywhere the waters are breaking
the labor of She Who carries and bears
and raises and rears is the first labor,
there is no other first labor.[28]

Like the grain that is cut down, dies, and is buried beneath the earth only to sprout anew, Persephone is the ever-rising, ever-renewable, ever-creative life force—the hope to us all, who battle even now with the renegade power still seeking to split us away from all that her world represents. These renegade forces are wielded by human hands now who recklessly play with their power, while ignoring their cosmic dimensions and bringing us perilously close to collective and personal extinction. Before we can move more deeply into how this drama unfolds in our cultural and personal stories, we need to return these death-dealing forces to their transpersonal origin and explore the faces and meanings of their ancient representative—the shadow god Hades and his kingdom below the earth.

Anne-Marie de Barolet, *Hades and Kore: The Myth Rewritten*, 1989.

❦ 5 ❦

The Shadow of Patriarchy:

Hades and His Kingdom

> Death was real. It could come on a beautiful au-
> tumn day, with no warning, no doctor's diagnosis,
> no lingering in a hospital bed to say goodbye and
> bravely face death. Death could come with no
> preparation. Death had spit its terror in my face
> and I could not forget.
>
> —JENNIFER BARR,
> *rape survivor*[1]

THE GOD OF THE UNDERWORLD in classical Greek myth was a complex figure; a multiplicity of names surrounded him, circling a
core image so frightening that it was almost impossible to address it
by name. This core image, called Hades, apparently evoked such
dread and terror in the ancient Greeks that most of the time this god
was approached only through euphemisms designed to appease rather
than invoke his power. Thus the Lord of Death was spoken of as
Trophonious "the nourisher," for example, or Pluto, "riches," and the
terror of passage to his underworld kingdom was contained by speaking of his "hospitality."[2] These euphemisms pretended that there was
a positive side to Hades but this pretense was apotropaic; his real
name, Hades, "remained barren, a word of taboo or teratology, of no
avail for the kindlier purposes of worship."[3]

Hades carried the unmitigated horror of death. Through him,

107

human existence was derealized, passing from the fullness and vitality of embodied life to the disembodied, ghostly existence of a shade. In the time of Homer, the dead were considered to be different from the living in that they lacked strength (a quality they shared with dreams) and full command of their faculties. A soul and image existed in the kingdom of Hades but the "wits" were gone, as was the personality. When summoned by the living with offerings of blood, they could not recognize their loved ones until they had drunk of it; then, briefly, they could feel fully human again.[4] They "are not of a nature to enjoy anything; they are feeble, impotent wraiths, mere semblances of men, all doomed to the same miserable travesty of life; the bodies from which they are now severed were their real selves, and there remain now only impalpable, joyless phantoms."[5]

When people died, it was believed that they were ferried across the poison river Styx to the part of the underworld kingdom called Tartarus, there to be judged according to their virtues. Those who were virtuous were assigned residence in the Elysian Orchards, a land of pleasure and sport. Those judged to be evil were sent to Erebus and punished with perpetual, fruitless tasks such as that consigned to Sisyphus, who had to roll a huge stone nearly to the top of an incline, be pushed down by its weight, and then roll it up again, only to repeat the process—or by perpetual torments such as those plaguing Tantalus, who endlessly craved food and water, both of which were perpetually held just out of his reach. A third judgment was also possible: that of neither good nor evil. Such souls were sent to the Asphodel Fields where, as Robert Graves so poignantly describes them, "they twitter like bats and only Orion still has the heart to hunt the ghostly deer. None of them but would rather live in bondage to a landless peasant than rule over all of Tartarus. Their one delight is in libations of blood poured to them by the living; when they drink, they feel themselves almost men again."[6] What is particularly striking about existence in the underworld is how static it was; everything happened over and over again and was perpetually the same. Nothing grew and developed, and nothing transformed. Nor was there meaningfulness to the cyclicity; everything simply repeated. Such was existence without Mother and body.

The dead lacked substance and personal definition. Even the realm that they lived in was not well defined. Kerényi describes the kingdom of Hades as "poor in form and without any contours, with no connecting lines."[7] Everything was fluid; nothing was demarcated from anything else.

Trapped in this boundaryless, wraithlike existence, insubstantial yet not totally annihilated, the shades yearned and hungered for reconnection with life. Blood offerings could give them a sense of revived substantiality but only temporarily. But there was one other way they could recover what they had lost, and this was through the transformative Feminine, through Mother and body. As with Hades, reconceiving himself through the pomegranate seeds eaten by Persephone, food provided the vehicle of this transformation through the Feminine. Those shades who were privileged because of the virtue they had exemplified while still alive could sometimes inhabit a bean, a nut, or a fish; these, if eaten by a living woman, could bring about conception and thus the shade could be reborn into the upperworld as a human being.[8] For the most part, however, existence in the underworld was permanent and no one who went there ever returned; this is one reason why Demeter was so frantic when Hades snatched Kore and took her to the underworld.

Is it any wonder that the ruler of such a place would be worshipped with aversion rather than invocation? Or that the offering to underworld deities was traditionally an offering that was holocausted, completely burnt and given over to the god, rather than the more usual practice of inviting the Divinity to share in one's bounty of food, as in the worship of the Olympians in their temples above?[9]

Hades himself was as uncanny and as fearsome as the realm he ruled. His taboo name meant "the unseen one," "the invisible," and he was the invisible-maker as well. Here he was in stark contrast to Helios, the sun, who not only was prominently visible but also brought visibility with his light.[10] In his rare appearances in Greek art, Hades was often represented with an averted face, suggesting that he was not to be looked at directly.[11] He was fierce, protective of his rights, and frequently described as grim. "He willingly allowed none of his subjects to escape," writes Graves, "and few who visit his underworld kingdom return alive to describe it, which makes him the most hated of the gods."[12]

His remoteness from the upperworld of natural life and even from Olympus, the realm of the gods, was profound. He owned no property on earth, although all the gems and precious metals beneath the earth were his. Amid the profusion of temples in ancient Greece, only one was dedicated to Hades. This temple was located at Elis and whatever worship took place there was shrouded in mystery, remote as the god himself. It was opened only once a year, and only a single priest was allowed to enter it.[13] Distant and isolated, alienated from life and even outside of the celebrations offered to every other god, Hades was completely cut off from the world.

"Hades never knows what is happening in the world above or in Olympus except for fragmentary information which comes to him when mortals strike their hands upon the earth and invoke him with oaths and curses."[14] Unaffiliated with the realms above, he rarely left his kingdom except when overcome with lust; then he raped or attempted to rape. His approach was violent, swift, and possessive. He did get permission before abducting Kore but only from Zeus; with Kore herself, he simply took what he wanted. His attitude was one of presumptive lust that sought not relationship but possession. He did not court Kore, did not try to win her, did not even ask her or her mother's permission; he simply desired and took. Ripping her out of context and away from her matrix, he put her into his own world, intending for that to be the end of the story. "I want; I will have; I will do with Kore whatever I want to. She shall be mine because I want her and she shall live with me forever": this is Hades' lustful message. (And Demeter is accused of possessiveness!) He approached the nymphs Leuce and Minthe in the same way— but in these attempts at rape, Persephone intervened, metamorphosing the nymphs into plant life. Leuce became a white poplar standing by the pool of Memory in the underworld, while Minthe became the plant mint which was used in funerary rites.[15]

Scholars have disputed the origin of the core image of this god with the central title Hades. Jane Harrison traces an earlier version—the underworld form of Zeus—back to aversive religious practices focused on appeasing the souls of dead heroes.[16] Louis Richard Farnell disputes Harrison's version, emphasizing instead the need for a god of souls that gave rise to the underworld Zeus, later called Hades.[17] Hades' connection with Zeus is well established since in classical mythology, Hades was Zeus's brother and, like him, received one-third of the world to rule when dominion was wrested away from the god Chronos. In addition, many of Hades' euphemistic names emphasized his connection with Zeus, such as Zeus Chthonious and Zeus Eubouleus.

Robert Graves, however, writing at a later date than either Farnell or Harrison, asserts that Zeus and Hades were patriarchal gods imposed on a previously Goddess-worshipping people.[18] Persephone's kidnapping and rape by Hades, according to Graves, "forms part of the myth in which the Hellenic trinity of gods forcibly marry the pre-Hellenic Triple Goddess—Zeus, Hera; Zeus or Poseidon, Demeter; and Hades, [Kore]."[19]

Graves contends that much of Greek mythology represents actual political-religious history.[20] Thus it may not be farfetched to speculate that Hades' rape of Kore may be a metaphorical representation of an actual historical invasion—one of many that took place around 2000–1450 BCE in which the southern European goddess worshipers were subdued and eventually assimilated by patriarchal invaders from the North. Hades then emerges as part of an invading patriarchal religious system whose objective was to subdue and overthrow the sovereignty of the Goddess in southern Europe—an objective that eventually succeeded with the establishment of the Olympian pantheon.[21]

In light of this picture, it is fascinating to discover that Hades—who is essentially oppositional to the Goddess and seeks to overthrow and possess her—is repeatedly linked to her through some of his euphemistic names. Several of these titles, used to soften and ward off his cruelty, are references to figures who sought *not* to rape the Goddess but to serve her. "Eubouleus," for example, was originally the name of a swineherd "in service to . . . the sow goddess who makes the corn sprout."[22] (The reader may recall that pigs were also sacred to Demeter and that she was the goddess of agriculture; so essentially, Eubouleus served Demeter. Chapter 2 presented a variant of the Homeric tale in which the pigs of Eubouleus were swallowed into the underworld along with Kore and in going after them, Eubouleus leads Demeter to the underworld to retrieve her daughter.) Fear of Hades, the rapist of the Goddess and violator of the Mother-world, was stilled or averted by addressing him as Eubouleus, a title essentially linking him back to her.

This linking is even more striking in the network of meanings surrounding Hades' most well-known title, Pluto or Pluton ("riches"). This name, euphemistic indeed for a hated god of horror and death, was derived from Plutous, the name of Demeter's son by her Titan lover Iasion. The name is also linked with Iakchos, another son of Demeter's (the one who danced in Baubo's womb and later led the Mystery procession); with Triptolemus, the thricefold warrior whom she initiated into the thricefold ploughman, teaching him her mysteries and sending him into all the world to plant her seeds; and with the Mystery child Brimos. Farnell adds to this picture with the mention

111

of an ancient Pluton cult and a Plutonion (entrance to the underworld) at Eleusis, predating the image of Hades, in which the name of the underworld ruler was Eubouleus.[23] Homer links Plutous with Demeter and Persephone, naming him as the "wealth" these two goddesses convey to mortals they love.[24]

"Obviously," writes Farnell, "a ritual name so uncanny as [Hades] 'the Unseen' had no such fructifying force for those who were praying for crops or a favourable sign as names like Pluton or Eubouleus. Nor would it be likely to be cherished by the Mysteries which aimed at brightening the conception of death and of the world beyond death."[25] It appears, then, that the horror and dread associated with this patriarchal image of death, removed from and antagonistic to the natural life of the Mother-world, were dealt with by softening the image of Hades through connection with the Goddess—people pretended he was linked with her like one of her sons or, from a more patriarchal perspective, attributed her riches to him in order to appease and keep him at bay.

One of my theses about this myth is that, with the rape and return of Kore-Persephone and the establishment of Demeter's Mysteries, what was before only pretense and euphemism actually became true. Hades did become linked with the Goddess, and that was one of the reasons for rejoicing. My hypothesis (and this takes us into a psychological realm again) is that beneath Hades' lust was an envy of feminine relatedness and a genuine need to be connected with the Goddess, and this connection was made, albeit through rape and trickery. It was Hades himself who was transformed in the rape; far from overcoming the Goddess, he only re-evoked her original connection with her death side—thus, linking himself to her, Death was reconnected to Life, and Hades was transformed from the patriarchal rapist and violator into the Plutous child. Relinked to the Mother, patriarchal death becomes once again a fructifying force. Although psychological interpretations have endlessly stressed the patriarchal triumph of separating mother and daughter, no one has adequately explained how it is that the Mysteries—Demeter's Mysteries—meant that the fear of death and annihilation had been conquered. No longer was death a terror but a link to life, toward which one could move with joy and hope. This was the marriage of Persephone and Hades, a marriage reconnecting a prepatriarchal Feminine wholeness and a Masculine service to that wholeness and to life itself.

Even Hades' later association with Dionysos, which renders him more positive, does not dispute his reconnection to the Goddess, for in his earliest form, Dionysos was a cereal god, the god of beer, son of the Mother Ceres (Demeter).[26] Only much later does the cereal son of the Mother give rise to the wine god who is separated from his maternal roots and grafted onto the Father for an unnatural birth— who then is himself both surpassed and appropriated as the new god Christ gains power and becomes dominant in religious history.[27]

Stripped of the euphemisms that surround him (and his later, more positive linkings), Hades' terrifying core becomes more visible. Even a relatively late version of the Persephone myth presented by Ovid in 8 CE reveals the unmitigated cruelty and annihilative predilections of this underworld god. As told by Ovid, the myth of Persephone's abduction includes another, subsidiary tale: the story of Cyane and her attempts to forestall the rape.

Cyane was a water nymph who encountered Hades carrying Kore away and tried to confront him as he passed by her holy fountain. Rising from the midst of her waters, she cried out, "You will go no further, Pluto! . . . You cannot be the son-in-law of Ceres [the Roman name for Demeter] if she does not wish it. You should have asked for the girl, instead of snatching her away."[28] She then spread out her arms to block his path. Hades became enraged and plunged his scepter into the depths of Cyane's fountain; when it hit bottom, it opened up a path into the underworld through which he and his screaming captive furiously dove.

Hades' brutality had a profound effect on Cyane. The water nymph

lamented the rape of the goddess, and the contempt shown for her fountain's rights, nursing silently in her heart a wound that none could heal; until, entirely wasted away with weeping, she dissolved into those waters of which she had lately been the powerful spirit. Her limbs could be seen melting away, her bones growing flexible, her nails losing their firmness. The slenderest parts of her body dissolved first of all, her dark hair, her fingers, her legs and feet. It needed but a little change to transform her slight limbs into chill waters; after that her shoulders, her back, her sides, her breast disappeared, fading away into insubstantial streams, till at last, instead of living blood, water flowed through her softened veins, and nothing remained for anyone to grasp.[29]

When Demeter passed by in her search for her daughter, Cyane wished to speak, to tell the goddess what had befallen Kore, but she no longer had a voice, a mouth, or even a tongue; she had completely dissolved. Nevertheless, she managed to send up to the surface of her fountain Kore's girdle, which had fallen in the water during her abduction; seeing it, the goddess knew her daughter had been in that place.[30]

The myth of Cyane illustrates Hades' cruel character, particularly his reaction to being challenged and held accountable for his deeds. It also exemplifies a response to his lethality quite different from Demeter's; here the woman faced with Hades' power is totally undone.

Hades will not be held directly accountable for his actions; he becomes enraged when confronted and "rapes" his challenger's domain. He plunges his shaft into the center of what is most essentially hers, the domain that she governs, and then uses it as a passageway into his own dark kingdom. Cyane loses her power once she is violated; she dissolves. Hades deals her a blow from which she cannot recover. She literally becomes undone, loses her cohesiveness as well as her voice. Hades' capacity to make insubstantial is here at its most extreme and complete—". . . and nothing remained for anyone to grasp." Hades' death blow can make one literally fall apart.

Cyane's response to Hades is strikingly different from that of Demeter. Cyane attempts to protect Kore but fails to "watch her back"; she cannot protect herself or guard her own world adequately. Further, she comes undone by the first attack on her stance (though it should be noted that Hades' attack goes to her core and is therefore very effective). Demeter also becomes enraged and active but, unlike Cyane, she persists; despite her considerable depression, she maintains her anger, never relinquishing what belongs to her and never letting her rage and protest dissolve into woundedness. Each time Demeter is thwarted, she gets angrier and finally turns the tables on the masculine gods themselves: she refuses to continue to serve their system or allow it to use her gifts (unlike Cyane who does not protect what is hers, enabling Hades to use it for himself and destroy her in the process). Demeter also punishes the gods (and their human subjects) until they relent and return her daughter.

In summary, the god Hades is characterized by hiddenness, physical and emotional distance, and a propensity toward violence. He prefers invisibility, shrouding a core nature so frightening and threatening that people used euphemisms to stem their terror and keep him at bay. He is generally disconnected from the upperworld except by curses; despised and feared, he is excluded from the rhythms of ordinary life, denied the celebrations and communion enjoyed by the other Greek gods in their interchange with humanity. Although claiming some of her attributes as if they are his own, he is essentially outside the Mother as well as separated from feminine relatedness, from Nature, growth, and cycle. Yet he is deeply drawn to disrupt the feminine world in order to transform himself through it.

Strikingly, he is also set apart from the brighter masculinity of his patriarchal brother Zeus and commands none of the Father god's honors; the shadow side of patriarchy is relegated to an underworld realm, removed from the power it mirrors so darkly, the power that hiddenly consummates in a split-off, patriarchal version of death. This form of death is static, repetitious, disconnected from life, unfertile. It is embodied by the character of Hades: wielding death's powers, he ungrounds, desubstantiates, depersonalizes, and possesses his victims.

Hades is also strikingly unrelational. Focused on his rights, intent on power over his victims, the closest he comes to relatedness is lust. His style of relating is violation; he rapes and possesses whatever his lust compels him to want. He refuses to be held accountable, at least by the feminine call to conscience embodied in Cyane; confronted with his cruelty, he becomes especially lethal, "going for the jugular" of his challenger, destroying her at her core. Yet, he chooses for his bride a goddess so essentially steeped in feminine relationship—as if to compensate for his own primitivity and one-sidedness. Therein lie the seeds of desire hidden even more deeply than the lethality in patriarchy's shadow: the secret, buried impulse to reconnect and transform. But before this hidden impulse can take root in his marriage to the Goddess and find its fulfillment in the power of her Mysteries, it is embedded in a context of fixedness and death.

When the archetypal forces embodied in the god-image Hades infiltrate the human realm, they may be encountered in different ways. A person (or group) may identify with the archetype unconsciously (i.e., be possessed by it), exhibiting aspects of personality and behavior quite in line with the god's and unknowingly playing out parts of the mythic drama. Or a person may have an inner aspect that appears in Hades form, such as recurring dream figures representing a shadow aspect of a man or animus of a woman (figures in dreams may also be introjects of Hades-like people in the person's history now implanted in his or her psyche). A person may also encounter Hades in another, that is, "out there" in relationship, and metaphorically or literally become Hades' victim, following aspects of the myth in his or her response to the Hades-carrier and undergoing some kind of symbolic death. These possibilities are not mutually exclusive, at least as played out between individuals: a woman who chooses and remains with a Hades partner, for example, may have a Hades imprint in her own psyche as well. In each of these human arenas in which this archetype may appear (identification, inner configuration, relational dynamic), aspects of the myth will be played out.

The man in whom the Hades archetype is dominant may exhibit personality and behavioral characteristics that are similar to the ancient god's but expressed within a particular social milieu and subject to individual variations. He may be someone who is emotionally remote from others, holding himself apart from the usual, everyday world of social exchange. He may see himself as superior and independent of what he considers too ordinary, or he may be set apart by others because of inadequate social skills (particularly true empathy and give-and-take) or a negative personality (or one may mask the other). Thus he is likely to be a "loner" and have few, if any, real relationships; the only kind of relationships he may get into are those in which he can establish some kind of power over the other as with employees, servants, children, students—anyone whom he can consider his inferior or dependents. Most likely this will include his partner; however, since the partner has the potential of being more equal, he may have to establish and maintain his power over her via psychological methods of coercion and intimidation (though he may also have an economic hold over her, especially if there are children).

In marriage and in the way he looks at the world, the man in whom the Hades archetype is dominant is likely to hold traditional patriarchal values of male supremacy, separation from and dominion over Nature, women, anything considered feminine (including the Feminine in himself), minorities—anything that threatens his power and the cultural status quo that supports it. Further, when threatened or challenged, he is apt to resort to violence or threats of violence, even if these are well hidden and are expressed only in put downs and intimidations of his partner.

Because Hades was a patriarchal god and much of Western culture has been steeped in patriarchal values and power arrangements, his human carriers, even now when much is in flux and cultural arrangements are changing, are likely to draw some support from the collective: there is still a tradition out there to support or at least tacitly allow his power to continue. Though by and large I will be focusing on the more extreme and full manifestations of this archetype to draw forth and explicate a picture of him, there is a piece of Hades in all of us; he exists at some level in nearly everyone's social conditioning and in the power arrangements of our dominant culture.

Hades is not simply power, however, or even all forms of power-over. Zeus represents patriarchal power as well, but Hades' power is hidden under Zeus-type patriarchy or accompanies it as its shadow. Moreover, Hades is hidden lethality, and this lethality attempts to unground, undermine, fixate, control, and utterly possess the other. This is Hades' core that in Hades-identified men as well as in the god is shrouded in the euphemisms with which he surrounds himself and insists on and may even, to some eyes, appear to embody.

Thus, the Hades-dominated man may see himself as extremely generous, gifted, "liberated," may even insist that he is basically a nourisher of others (Zeus Trophonious). He may "play poor," readily trumpeting his own inadequacies or modesty, disavowing any motivation in his relationships with others except to "help" or support. He may even exhibit behavior that appears to support his claims, being lavishly generous to employees during the holidays for example, or taking special pains to encourage the work of a subordinate. But should that subordinate rise to a level of true independence (the one-in-herselfness of Kore), he or she is immediately undermined, denounced as "disloyal," or hiddenly dealt a killing blow. People more intimate with a Hades-oriented man, his wife or partner or children, are more likely to experience his passion for power more directly. But even here, he may be a consummate shape shifter, charlatan, or dissembler, continually reframing his behavior as positive and insisting that others' perceptions of hurtful intent, falseness, disdain, or even violence are wrong or "misguided" (or deserved).

The extent and skill of this shape shifting, all aimed at concealing the Hades core, can take on extreme dimensions. (Dreams or fantasy images of such a man in his wife's or child's psychology may picture this aspect of him as a black magician.) Especially if his captive audience is very young, emotionally or literally isolated, psychologically fragile, or conditioned by her own background to endure this kind of

117

personality (e.g., has been abused in her childhood), this shape shifting can go to the level of literal brainwashing and evoke profound confusion, even dissociative states, in its targets. If the dissembling is coupled with overt or subtle threats of violence, whether literal or psychological, even more harm may result. Thus a person who is playing out Hades can literally unground the other, sending her to a hell within her own psyche as well as within the relational field.

The characteristics and dynamics of the Hades archetype can infuse human life not only in shadow aspects of male psychology (or the patriarchal collective) but also characterize a woman's animus. This aspect of a woman's psychology, appearing in dreams, fantasy, and creative products as an "inner man," is often experienced by the woman half-consciously as a masculine voice or running commentary within her head; it colors her experience of herself as a woman as well as entering into her outer experiences of men. If her animus bears the mark of the archetypal Hades, it is likely to appear and to function as some form of rapist or death-bringer, constantly pulling her down and ungrounding her and her relationships.

The animus has both archetypal and personal origins; in the case of a Hades-type animus, it also carries an introject of patriarchal values and patriarchal power dynamics. Thus it is a repository of patriarchal views *within* the woman and partly echoes the dominant culture outside her—but operating in an *inner* form. So, for example, the assumption of male supremacy may work from within. A woman may constantly be reminded inwardly that she is "nothing without a man" or that her work is not as accomplished as her husband's or that her body and its rhythms are a handicap she has to transform and transcend. This voice inside does not simply express its opinion, nor is the woman likely to be able to receive it as such; instead it seeks to overpower and estrange her from her sense of self, from her rhythms, from whatever seems truly natural to herself and what she would call "home." And if she resists or tries to stand against the power of this voice, it grows stronger, more forceful, and more overwhelming.

In dreams, the nature of this kind of animus is pictured more deeply. He appears as a murderer, rapist, magician, con man, or robber—secret, elusive, or partially invisible. He threatens some version of death or its psychic equivalent. Even as inner figure, his power over the woman may reach the Cyane level and not only unground but undo her. One woman dreamed the following: an emotionally fragile,

118

terrified woman was being relentlessly verbally berated by a man. She became more and more mute and frightened. He wouldn't let up until finally she had a nervous breakdown and then he was satisfied. Here the woman could not defend herself against a sadistic power drive that had to win and, in winning, annihilate the other. She had married a man who was a highly competitive businessman and constantly lorded himself over her, but there was also a part of her that put herself down from within. This type of animus continually seeks to undermine a woman's ego; on a deeper level, it also prevents or disrupts her bond with the feminine Self.

A woman may relate to a Hades-like animus in one of two ways (or move between both): she may become its victim, as implied in the description above, in which case her feminine ego is continually Kore, pulled under and raped from within. Or she may identify with her animus and merge into it; in this case she is likely to victimize others much like a Hades-identified man would. In this latter form, the entire myth may be played out between women as lovers, friends, sisters, or mother and daughter with one woman's animus in the Hades role.

One mother, for example, profoundly overvalued the men in her life and identified with the values of traditional male conditioning. This woman worked for a large corporation and was particularly proud to be seen as "one of the boys" among her male colleagues; like them, she saw the other women in the office as less interesting and less worthy. Having grown up in fear of a dictatorial, abusive father with whom she secretly identified and admired, she continually "gave" her young daughter to her husband, attempting to give her daughter what she herself considered to be of most value—connection with a man. Stressing traditional male values of self-reliance, independence, and emotional toughness, she nipped in the bud her daughter's longing to bond with or depend on her and constantly exhorted her to stop any show of pain or tears.

At the same time, this mother was deeply involved with her daughter but from a possessive, power-over perspective. Filled with envy, deeply competitive with her daughter even around the father's attentions, she savaged not only the daughter's attempts to bond with her but with any woman, verbally slashed whatever gave the daughter joy, and refused to be held accountable for any of the considerable pain she inflicted. The depth of her unconscious savagery was profound.

119

When in adulthood her daughter became pregnant with an eagerly wanted first child and was threatened by miscarriage late in the pregnancy, the mother responded to her daughter's terror by saying, "Oh, there was a woman in my office last year who went all the way through the nine months and then had a stillborn." Years later when her daughter went through a painful divorce, the mother blamed her daughter for not being able to "hold her man" as she, the mother, had. In therapy the daughter relayed that she had often thought that only if she died would her mother be sorry—and then felt that at some level this was precisely what the mother unconsciously wanted. Only then could the mother finally win—by wresting even life itself from her daughter's grasp. As we worked over time and the mother continued to compete with and triumph over her daughter, this client learned to stop euphemizing her mother's behavior by saying "oh she can't help it" or "she doesn't really mean it" and saw the lethality head on; she also waged a deep and long struggle against intense suicidal feelings when, goaded on by her mother's voice inside her head, she felt compelled to end her life. This woman had a long struggle to find a Demeter inside of herself, to claim and value connections within herself and with others that could support her life instead of cut it down and attempt to destroy it.

Whether carried as masculine shadow or feminine animus, the Hades dynamic goes for the jugular of the woman. He spoils her joy, undermines her one-in-herselfness, savages bonds with other women or with the Self, and pulls her under precisely when she reaches for something she wants. His methods are lethal and he is most likely to thrust his staff into whatever she considers most "hers." This power dynamic is masterful at finding weak spots and exploiting them in order to gain and maintain control. It may come in the form of a killing perfectionism, deep envy (which seeks to undermine what the other has or even annihilate it), or outright attacks from within or without the woman.

Several examples from my practice come to mind. One woman was struggling courageously to confront her sexually abusive father with his past acts of molestation, ongoing seductiveness, and attempts to keep power over her in her adult life. The father continually denied what he'd done to her as a child; continued to behave seductively, pretending, for example, that pressing his erection up against her was an accident; and when she finally threatened never to see him again, faked nervous collapse. This woman had come into therapy obsessed with death and feeling that she had no inner permission to have a life, especially one that included joy. Slowly, drawing strength from our bond in therapy, from a basically happy marriage, and from a deepening sense of the Goddess acting through her life, she became strong enough to see through her father's euphemisms and confront him directly.

In the midst of the time we worked together, she and her husband bought a wonderful piece of land in upper Michigan. She began to make weekend trips there to meditate, to feel herself deeply in touch with Nature, and to be by herself and restore her sense of value and wholeness. For months, she instinctively knew not to mention this land to her father. When she finally could not contain her joy and shared it with her mother who in turn told her father, his response was quick and incisive: he knew she was deathly afraid of snakes and told her she had better watch out for the snakes in the grass on her land. In the past, this would have worked masterfully, sending her into a Cyane-like response; she would have dissolved in terror and let go of what she had newly claimed as her own. This time she could hold against her fear, grounded in a Demeterian capacity to see clearly and confront the truth: the "snake in the grass" that had terrorized her was and had always been her shape-shifting father.

As in the myth of Cyane, such attacks come most often when the woman has mustered some strength and attempts to confront the Hades dynamic in the other or even within herself. Feeling the threat to his power, he goes for her throat. One woman, for example, married to a controlling, narcissistic man who continually put down even her ideas and opinions as "nothing" next to his own, finally got angry enough to threaten to leave him if he didn't stop saying hurtful things. This woman had grown up in a series of foster homes and had been separated for long stretches of time from her mother; when she was finally grown, her mother died a premature death. All of this had left her terribly wounded and once she had children of her own, three little girls, she had vowed that they would never feel the kind of pain from maternal abandonment that she had grown up with. Her husband responded to her confrontation of his verbal abuse by telling her that if she left him, he would fight for the children, prove her an unfit mother, and never let her see her children again. Terrified, she dissolved, vowed to be a better wife to him, and begged him to let her stay, saying she would do anything if only he didn't threaten to separate her from the children. It didn't occur to her to question the power over her that he claimed; when her sister mildly suggested that she could go to a lawyer for a consultation to get a different perspective on his power, she became hysterical. His "death threat" had found its mark; the very thought of her children being separated from her was enough to undo her. She became a "Stepford wife," making herself over into whatever the husband wanted, like the ancient Greeks who forever propitiated the lethal god with holocausted offerings. Only here it was she who was holocausted in service to the threat of death of the mother-daughter bond most dear to her.

In my observation, Hades in human dynamics often targets a woman's creativity, perhaps because this doesn't truly derive from or depend on him, or perhaps because creativity always brings to birth something new and this in itself is a threat to the power of the status quo that Hades strives so mightily to maintain. Or perhaps the Hades-laden man or animus subconsciously feels an echo of the ancient myth, for it is precisely Persephone's power to introvert and create that determines the Mystery transformation that relativizes even the death threat of Hades. Whatever the reason, Hades in human life seems particularly tuned to a woman's creativity and particularly out to do it in. This may come in the form of a husband or partner who competes with everything his wife does and has to do it "bigger and better." It may come in the form of literal appropriation of her work, using it in some way as an adjunct of his own or even taking it over and taking credit for it. It may come as a continual lack of emotional support or validation for what she creates or her joy in it, or in the form of devaluation so intense that she finally gives up and abandons what she loves altogether.

When the Hades dynamic comes from within, it is the animus that provides the constant cutting down of a woman's joy or creativity as a nagging voice in her head that devalues whatever she cares about. Such a voice may also be an introject from a past experience of someone else's Hades-like animus—a mother's or grandmother's or aunt's, for example.

In her poem "The Hex" from *The Book of Folly*, Anne Sexton describes an introjected Hades animus.[31] The poet recounts that every time she felt joyful and optimistic about life or full of her own accomplishments, an inner, savage voice would tell her she was evil. This

122

voice, which she called the "Nana-hex," echoed precisely a great-aunt's psychotic ravings at her when she was a child.

Sexton had been close to the great-aunt she called "Nana," finding with her the comfort and closeness she did not experience with her mother. This Demeterian source continued in her life until she was thirteen years old, when suddenly her great-aunt disappeared into psychosis and began savaging Sexton and their bond. Here Hades came through madness (another effective "being pulled under" to depersonalization, disembodiment, and psychic death); once a beloved nourisher, Nana now hurled accusations and suspicion at the bewildered girl, who was too young to grasp how this shift could be happening and figure out how not to take it into herself.[32] As the poem testifies, it left a powerful mark in Sexton's psyche, operating in her adult life as an inner savager who attacked especially her joy.

Sexton's great-aunt probably did not have enough of an ego left to experience triumph over killing off her young niece's joy. But usually the person in whom the Hades archetype is dominant experiences not only satisfaction from metaphorical killing but also heightened power, an inflation into the archetypal Lord of Death who wields life and death power. Mixed with a kind of sadistic lust, this "high" from merging into the archetypal realm comes not necessarily from the literal killing of another (although it may come from that too) but from the experience of power over them, particularly when it is flavored with threat or violence.

The appropriation of archetypal death power and the "high" human beings get from wielding it infuse their relationships as well. The death-marriage, for example, from the perspective of a Hades-identified man, is an arena of power. He has to win, to establish and maintain power over the woman at every turn. He is perpetually concerned about his rights in the marriage and all riches are appropriated as his own. In some cases this is played out on a literal level: the house, the bank accounts, the car are all in his name alone. Even the children are "his."

This remnant of extreme patriarchal rights still goes on; as I write, I can think of at least two marriages I know of where this is the case. Reflecting centuries of patriarchal tradition, the "man of the house" *owns* everything, and everything accrues to him. With regard to his wife, however, his appropriation may also be more subtle and more psychological. He may also insist that his thoughts, his interests, his values, his preferences are all superior and more important than hers, or that all her accomplishments or even her positive qualities as a person accrue to or depend on him. Even her illnesses are not as important, as real, or as deserving of care as his. At the same time, he may consistently assert that anything good about her comes from him; even her viability as a person may be seen as dependent on his power. In one of the most extreme examples I have heard of this dynamic, a man who was bedridden and dying insisted that his wife could never make it without him. She was working full time and supporting the family financially, tending to his considerable nursing care needs, including weekly trips to a doctor seventy miles away, and raising their two young children, but he continually berated her capacity to manage on her own. Incredibly, she believed him, and only years after he died did she begin to recognize her own considerable strength and competence.

Secretly (as is the case with any oppressor vis-à-vis those he oppresses), the Hades-bound man projects enormous power to the woman and is constantly attempting to keep it from rising up to thwart him. Particularly threatening is her power to exclude him; both her bonds with others and any indication of self-cohesiveness that is not dependent on him threaten his sense of absolute control. He is constantly killing off her relationships, may even insist that she drop all relationships, and interrupts/interferes with any domain she might claim as her own. Essentially, he wants to possess her relatedness (and envies her capacity to be related), to have it only for himself and under his control. Often there is a poignant but hidden dependence here; like the underground god who has no access to the upperworld of life and love, the Hades-bound man may have no one else who is voluntarily related to him and is not his employee or servant. His one chance of care may be with his wife, though he is continually terrorizing her into staying under his thumb, never dreaming that perhaps if he stopped his controlling behavior and learned to relate to her, she might *choose* to stay.

On a human level, self-hatred and profound feelings of inadequacy and inferiority often underlie the manifestations of this isolated, hated god. If these aspects of the man are visible in the relationship at all, they too will be used to control his wife or she herself may weave them into euphemism to explain or excuse his abusive behavior— "deep down he really feels bad about himself," "he had a terrible childhood." One woman I knew even said that since the culture still sanctioned some of this power-over behavior in a man, her abusive boyfriend could hardly be blamed for it.

The point, however, is not simply blame but rather accountability for power abuse and the capacity to confront the Hades dynamic in oneself or another. This requires the clear eyes of Demeter and her passion for her daughter's life. In human terms, this means that to deal with Hades in herself or another, a woman must be grounded in an authority deeper and older than Hades, a matrix not derived from or dependent on the patriarchal Masculine. Even the goddess as Kore could not by herself overcome the power drive of Hades. Even Demeter could not prevent the rape, just as the early goddess worshipers apparently could not stem the tide of the northern invasions. But Kore's loyalty to her mother's world and Demeter's passionate, clear-eyed stance that did not for a minute buy into the euphemisms surrounding her daughter's abductor were enough, in the end, to transform the kind of death that Hades threatened.

For modern women, as we will see in subsequent chapters, this Matrix and feminine bonding must be discovered (or perhaps uncovered—images of excavation sometimes come up in dreams of this journey to the feminine source ground); the Goddess and her power to stand against the patriarchal death god emerge from or must be dug out of the collective layers of the psyche that both predate and transcend patriarchal culture. Until then, women are likely to give credence to the Hades voice and grant the Hades-carriers the authority they claim.

While a woman who has gone under to Hades needs a profound encounter with the matriarchal Feminine, a connection with the Goddess's power (in psychological terms, an experience of the Self), a Hades-identified man is linked back to life and the recycling Goddess in the Mysteries through a forced or voluntary sacrifice of destructive aggression, a learning of empathy for what the patriarchal shadow has savaged, and finally, a new and voluntary service to the Goddess as seed bearer and son. Before we explore the difficulties of such a journey for the Hades-bound man, we must look more deeply into how the goddess and her daughter in this myth and in general may exemplify the female Self. We must also look at the nature and meaning of the bond that the Hades archetype attempts both to disrupt and rupture.

125

Judith Anderson, *As I Am So Shall You Be*, 1990.

∾ 6 ∾

The Intrapsychic Experience:

The Mother-Daughter Archetype as Representative of the Feminine Self

Our other half is not only of another sex. The union of opposites—male with female—is not the only union for which we long and is not the only union which redeems. There is also the union of sames, the re-union of the vertical axis which would heal the split spirit.

—JAMES HILLMAN,
"Senex and Puer"[1]

The Great Goddess . . . is the incarnation of the Self that unfolds in the history of mankind as in the history of every individual woman. . . . [Symbols] of the archetypal Feminine in all times and all cultures, that is, among all human beings of the prehistorical and historical worlds, appear also in the living reality of the woman, in her dreams and visions, compulsions and fantasies, projections and relationships, fixations and transformations.

—ERICH NEUMANN,
The Great Mother[2]

Y EARS AGO, in a moment of deep inspiration and vision, I wrote a song. The words were "Let my life / a mirror be / of the Imprint given to me / Marked by Her, / my life shall be / bound by Love / yet also free.[3] The image behind this song was of an inner, personal, and transpersonal imprint given by the Goddess to my psyche, an image whose fullness is beyond my comprehension yet nevertheless seeks to be fulfilled through me. It comes to me in intimations that I glean from dreams, from outer events that appear to coincide in meaningful ways with my inner life, from self-observations over time of patterns of my own behavior that I struggle to be conscious of and responsible for in my quest for self-knowledge and self-fulfillment. The imprint unfolds in inner visions, answers to prayers, and through the stories, characters, and images that sometimes spontaneously just appear in my creative work. For me, trying to attend to this, to see what this imprint *is*, is inherent in my passion to become most truly and fully myself; it is the essence and the backbone of my spiritual quest.

What I visioned in my song from a religious perspective, as a divine imprint on my being, is what Jung years ago, writing from a psychological perspective, called the Self. The Self is a hypothetical construct, inferred from a seeming intentionality in the unconscious. It is "as if" there were a Greater Personality behind and beyond consciousness, ordering its behavior and perceptions, influencing it and even attempting to guide it through dreams and other inner phenomena. Jung observed that this deeper organizing Center even appeared at times to be behind the ordering of outer events in an individual's life; sometimes even the outer world interfaces with our inner lives in a remarkably parallel but acausal way, as when a dream prefigures outer events.[4]

While the ego—our usual sense of identity, of an "I" that is continuous over time and space—is the center of consciousness, the Self is the center of our wholeness (conscious and unconscious) and, paradoxically, is wholeness itself. It includes everything beyond our consciousness, parts of ourselves that we may have some inkling of like our shadows or animus/anima, as well as collective and transpersonal aspects we may know little about.

The Self, when it appears to consciousness at all, makes itself known most often through symbols in dreams or creative vision: magical animals or idealized human beings, geometric symbols such as the square, sphere, circle, or various combinations, plants and flowers, mandalas, images of Divinity, and mythologems.[5] It often appears as a complex of opposites, simultaneously expressing young and old, good and evil, light and dark, positive and negative. Its symbols are likely to be distinctly and powerfully numinous. It may also appear nonvisually, in a pattern of events or behavior, in movement or music. Thus, for example, when I wrote the song above, I was astonished to see that the inspiration that compelled me to write the words and music to my prayer also manifested in a certain outer form; the song was a perfect round, something that I have no idea, consciously, how to write. Since its appearance could not be explained by my conscious musical competence (I have only a little background in music and have rarely composed anything) and to my knowledge, the tune is original, I took it to be a manifestation of the Self, a musical circle coming into my ego's desire to make a song from my prayer.

The song that I wrote was a prayer to the Goddess, a prayer that my ego life might reflect her design for me as fully as possible. While I sense that there is such a design and the passion to live according to it is perhaps my deepest religious desire, my life is full of obstacles that get in the way of this, including my own stubbornness and resistance. Sometimes I lose touch with the Goddess completely or she seems to recede from my vision; sometimes I am stuck in old neurotic patterns and try to live out more secular ideas of what I am or should be; sometimes I am terrified of change and risk and feel she is asking too much of me; sometimes I simply don't care or am angry and want to go my own way. In Jungian terms, I live between the limitations and predilections of my ego and the greater expanse and knowledge of the Self. When I can manage it, I feel myself in a kind of partnership with Something greater, attempting to stay aware of its presence in my life and to look for its signs, yet I am also unable to comprehend this partnership in its fullness and perpetually fall away, thinking that whatever I am aware of at any given moment in myself or outside me is really all there is.

Jung writes at length about the ego's perpetual dance of approach and avoidance, connection and estrangement vis-à-vis the greater Self. The ego is included in the Self, yet experiences itself as separate and even has the illusion of being independent, the master or mistress of the house, though it is only the center of what we know at any given time. The ego is shaped both by the archetypal imprint that stands behind it and by the person's particular outer circumstances (e.g., parental demands, childhood experiences, cultural conditioning); these influences, however, may clash. Thus what the Self calls one to be may be at great odds with what parents or culture consider the right way to be and may even go against one's own ego preferences and conscious values.

Living according to the Self is not an easy or romantic thing to attempt; it often involves suffering, feelings of estrangement from one's family or peers, and long years of searching. In addition, because the Self is rooted in the archetypal realm that is not bound by time and place, it appears sometimes to be completely unaware of human limitations; the Self manifesting as creative passion, for example, may compel one to live not only with the disapproval of one's family but also be so demanding and relentless that it gives one no time for food or rest or making money to support oneself. It is as if the Self simply seeks to manifest but doesn't recognize the limits of the human vessel it seeks to fill; it is up to the human ego to stand for what it can and cannot tolerate while at the same time struggling to tune into and embody the transpersonal call.[6]

Optimally, the person longs for a sense of connection with the "Greater Personality" beyond his or her ego and thus wants to tune to the Self and realize its demands; with this comes a richness of meaning, a depth, and an authenticity to one's living. This longing and willingness to serve the Higher Power in one's life requires an open and fluid ego. At the same time, the ego (according to Jung) is not to be overthrown or transcended; it provides the grounding for the Self in a human existence, the Self's feet on earth, so to speak, and as such is limited by time, space, and the ego's capacity to comprehend and realize what is beyond it.

While the Self-directed ego will strive to serve and embody the divine imprint, it may also at times have to stand against the Self's demands in the name of human responsibilities (e.g., responsibility to the culture or one's family) and human limitations (e.g., needing time to eat and sleep).

If, however, the ego goes to the other extreme and sets itself up against the Self altogether, asserting that it—the ego—is the only center of life or insisting on living according to cultural or family demands that are inimical to the person's deeper nature, the Self may manifest as the enemy of the ego, the archetypal Antagonist, and threaten the ego's continued existence.[7] Ferocious, powerful, numinous beings or animals may haunt one's dreams then, bringing with them the threat of death or dissolution. Outer events in one's life may appear to arrange themselves in ways that consistently threaten or terrorize the ego, exacerbating the limits of its power and control. Even these terrors may be intimations of the Self, seeking to rebalance a life that has become too one-sidedly ego-oriented and not adequately aware of the transpersonal forces coursing through its depths that can be tuned to but neither completely ignored or controlled.

Attempting to serve the Self is a lifelong endeavor that can never be fully accomplished; there will always be some aspect of the Self that remains unconscious and unrealized. Yet it is precisely this Mystery, this transpersonal "Other," that stands forever as a lodestar for our lives, spurring us on to deeper comprehension of ourselves and infusing our human existence with a greater-than-human imprint and meaning.

In the present context, my interest in the Self is focused particularly on its manifestation in images of human or humanlike figures and god-images within the human psyche. Jung wrote:

> Apart from the geometric and arithmetical symbols, [the human figure] is the commonest symbol of the Self. It is either a god or godlike human being, a prince, a priest, a great man, an historical personality, a dearly loved father, an admired example, the successful elder brother—in short, a figure that transcends the ego personality of the dreamer. There are corresponding feminine figures in a woman's psychology.[8]

Taking the last statement seriously: for a woman, a goddess or goddess-like human being, a princess, a priestess, a great woman, a historical personality, a dearly loved mother, an admired example, the successful elder sister (and surely the female therapist) can all serve as images of the Self. Such images may appear intrapsychically in a woman's psychology, in dreams, fantasy, creative work or religious visions, (e.g. a priestess figure appears in a woman's dream) or relationally (e.g., a woman experiences another woman as "priestess").

While both Jung and Erich Neumann (see the second epigraph to this chapter) asserted that the Self appeared as a Greater Personality or god-image of the same gender, neither developed this idea extensively in clinical or spiritual terms for women. Some of the foremothers of contemporary Jungian psychology such as Marie-Louise von Franz, Esther Harding, and Irene de Castillejo, began the work of explicating feminine psychology within the framework of women's own experiences of the transpersonal Feminine, but it has only been in the last fifteen years or so, with the flowering of the Women's Spirituality Movement and a parallel blossoming of more extensive work on feminine psychology by women Jungians, that the implications of the Goddess as a Self-image for women have begun to more fully appear.

To me, these implications are profound and wide-reaching. The vast variety of images of the Goddess derive from earlier cultures and times that were more female centered, at least in their religious apperceptions, than our own; these figures of the Goddess from the past offer broad, deep, and complex pictures of all it can mean to be female. Moreover, they exist beyond and before patriarchal visions of what is feminine and carry powers, attributes, and stories that have been lost to most women growing up in patriarchal cultures. Both I and many others have written about the deep possibilities of sociopolitical, psychological, and spiritual liberation that can take place when we recover Divinity as Feminine and consciously draw from and dream forward these ancient goddess figures. Even viewed from a secular perspective that does not see them as holy, these ancient images offer a vivid vision of the variety of styles, attributes, and powers that have been considered female, far beyond what our culture prescribes as possible and right; this in itself has been empowering for many women who can now name and claim aspects of themselves considered sinful or deviant by patriarchal standards (e.g., joyous, assertive sexuality not connected with sin, an inner wildness of spirit not to be made domestic, passion and rage, a variety of body types).

My interest here is in the further possibility that the Goddess in her many guises and stories may also, for some contemporary women, function as the Self. That is, the Greater Personality, the archetypal matrix of a person's wholeness that appears to organize, determine, and seek manifestation through the human ego, may appear in the dreams, behavior, and relationships of a modern woman as a goddess story or goddess image or pattern. Studying these mythologems both in what we can know of their ancient forms and contexts and through their direct, distorted, or reshaped appearances in the psyche today, we may be able to better grasp and recognize the topography and

132

nature of one of the forms of the female Self. From this study we can also speak in more depth of the ego/Self relationship and its dynamics in women today, including the challenges posed to a woman's ego life when the 'god-within-her' is female and the patriarchal culture she lives in not only fails to acknowledge a female Divinity but has played and continues to play an active role in its misrepresentation, exile, and repression.

The body of literature focused on the Goddess that exists today, perhaps especially the work of the late Marija Gimbutas, the archaeologist who has often been heralded as the "grandmother" of the Women's Spirituality Movement, details both the fullness and multiplicity of the Goddess as she appeared in ancient times and as she reemerges in the contemporary feminine psyche. Gimbutas's archaeological work and subsequent interpretation focus in depth on one of the oldest manifestations of the Goddess, the widespread Goddess of Old Europe as she appeared in Neolithic times and interfaced with later goddess images throughout the region even after the Christian era began. By considering the functions and images of the Great Goddess of Old Europe, we can clarify how and in what forms she could appear in the collective unconscious today and in what ways she may function as an image of the female Self.

Her appearance as carrier of opposites and as a figure of feminine wholeness is clear. The Neolithic Goddess had both lunar and chthonic aspects; she embraced both heaven and earth and all that existed and moved within them. Gimbutas asserts that the Goddess had two global functions: life-giving/death-wielding/regeneration (under her lunar aspect); and fertility/multiplication/renewal (under her chthonic, seasonal aspect). Within these functions were various subfunctions as well as a plethora of images that served to express them.

As life-giver, the Goddess was giver of all. She gave birth to the world, to humanity, to the animals and plants. The primeval Mother as bear, doe, and female elk as well as various anthropomorphic givers of birth gave expression to the Goddess in this form. As giver of all, the Goddess was also the origin of life, water, and health—standing stones as guardians of life water, anthropomorphic or bird-shaped vessels, and aquatic images all pictured this aspect of the Goddess. The season of spring and the capacity to tell the future were also connected with the Goddess as life-giver; young female figures represented these aspects as did the spring birds—orioles, cuckoos, swallows, larks, and doves. She also embodied life energy as healer and regenerator, protector of the household, and the power behind the increase or decrease of material goods. An abundance of images expressed these various functions: the snake or snake-woman expressed her capacity to heal and regenerate; the nurse with a baby pouch or madonna/child figures in human and animal form emphasized her protectiveness; epiphanies as water birds or water-bird-woman combinations connoted her connection with material well-being. In modern dreams, any of these images may express this aspect of the Goddess—or, put psychologically, may express the feminine Self as life giver and sustainer, the vessel and matrix of psychic energy.

Giver of life, the Goddess was also the harbinger and agent of death. As owl-woman, snake-woman, raven, crow, vulture, and bird of prey, as frightening mask with poisonous snakes, or as stiff "White Lady" figures, she killed and reclaimed all she had once given birth to, only to regenerate it all. Never simply dichotomous, never only a carrier of opposites, she also transformed life and death through her greatest and most essential power: the power of regeneration. The sacred triangle of her vulva, reproduced over and over in ancient times; her uterus and the animals and animal-women who symbolized it—frogs and toads, hedgehogs and hare, turtles and fish; as well as the insects of transformation—bees, butterflies, and moths—vividly expressed this most essential of her aspects. Here too the appearance of these images and symbols in contemporary material may express the dark side of the Self, its capacity to limit and even kill the life of the ego as well as transform and regenerate it.

Life-giver, Death-bringer, and regeneratrix: these were the Goddess's links to the moon, which also served in ancient and in later times as a quintessential visual reminder of her presence and continual in-process transformation. Her chthonic aspects linked her to the earth as giver of the seasons and fertility and Mother of the dead. The sow was the sacred representative of her chthonic side (later linked with Demeter and the piglets brought as sacrifice to honor Kore in the Mysteries). Seasonal rising, growing, ripening, and dying; all links to pregnancy, direct and symbolic (e.g., hills and mounds of earth and stones, ovens, protuberances on female bellies); all representations of rising in the spring expressed this aspect. And the opposites most carried by her chthonic side were young and old (including the combination "old and pregnant"), mother and daughter, summer and winter—these were expressed in doublings of the Goddess that will be considered in more depth below. Caves and graves, including the shaping of the latter as egg, vagina, uterus, or pregnant body of the Goddess, exemplified her presence and dynamic as the Mother of the dead.[9] Caves and graves have long been linked to Mother symbolism in modern psychology; within the context of the Old Religion, they also connect life's origins in the Feminine with its final destination.

The powers to give life and sustain it, to limit and kill, to transform and regenerate, all written large and profoundly numinous in a feminine being as vast as the sky: what if *these* were behind the Greater Personality Jung writes about that seeks to be realized and fulfill itself through the lives of individual human beings? What if this ancient figure in her many vibrant facets and multiple symbolic forms was alive and well and pressing toward expression in contemporary women today? What if her myths were playing out in individual lives, in individual ways, in old forms and new, struggling to correct and rebalance a depletion, constriction, and devaluing of the vastness of the Feminine at the hands of a controlling patriarchal culture?

Consider the following: Rosa (a woman whose personal mother appeared as the goddess Kali in a dream I wrote about at length in my previous book)[10] was in her fifties when she came to me. She spoke of herself as a "collapsed old woman," "over the hill," "nothing without a man." Growing up in the 1930s and 1940s, she had served the feminine image that had been prescribed for her extremely well. She had worked diligently to augment her husband's powerful personality and career, carried forth his values, entertained his friends—but he had left her. Already past midlife (an issue she felt so keenly that she constantly lied about her age, even to me), alone and feeling empty, betrayed, and depressed, she felt that life was over; she was bitter and angry and struggling to reconstitute her life around the values she had served.

The centrality of "the man" as a feminine focus had been etched into her in extreme by her family. Though the women in her family all had powerful, devouring personalities, the central figure was her father, whom all of the women, her aunts and her mother alike, held up as a god. Rosa worshiped her father; pleasing him and living in his light constructed a nearly mythic sense of meaning in her childhood.

Even at the point at which she came to me, she could scarcely speak of him without becoming reverential and almost maudlin with emotion. The truth of her father was that he was a petty thief who had been sent to prison during Rosa's early years for embezzling funds from his company; this was literally hidden from Rosa, her mother and aunts pretending for months that he was away on vacation. Rosa was in grade school at the time. Somehow the other children found out the truth about her father and teased her mercilessly; shattered and crazy-made, not knowing what to believe, she simply withdrew into herself and, along with her family, maintained the fiction of her father as a large-than-life "golden man." It was not until her adult years that she was able to unbury and confront the truth.

When she began therapy with me, she was struggling on an ego level to reconstitute her role as handmaiden of the Great Man, the patriarchal vision that had given her life its major sense of meaning. She was now a struggling artist and traveled in the entourage of a well-known, charismatic male artist who commanded a national following. She lived for his attention and approval, was envious and angry when younger women appeared to get more from him than she; apart from him, she languished in feelings of low self-esteem and resentfully eked out a marginal life as a graphic assistant.

Her initial transference to me was immediate and negative, reflecting both her devalued sense of self as a woman and her estrangement/ suspicion around women in general. In the first session, I was moved by her childhood story, by the little girl and woman who had somehow survived the intense loneliness and lack of support involved in a family system and environment that gave her only a fiction to believe in. The image of a small green sprout came into my mind (a Kore image, I realized later, the plant vitality so vibrant that it pushes even through stone); I was picking up unconsciously an energy that compensated her conscious sense of the "collapsed old woman," though it would be many months before it surfaced consciously in her. I took the risk and shared the image with her; she immediately trashed it, enraged. "That's ALL you see?" she asked.

The work began. I was considerably younger than she was, which fed into her issues with aging; she bought in very strongly to what I've called our culture's "cult of the Maiden." Any younger woman, including her daughter, was a painful source of competition and comparison for Rosa. We had all the advantages, she believed—youth, skills, the greater capacity to attract a man, increasing support from the Women's Movement as it flourished around us in the late 1970s; she had none of these, she felt, and her envy was intense. I felt estranged when I worked with her in those early months; stung at times by her relentless devaluing and envy, set apart repeatedly by the competitiveness she'd been taught, I held back from expressing my compassion and care as fully as I felt them. I wondered if I could go on working with her and why on earth she had come to me; given her conscious viewpoint and values, a woman therapist was a most unlikely choice.

Yet something had pushed her to me and continued to push her toward connections that challenged her conscious views and surprised even her in the beginning. She fell into a women's support group, made up of mostly younger women; this brought out all her distrust and competitiveness until she noticed with astonishment that not only were the younger women genuinely interested in her life but supportive of her efforts to recover from her divorce and make her own way in the world. Some even looked to her as a role model, an older woman they admired and were fond of. In therapy she softened a little toward me, beginning to trust my care, though often still holding me at arm's length and controlling my contributions to our work and her life.

We spent many hours focused on seemingly endless dreams of and conscious obsession with "the man"—the male artist who carried her sense of value and from whom she still desperately wanted recognition—and of course the earlier incarnation of him, her experience of her father. Repeatedly and increasingly, her dreams of both men and of other negative animus figures conveyed the same message: her ego's elevation of the man to the Great Personality was directly linked with her devaluation as a woman and a person. The service that part of her still consciously wanted to maintain, the patriarchal role of being a reflected light of a powerful man who would give her validation and meaning, was profoundly at her own expense; this elevation of the man, coupled with her own lack of self-worth, was furthest from her conscious beliefs about her life and conflicted directly with what the most conscious aspects of her ego wanted to reconstitute. It took a long time for the message of these dreams to filter through her ego attitude and values.

Nevertheless, something drove her toward change. She worked hard on her dreams, struggling to take in their points of view as they became clear to her. She continued her new connections with women, slowly learning to take in their support and let it nourish her. She became involved with a meditation group, another community that had at its center a powerful man. But this time she struggled against her idealization; she felt drawn to and wanted the centering and inwardness that meditation could give her but began to want it for herself, not as part of a way of being validated by and looking good to others. When some people in the group pressed her to join their religious community she resisted, even though she was torn by her need to look good and fit in and by the magnetic personality of the male guru. Instead she carved out for herself a place on the periphery of this community where for the first time in her life she could take what she wanted from a situation rather than having to give herself up to serve the "great man."

Working on her dreams, learning to meditate, and taking up yoga became focal points of a developing sense of vitality about herself. Her dreams began sending powerful female figures, at first in personal form, women she knew in reality and saw as pushy, aggressive, self-centered, and arrogant; increasingly these dreams opened toward an image of the Death goddess and her potent dark powers to limit and kill. Rosa's mother appeared all in black with a crow's wing for a hat and disrupted a regression to her "looking good for the man" days; in a variant of Kali's necklace of human heads, her mother wore a single chain around her neck from which dangled a helpless human figure. Even more powerful in Rosa's mind was another dream in which she was on a ship, intensely engaged in conversation with a woman who liked and supported her. A man approached them and tried to disrupt the conversation; they ignored him. But then, as had happened so often in other dreams she had had, he began to berate her, referring to Rosa as that "useless old woman" (precisely her vision of herself when she had first started therapy). Casually but decisively, the woman whom Rosa was with pulled out scissors and stabbed the man to death, then turned and continued with her intensive conversation with Rosa, while from the man's stab wound spouted a rush of orange paint.

What struck Rosa most about the dream was the matter-of-factness with which the other woman, who valued her, got rid of the devaluing man: a stance that was cold and unthinkable in her former deference to men, even toward those who betrayed and abused her. But even more telling and striking were her associations to the orange paint released at his death. She spoke of a time in her marriage when she had suddenly been desperate to have something of her own, a space that was hers, something that reflected and belonged only to her as an individual. Driven to make such a space, she'd declared the sun porch hers and painted its walls a bright, vibrant orange. What she saw in the dream was that the devaluing man had carried her lifeblood, her individuation drive for a "room of her own," a life of her own, and it was only when someone darker and bigger than her conscious sense of self, a woman wielding the powers of the Goddess most taboo in patriarchy—the powers to limit and kill instead of perpetually serve what devalues the Feminine—could stand up for her, that the Self value carried by the man could be released from identification with him. Yet, as ever with the Goddess, the killing was but a necessary step toward transformation; the negative animus reappeared in Rosa's later dreams—a familiar figure that came back to taunt her—but in these dreams she herself stood up to him and, like Hades reborn from the raped-woman-turned-Death-Queen, this man changed his attitude. Confronted with her newly found power to stand up for herself and no longer accept his devaluing, the male figure changed and vowed to help her for the rest of her days with her art.

Though consciously Rosa felt the strongest identification with Kali, a goddess both old and contemporary whom she now consciously sought and began to study, the death side of the Goddess was not the only figure that appeared to Rosa in personal and transpersonal form. Late in our several years together, she came into a session visibly different, more open, transformed, and told me the following story. Her meditation that week had opened into a powerful experience, one that had touched and shaken her to the core. Deep in meditation, an image had come to her: the image of a huge clay jar, "You know, the kind with openings all over it that look like vaginas," she said. The jar was enormous and potently numinous; in a leap of raw courage, she put herself into the jar and felt the most profound sense of peace and centeredness that she had ever felt. For the first time in her life, she felt herself held by a powerful mothering Presence; this "wildly unmothered" woman who was so estranged from other women and had been handed over to the father repeatedly by her rejecting and unempathic personal mother, for the first time experienced being inside a womb. She felt it as transpersonal; it was bigger than human and holy. For many weeks, she returned to the jar, each time experiencing a profound sense of containment and of peace.

This image of the Goddess, the jar as transpersonal womb (and also as tomb), goes back as far as we know, abounds in the Neolithic images of her uncovered by Gimbutas and others from the farthest reaches of our human history. It returns today in spontaneous form to a modern woman, infusing her being, transforming her consciousness, her understanding, and ultimately what she will value and serve, out of the narrow, constrictive container of her personal and cultural past, into a vaster and older feminine space, a room of her own as spacious as the sky. This is not unique nor is it taking place only within the context of deep therapy; it is happening everywhere around us and taking hold. The Goddess is repeatedly returning and re-forming as an image of the feminine Self.

A later image of the Goddess even more accessible to consciousness and even more obvious as a model for the Greater Personality in a woman's life is the Triple Goddess. Maiden, Mother, Crone: these goddess images mirror the stages of a woman's life in a rich, powerful, and meaningful way. The contemporary artist Judith Anderson illustrates and suggests the power of the Triple Goddess as an image of the female Self in her lithograph *As I Am, So Shall You Be*, the frontispiece of this chapter. Personal and transpersonal trinities reflect the artist's appreciation of the many ways the Triple Goddess can appear in women's lives today while the title itself conveys the ego/Self dynamic: the promise that the human woman can grow into the Goddess's image and participate in her strength, movement, and power.

The central figures, Maiden (a young Vietnamese girl holding a lily), Mother (Anderson herself, a middle-aged woman holding an open pomegranate), and Crone (an old woman holding a skull), are superseded by the Crone as Vulture and surrounded by her birds of prey, thus giving visual form to the supremacy of the Crone as ultimate power. Below, the pelvic triangle holds an ancient doubled Eye goddess; the triangle suggests the Neolithic basis for her triplicity, while the twinning motif, to which I shall return below, reappears in the two lionesses that a occupy strikingly ovular positions relative to the triangle below. On either side are more familiar and more personal expressions of this trinity. On the left, the Virgin and child with Saint

Plate 1. Demeter, Persephone, and Triptolemus.
Greek votive relief, 5th century BCE.

Plate 2. Head of Demeter. Terracotta decorative panel.

Plate 3. The goddess Demeter holding Kore on her lap.
(Note that Kore is presented here as a developed adolescent.)

Plate 4. A Kore (proffering a pomegranate?).
Greek, Archaic Period.

Plate 5. Demeter and Core, "Exaltation of the Flower,"
470–460 BCE.

Plate 6. Persephone and Hades enthroned.

Plate 7. Demeter and Kore. Votive relief, 5th century BCE.

Plate 8. Persephone as Queen of the Dead (note snake hair).
Drawing from an Etruscan tomb, 4th century BCE.

Anne, fashioned after Leonardo da Vinci in which the Virgin with the child on her lap is herself seated on the lap of her mother, which Anderson suggests hearkens back to the image of Goddess as Throne. On the right is a personal trinity: the artist's grandmother, mother, and herself as a ten-month-old child. "The background of this print," writes Anderson, "is all movement, a storm-tossed sea beneath which this birthing of the Triple Goddess seems to take place in stillness and darkness. The choice of blue-black ink for the print [in its original rendering], rather than a warm sepia, underlines the feeling of darkness and solemnity and the vision of death in the presence of new life."[11] The sea reappears in the wavy lines and around a fish in the pelvic triangle, while Neolithic barrows that in reality open into a space shaped like the body of the Goddess appear at the bottom of the print, their calm solidity balancing and perhaps compensating the turbulence of the sea.

"As I am, so shall you be"; thus is the female viewer invited to imagine and enter into the grounding, the dynamic, and the personal/ transpersonal infusions that comprise the appearance of the Triple Goddess today. Maiden, Mother, Crone: the entire life cycle is here, and each woman can see each stage of her life as reflecting and growing into the Greater Personality that stands before her as her matrix in heaven and on earth. So, for example, deeply taught by the Death goddess Kali, held in the Mother jar, Rosa began to own, value, and embody her age, coming at last to value the Crone stage in herself and the larger transpersonal power it mirrored. And through acceptance of the Crone, the Maiden energy that I had perceived as so vital in her survival of her childhood, the true Kore energy that she had for so long given over in service to "the man," was reborn, reinfusing her now as an older woman.

In summary, one way the Goddess functions as a transpersonal image of wholeness for a woman is as holder of all of the stages of life: girlhood, maturity, and aging. The Self in this form holds the lifespan beyond its literal and physical manifestations; so, psychologically and spiritually, the Maiden may be part of old age, the Mother may be found by a woman far beyond biological mothering herself, the Crone may appear as a guardian or lodestar to a much younger woman or even a child. And all may appear together, dynamic and intertwined, as they do in the Goddess: Maiden, Mother, Crone, the feminine three-in-one. They may also appear sequentially, following the natu-

141

ral cycle: flower, fruit, and rot that makes compost for the Maiden hidden in the fruit—the seeds that will sprout again into new buds and flowers.

Thus the Triple Goddess can be said to symbolize the feminine Self as a three-in-one wholeness or as a dynamic, ever-repeating cycle; women who become conscious of her presence in their psyches can catch glimpses of a multifaceted Self that embraces and gives value to their entire lives and expresses itself as sequential, predictable energies that continually cycle and recycle in the innermost soul.

Mother and Daughter or Mother and Maid, the generic forms of Demeter and Kore, are part of the Triple Goddess—yet they also stand on their own and form another image of the female Self. There is no strict differentiation here; duality and trinity are both separate and simultaneous, part of the fluid and paradoxical vision of early pagan thought. This is clear both in the myth and in the history of the Mother-Daughter dyad.

On the one hand, the Crone aspect of the Goddess in the myth of Demeter and Persephone is initially effaced or even lost, reflecting perhaps the impact of the historical patriarchal influence which would eventually "diabolize" and attempt to erase the power of the Crone altogether.[12] Thus the Mother and Daughter as the Two may reflect a loss brought about by historical suppression; viewed from a matriarchal accent, the incursion of Hades may mean not only the splitting of the Mother and Daughter archetype but, paradoxically, set in motion the dynamism that can bring about reunion and reintegration not only of Mother and Daughter but of Crone as well. At the same time, the two-ness of the Goddess has a history predating the patriarchal invasions and thus suggests a separate meaning of the Mother and Daughter in addition to their interconnection with the Crone.

Twin goddess figures date back as far as 6500 BCE; they appear as Siamese twins, which may be double-headed and double-breasted but share a common base, or as Mother and Daughter figures, differentiated only by height or size of breasts. Even temples shaped like the Goddess's body, one larger, one smaller, have been unearthed by archaeologists.[13] Gimbutas suggests these may represent major and minor aspects of the Goddess or her presence as Sisters or Mother and Daughter. The "power of two" in ancient artifacts also conveyed potency, both as expression and invocation of fertility, and in some cultures, the opposites of life and death or summer/winter.[14]

Though the figures of Demeter and Kore appear much later in time and as highly articulated images, remnants of this more ancient twinning of the Goddess remain. At times they appear clearly as separate, mature woman/mother and young woman or girl/daughter. At other times they are both mature women, nearly indistinguishable from each other. Their qualities overlap; Demeter has a Kore side, Demeter Chloe; Kore becomes the Mother in the Mysteries. Both have chthonic connections predating and reappearing in the myth as we know it. And, though also possessed of different attributes and different names, in some places they were also called by a single, generic name, *Damatres* (the Mothers) or, simply, "the Two Goddesses." Again there is paradox and fluidity: Demeter and Kore, Mother and Daughter, are separate yet one. So too psychodynamically; as image of the feminine Self, they represent separable figures within an underlying unity, a common ground in which they become part of one another. But in the myth of Demeter and Persephone, Mother and Daughter are split apart and then reunited but in altered, deepened form. As a drama of the splitting and reintegrating of the female Self, this myth is especially profound. But before we can grasp what this splitting may mean for contemporary women, we have to consider what each of the poles in this archetype represents in the feminine psyche.

At a transpersonal level, the Mother is the source: of life itself, of nurturance for that life, or is its rejector and killer. The transpersonal Mother as an image of the feminine Self is obvious; what could more aptly represent source-ground, matrix, base for a woman? The Mother is an image of maturity, fruition, fullness, especially in the plant realm so vital to Demeter and Kore. It is the Mother the Daughter grows into as a mature woman. The Mother is the Daughter's telos, her future.

This is difficult to grasp in a culture in which the Divine is not imaged as Mother and Matrix of All; in our culture the archetypal dimension of Mother is not consciously named as such; as a result, its potency and bivalence overloads the human being who becomes its unwitting carrier—the personal mother. On the one hand, this means that if we looked deeply enough into our personal mother experiences or our transferences to other women, we might see through to the Goddess level and in this sense even the personal mother may mediate the Self.

In my experience, the personal mother rarely carries the Self consciously for a woman in our culture, at least not past earliest childhood, though unconsciously our enormous expectations and mother blaming mirror the bigness that is laid upon her. With the exception of the Virgin Mary—the human mother of a divine Son—there is no proper place to refer the archetypal Mother in our culture (I have written about the consequences of this at length in my book *In Her Image*). So she operates unconsciously, extending our childhood dynamics and entanglements with "Mom" far beyond our early days for some of us, keeping both us and our personal mothers bound by the weight of the archetype. Rather than see the experience with the personal mother as the prima materia for a spiritual journey toward the Great Mother, too often we do not apprehend that the object of that journey is not human but divine—or, in psychological terms, we fail to perceive the Greater Personality that stands behind the human mother—and we spend our lives futilely trying to get enough from our personal mothers. Behind the drive to keep trying is an archetypal picture we are caught in (as I will argue in chapter 7): Kore without Demeter, the motherless daughter we have all become, transpersonally speaking, under patriarchy and its impact on women and the feminine psyche. Without the Mother aspect of the Self, a woman is without connection to her source, without grounding, without an authentic body, without a Matrix.

But Demeter is more than generic Mother. She especially is connected with fruition, with learning how to seed our lives and bring those seeds to harvest. She is connected with nurturance, so deeply that when she punishes a man with perpetual hunger, she cannot approach Hunger herself but must send an emissary. She is also the Daughter's Mother, the matrix and sustainer of our younger self. Split from Demeter, we are without a feminine source ground, without a primary feminine bond, without maternal food for our psyches and our souls, without futurity—a model of female maturity that we can grow into—and often, without substance or body. Like Kore held in the underworld, we long for resubstantiation, for the upperworld of affection and connectedness, for the Woman who would be an archetypal home. But for most of us, the patriarchal underworld is the only home we have ever known, the Mother is always missing, the spiritual drive toward her is difficult to make conscious and to name, and we

144

long for a matrix we haven't known or have been divided from so early on that we no longer know what our soul-life is seeking.

Jenny was a woman in her early twenties whose unconscious pushed her repeatedly toward a profound connection with the Mother archetype. The Mother as Self was potently present in her psyche even though for a very long time her consciousness could neither recognize nor receive this. She had not been in therapy before and sought it now out of a vague sense of unhappiness with her life; she said she'd decided to work with a female therapist because she knew she had "mother issues" and thought it would be harder but richer than working with a man. (This is a case told to me by a colleague of mine, a portion of which appears in *In Her Image*.)[15] Her husband was a psychotherapist and it was because of him that she had begun to read Jung and decided to try therapy. She was readily engaged intellectually with the therapeutic process, was interested in her dreams, and often had considerable insight. Emotionally, however, she was frightened and uncomfortable, particularly by what she saw as inappropriate feelings toward her therapist. Although she presented herself as highly independent and self-sufficient, she felt threatened by feelings that would come up whenever she experienced her therapist as warm and compassionate. Then she felt a great impulse to reach out and touch her, longed to be near her; sometimes she even imagined being a little girl and sitting on her therapist's lap or being held or lying down next to her and going to sleep. These feelings and fantasies were extremely uncomfortable for her; she had been raised by a cold and emotionally abusive mother who was extremely homophobic. Her mother couldn't stand to be touched by her daughter and had conveyed that all touch between women was suspect and "dirty," even going so far as to repeatedly attempt to break up Jenny's childhood closeness with a best friend.

Several months into therapy, Jenny dreamed: A girl, perhaps eighteen or nineteen years old, was walking up a road. A pigeon appeared in front of her; she was frightened by it. She went home, where her mother had just closed the door of a room in which there were younger children. This family had somehow lost its substantiality, but there were cousins in Berlin and if they could make contact with them, they would regain substance. The mother was going to try to call them on the telephone. At this point, a narrator broke into the dream and said of the mother, "But if she tried the telephone, she would never reach them." The daughter, however, detained the mother; she seemed to know that calling was not the right way. She put her arms around her mother and held her very close. She indicated to her mother that this was the way they must go and pressed harder against her mother's body, perhaps even beginning to move with her, as one would in lovemaking. It was as if she wanted to make love with the mother or maybe merge with her, and this would be the way to contact Berlin. The mother did not push the daughter away and yet was very uncomfortable; she didn't want this to go any further.

Jenny felt this dream to be important, though it also made her uncomfortable. The dream reminded her of a fairy tale, complete with narrator; she herself was not directly in the dream, although she said she could identify with both the mother's and daughter's feelings. Although the dream held personal associations for Jenny, its impersonal form suggests that it was also coming from a deep layer of the psyche, a layer closer to the collective unconscious than to consciousness. Subsequent material confirmed that for Jenny in particular, mother issues were a pathway to the Goddess and a profound layer of meaning. But this awareness was still very far from Jenny's consciousness.

The dream opens with the encounter with the pigeon and the girl's fear of it. "A pigeon is a particularly common bird, often hated because it is so common," Jenny wrote in her associations to the dream. She also thought of homing pigeons who carry messages and know how to find their way back home. In ancient times, birds were often believed to be oracular and carried messages to and from the Goddess. These ancient birds also represented a homing instinct; some commentators have seen this drive toward homing as a vital part of the longing of Kore for her mother—the yearning to breach the chasm between the mother and daughter when they are separated from one another. What's added from Jenny's association is that this also represents something that is common and hated; according to the dream, it is also something Jenny feared. In her particular psychology, the homing instinct, the simple and ordinary longing of the child to be close to the mother, had been filtered through her rejecting mother's rigid and stereotyped homophobia. The basic connection between mother and daughter as well as all other relationships between women and girls had been narrowly sexualized and then treated phobically. Consequently Jenny consistently misread her wounded child's longing for

146

a corrective experience as sexual desire. More deeply, she confused the personal level with the archetypal, as we shall also see.

The problem in the dream is that the family of mother and children (there was no mention of a father) had lost its substantiality; there was no sense of how this had come about or why. In Jenny's conscious life, mother and child had never had substance at all and because Jenny's mother was so phobic, all relationships between women in her life lacked substance and definitely lacked body. Jenny herself was never in her body; in sessions she presented herself as highly verbal and competently intellectual. She worked hard on her dreams, read books on psychology, but was so frightened of her feelings that for months she wrote out and read them to her therapist, terrified of embodying them and speaking them directly. This was particularly true of feelings of warmth and longing toward the therapist, especially a longing to touch her; Jenny feared if she expressed more of these feelings or wanted to act on them, she would be annihilated. As she described it, "It's not so much that I am afraid of being annihilated by you [the therapist] as of letting go of my demand to know and going with what seems to be essentially unknown and a mystery."

In the dream substantiality can be regained by contacting the relatives in Berlin. Berlin had powerful meanings to this client. Her mother had lived in Berlin when she was younger and Jenny had visited it when she took a trip to Europe after college. She saw Berlin as the divided city (the wall was still standing then) and had experienced the pain of a woman she met whose female relatives were on the other side of the wall. She was also struck by what the war had done to Berlin, spoke of "devastation and having to rebuild from scratch." This was precisely what was required in her inner Mother-world. Yet, for Jenny, "Berlin" also contained what Jung called a "reconciling" symbol; what had moved Jenny most when she visited was the sight of a church that was half contemporary (a part of it rebuilt after the war), half old and war-savaged. The integrated vision of old and new, bombed-out and rebuilt, stayed with her.

In the dream, contacting the cousins in Berlin was the way for the mother and daughter to gain substance again: in other words the war-torn, divided maternal legacy that connected with Jenny's experience, along with its potential for the new construction that could coexist and be integrated with the wreckage, had to be addressed. The way to accomplish this integration was precisely through the feelings that

147

Jenny consciously feared most: the urge to make love with or merge with the mother.

Jenny was struck by the contrast between the mother's and daughter's ways of contacting Berlin. She spoke of the impersonal, distant quality of connecting by phone and noted that the contact then would be totally dependent on words; it demanded little involvement between people, she said, whereas the daughter's way was nonverbal and meant total involvement. The daughter's actions in the dream and the references to making love with the mother or merging with her through physical intimacy reminded Jenny of feelings that she had for her therapist and made her acutely uncomfortable. She was much more familiar with and felt safer in the mother's preference for distance and words than with the daughter's urge toward intimacy.

Very slowly she began to risk her feelings and even more slowly came to see that behind them were not only the pent-up longings for closeness with a caring mother that had been so twisted by her personal mother but also the deeper, archetypal level of connection with something huge and numinous. Jenny's therapist felt she could benefit from some kind of body work and sent her to a woman who coincidentally happened to be German. Jenny was terrified at first but also felt deeply drawn to the therapist. Two experiences, one with each of her therapists, enabled her to begin to realize that behind her longings, which had seemed only personal and reductive to her, was a deeper and more inner image: the Mother as Self, the Goddess level.

Jenny's body therapist did body awareness exercises with her as well as yoga and some massage. She was so frightened at first that she had to talk compulsively for at least an hour before she could do the body work; the therapist accommodated this and gradually her need to talk abated. The massage was especially powerful for Jenny since she had so rarely been touched and she quickly realized that the feelings she felt were sensual, not sexual; until this time, deprived of ordinary, uncomplicated touch from a mother, she had not known there was a distinction. Nor had she realized that the powerful feeling of taboo that she had had around touch connoted its ancient as well as modern meaning: something not only forbidden but also set aside as sacred. Increasingly she identified this as what she felt and powerful images of being in a sacred space when she entered the massage room as well as numinous experiences of her body therapist's compassion and ease in her own body were present.

What her body therapist saw as ordinary, Jenny experienced as bigger-than-life, holy, charged with numinosity. One experience in particular pushed her past the narrow homophobic frame her longings had been held in. Jenny's body therapist wore a body suit throughout the sessions, just as Jenny did. One day the therapist remarked that Jenny never looked at her; she looked at the floor or out the window but never seemed to look at the therapist. Painfully Jenny described that she was afraid to; she was afraid because she wanted to and might see the therapist's body and this somehow felt wrong and dirty. The therapist encouraged her to try it; Jenny was terrified but risked it and when she did, her feelings opened out into something totally unexpected. She described it later to the psychotherapist: "Instantly I felt like I was three or four years old, and it was like I was seeing Woman for the very first time. It was like there had never been an image of Woman, like I never saw a woman's body before so I never knew what that was so how could I know what my own was? I could never look at my mother but this was more than that; it wasn't just G—— I was looking at but Woman." This experience calmed Jenny and she carried it inside of her for a long time; she felt as if finally she had an image her child self could grow into, a vision of a mature female body that she too could begin to claim.

Meantime, she also began to risk more with her psychotherapist, allowing the touch I described in *In Her Image* that enabled Jenny to experience her therapist as "real" (i.e., substantial) for the first time, as well as allowing herself to access and share some of her child feelings. She worried at times that her feelings were somehow sexual, but each time she risked them, they inevitably took her to a child level instead of adult desirousness and sexual arousal. One experience of this was especially dramatic and moved through the child level directly to the archetype. At times Jenny had vague feelings of what she identified as a "lustful" wanting to nurse and to get up on her therapist's lap and be close to her; she still worried at times that what she really wanted was to make love with her therapist. Her therapist encouraged her to imagine this through, let her feelings be in fantasy and see what would happen. It took many sessions for her to become brave enough to do this, but at last she did. She imagined getting up in her therapist's lap and "lustfully" wanting to nurse. But as she got into her lap the image suddenly, strikingly changed; the woman whose lap she was on was no longer her therapist but a woman made

149

of cornstalks, dressed in a pink dress, a sort of "corn dolly" like the dolls made in rural Britain and other places from the last sheaf of wheat from the harvest. These dollies are remnants of pagan agricultural rites in which the last sheaf of the harvest was known as the Corn Mother and either buried and observed to be sprouting in the spring or charged with all the fertility energy of the harvest that would ensure the future crop.[16] Jenny knew nothing of such figures at the time. What was also striking about her corn mother was that the pelvic triangle—the quintessential symbol of the Goddess's fertility—was empty. Following her longing to make love with the mother, Jenny had the sense she could fit into this empty space in the corn mother and slide through it, that it was like a passageway. But at this point she got terrified and broke off the fantasy. Relaying this fantasy to her therapist, Jenny couldn't help but be aware that far more was at stake here than the sexual dimension she feared. She had never heard of corn dollies but was moved by the pictures her therapist showed her; very gradually, Jenny found her way toward the Goddess and realized that behind her need to heal her experience with her personal mother was also a call to move into connection with the transpersonal level of the Mother and her fruitfulness as well.

Jenny's journey to the Goddess took years of deep therapeutic work. This work was both multileveled and multifaceted, involving a resubstantiating of the Mother-Daughter bond on both a personal and transpersonal level. Some of the work was profoundly intrapsychic, infused with images of the Goddess that came to her in fantasy, dreams, and imaginal work. Some of it was relational and involved both regressive work with her therapists to re-parent her wounded child and the recognition of how the Goddess was also coming through these mothering relationships. Slowly Jenny followed her homing instinct out of the underworld experience of estrangement from the Mother, from her body, and from other women and grew slowly toward the sense of a matrix she had both feared and been drawn to for so long. Slowly she came to realize that depathologizing the ordinary upperworld of relationships with other women as well as tending to the deeper vision of the Goddess was a lifelong endeavor. She felt like she had found connection with the Mother she so longed for all her life.

For some women, it is the Daughter side of the archetype that carries the Self. Intrapsychically, the Daughter represents our younger

selves, our historical girlhood, and even more profoundly the perpetually renewable virginity our souls require: the sense of belonging to
no man or role or institution but first and foremost to ourselves. The
Daughter carries springtime and verdure; she is the perpetual greenness that moves toward flowering and also toward death but is ever
renewable, ever returns. She is the life force itself in feminine form,
and without her we get dry and depressed and wither before our time;
like Emma grieving for her younger self May, we mourn what used to
be and is no more—our girlhood, the springtime of our bodies, the
vitality, play, and creative beginnings we were once in touch with.
The Daughter is also the Mother's futurity, her extension into time,
the future generation that carries the Mother forward as a memory, an
imprint, extending her own life into another time.

A profound inner dynamic, this face of the Goddess and aspect of
the feminine Self is sometimes projected by women onto their personal daughters. The Daughter may be idealized and carry unclaimed
aspects of the Self of the mother, appearing as the magical child. Or
the mother may seek to live through her daughter, literalizing the
symbolic futurity. But the full weight of the archetype cannot be carried by a human daughter any more than it can by human mothers;
inevitably there is loss and mourning as the daughter bends under the
transpersonal weight and either throws off her mother's projections or
breaks under them. For both mother and daughter, this may initiate
an experience of the Demeter-Persephone myth in patriarchal form,
positive here, with its emphasis on separation and the daughter's release from a matriarchal binding. On the other hand, if the mother is
able to recognize that what she has projected to her daughter is part
of the Mother-Daughter archetype, she may be able to separate the
Divine Child from her human daughter and discover its richness, vitality, and potential for her own renewal through a more direct connection with the archetype (my midlife dream of the baby Anna
Perenna and the need to mother what this goddess symbolizes is an
example of an introverted encounter with the Divine Child).

If the archetypal Daughter is experienced as lost on an inner level,
however, instead of projected, the matriarchal accent is likely to predominate. For example, if we go back to the case of Rosa, we see a
woman who has lost her inner Daughter. When a woman is living
through this side of the split archetype, she feels herself to be just the
way Rosa presented herself at the onset of therapy: a "collapsed old

151

woman," "beyond the gifts of Aphrodite" as Homer put it, raging and grieving over the lost younger woman in herself, experiencing her life as a wasteland from which nothing will ever sprout again. The feminine springtime is experienced as over and it feels like nothing will ever bring it back or revive all the value and vitality that went under with it. Some women experience this in the empty nest syndrome or in what used to be called involutional melancholia—depression during menopause. Some women experience it during difficult separations from a daughter who has carried the vitality of the archetypal Daughter. For Rosa, it was triggered by the loss of value and youth she experienced when her husband left her.

I am suddenly reminded now of a turning point in Rosa's therapy. I had not spoken to Rosa about the Demeter-Persephone myth, but one day she came into her session excited about a paper she had heard about at one of the meetings of the male artist and his entourage she was so taken with. She was still immersed in trying to get his attention and please him so this incident and what it meant to her were even more striking. At this particular meeting, a young woman had spoken up strongly, disagreeing with the artist's views on women and referring to a paper she had in hand, written by a woman whom she knew. The artist responded badly, resoundingly putting her in her place. Something about this stirred Rosa and she went over to talk to the woman afterward, who showed her the paper; it was on the Goddess and included a lyrical retelling of the Demeter-Persephone myth. Rosa subsequently brought the paper to her therapy session but didn't say anything about this experience until the very end; then suddenly she told me with intense feeling of how this young woman had been dismissed and gave me the paper as a gift. It was a kind of ritual gesture of extending value to what the artist, whose shadow she was just beginning to see and feel, had dismissed of the Feminine.

I had forgotten this until this very moment; it was one of Rosa's first moments of bonding with me by identifying us both as women who would feel together for what had been trashed by her idol's Hades shadow. It was also, for her, the germinating moment in which a genuine concern for the Daughter—beyond her value as a patriarchal anima who could attract a man—was born; she had admired the young woman's courage to stand up to the artist, felt pain for her when she was dismissed, and had been impressed by the content the young woman had been trying to convey—the myth that Rosa too was at some level finding her way back to.

Rosa was so deeply immersed in a patriarchal mind-set that for her, even the Daughter had to be transformed—rescued back from being of value only to the man. The entire female trinity had to be discovered and claimed in Rosa's life. She had experienced the Daughter aspect of herself only in service to the idealized Father; she had to experience becoming the Mother's Daughter, which she did when she put herself into the numinous womb-jar. Simultaneously, she had to reclaim her aging, discovering the power of the Crone in her life. Then, just as in the myth, she could become the transformative Demeter, standing up to the Hades animus and refusing to be devalued—then and only then did the animus himself relent and, like Triptolemus, put away his weapons of war and offer to serve the feminine Self.

Not only does the Mother-Daughter Goddess, the two-but-one archetype, appear intrapsychically as the feminine Self in some women or have to be pulled off an actual mother-daughter relationship; it can manifest between adult women as well. The following chapter explores the incarnation of the Self as Demeter-Kore in relationship between women and the negative animus that attempts to ravish the mother-daughter bond.

Sue MacDougall, *Searching for Persephone*, 1986.

~ 7 ~

Relational Dynamics:
Women Who Live the Myth Backward

Revolutionary thought has always been based on upgrading the experience of the oppressed. The peasant had to learn to trust in the significance of his life experience before he could dare to challenge the feudal lords. The industrial worker had to become "class-conscious," the Black "race-conscious," before liberating thought could develop into revolutionary theory. The oppressed have acted and learned simultaneously—the process of becoming the newly conscious person or group is in itself liberating. So with women. The shift in consciousness we must make occurs in two steps: we must, at least for a time, be woman-centered. We must, as far as possible, leave patriarchal thought behind.

—GERDA LERNER,
The Creation of Patriarchy[1]

THIS QUOTE FROM FEMINIST HISTORIAN Gerda Lerner reflects her thesis that for women to see themselves as central to history, as history makers, they must become aware of their own life experience, define themselves and the world from a woman-centered position. Then and only then can patriarchal thought be left behind. I believe this same process is also vital for individual women who seek to reclaim their deep inner lives from the ravages of the destructive aspects of patriarchy. The imperative to become "at least for a time . . . woman-centered" and to "leave patriarchal thought behind" has been played out in the *temenos* of therapy over and over with women seeking to redefine themselves from the raped Kore position vis-à-vis a Hades-like animus, father, partner, or patriarchy itself to a cherished daughter of the Goddess, the Mother of All.

While the last two decades have seen an explosion of both scholarly and popular literature reflecting the formulation of feminine psychologies that are increasingly women-centered and derived from women's experiences of themselves instead of male visions of them, it takes time for this shift in axis to penetrate collective consciousness and even longer perhaps to widely reshape cultural arrangements. Until the day when feminine psychology rests soundly on a base of woman-derived experience and this has permeated the popular culture as well as academia, individual women will still live in and be affected by patriarchal definitions and arrangements at least to some extent. These women will be our mothers and sisters, our friends, our clients, and ourselves. Enlightened or not, we have all been marked by the imprint of patriarchy's power and its Hades shadow.

Though the journey to the transpersonal Feminine, the discovery of a feminine Self, can sometimes be accomplished intrapsychically, it often requires relational companioning. As the example of Jenny in the last chapter suggests, there is no strict line between intrapsychic and relational here; the vessel of archetypal transformation takes place as much in relationship as within the psyche. Thus the myth of Demeter and Kore-Persephone with all its intense dynamics plays out as much between women as within them. This is particularly true but not limited to deep therapy in which both therapist and client are female.[2]

Deep and open relationships between women as friends, lovers, mothers and daughters, sisters, as well as therapist and client can unfold new dimensions of both personal and archetypal experiences of the Feminine and bring balance and healing to women still suffering from the constrictions and distortions of patriarchal vision.

Many women still grow up "male-identified" or with "animus egos";[3] their sense of self is derived not from their own experiences as women and individuals but is dominated, often unconsciously, by men's ideas of what a woman is or should be. Or an inner masculine standard predominates, representing and measuring the woman by images set by her father or husband or brothers or by her mother's animus, all asserting a more general sense of what's been defined as valuable and even viable by a patriarchal culture. Deep friendships, love relationships, or therapy with other women may dissolve this "false self" identity and plunge a woman into participation in women's mysteries, especially death and rebirth (this archetypal theme underwrites all rites of passage and involves the death of an old and, in the context of therapy, usually false self and birth into a new and more authentic or true self). This may be initially frightening, confusing, and disorienting but from this relational encounter a female-identified ego may emerge, grounded in a matrix of women's experiences with each other and the world.

If the experience of women's mysteries through relationship with another woman goes deep enough, it will inevitably lead to an experience of the feminine Divine; thus another woman may for a time mediate the Goddess to her woman friend or partner or client. This may lead to problematical relationships if neither woman understands that something beyond human dimensions is being carried by the relationship, but it may also be utterly transformative for one or both women. In psychological terms, relationship with another woman may bring with it an experience of the Self, the richness of the "Goddess-within" experienced relationally and in the transference.

If we look at Demeter and Kore-Persephone in terms of relationship, we might speak of several phases: the original bond before Hades, the experiences of separation and loss, the transformation of both goddesses, and the heuresis or reunion. In the myth these phases are presented as a linear (and, later, cyclical ritual) sequence played out against the backdrop of an Old Religion grounded psychologically in the archetypal Feminine that is disrupted and split by the shadow side of a New Religion that elevates the archetypal Masculine. In our culture, however, what was a "new" religion at the time of the myth has been in place and colored our personal and collective psychological experience now for over thousands of years while the Old Religion has been largely unknown. We might expect that for us, the sequence of the myth will be different, as I will illustrate below.

The original relationship between Demeter and Persephone re-

157

flects a pattern that I have come to characterize as "matriarchal bonding"; the feminine bond is primary while the presence of the Masculine is peripheral or effaced. Matriarchal bonding between women, as I have seen it emerge in the therapeutic container, is characterized by an intensification and emphasis on the feminine connection between client and therapist and the relegation of the Masculine as an actual man (the impact of the father, husband, lover) or as animus to the periphery. Theoretically, this does not necessarily mean lack of relationship to men or to the animus or even a negative valence (remember Demeter's joyous relationship with her Titan lover, Iasion), but masculine values and masculine perspectives, even if positive, are at least temporarily experienced as less central.

Psychologically speaking, the upperworld of Demeter is characterized by an experience of the archetypal Feminine as Source and Matrix, positive feminine bonding, an acceptance of change and cycle as the natural order of life, and embodied, sensate living. Spirituality in this world is not separate and pitted against Nature and body but rooted in them.

If a particular woman had grown up in this world literally and psychologically, she would be likely to have a predominance of positive feminine bonds in her history with mothers, sisters, grandmothers, and aunts and a sense of groundedness within a network of female relationships. Optimally these relationships would be internalized as she grew and would develop into positive feelings about herself, her body, and her gender. The fruitfulness of womanhood would be desirable and clear to her and she would have the sense of multiple role models from which to draw in constructing her own identity as a woman. More abstractly, this woman would be attuned with the natural realm: connected with and accepting of process; of ripening, decay, and renewal over time; of her own bodily rhythms. She would have learned this from other women and their nurturance and acceptance both of her and themselves; what is given by Nature expressed both in the rhythms of her body and of the world around her would be experienced as the underlying order of human and other life, to be lived from and with instead of fought against and artificially controlled.

In an optimal upperworld experience, the positive archetypal Mother would predominate and a woman's ego would be well-grounded in a positive relationship to herself and her body, learned from her mother's and other women's care and regard for her. In a

Demeterian-like world, a woman might include men and the archetypal Masculine as part of her life, but they would not be primary or
her locus of identity and self-esteem. Both she and her female relatives and companions might relate to men positively but not define
themselves through them, deferring instead to an outer and inner
feminine matrix and the authority of woman-derived conceptions and
experience. Through grounding in her female lineage, the young girl
and young woman would belong to herself first in Esther Harding's
sense of the Virgin and only secondarily give herself to relationship
with a man. Relationships with men would not violate this intactness
but rather would be a further expression of her capacity to connect.

Some women have had this kind of positive upperworld background in their personal histories and can trace their psychological
lineage through their identification with positive female figures in
their past; others, under the influence of feminism, are attempting to
create such a lineage and a woman-centered base for themselves as
adults. Nevertheless our culture, particularly the dominant Eurocentric aspect of it, is far from the original world of Demeter and Kore.
Even women who have had a positive experience of a female-centered background grow up to face a decidedly different context in the
dominant culture, one that still asserts power over the Feminine.

In patriarchy, the archetypal Feminine and all that connected with
it was both diabolized and oppressed; what characterized the upperworld of the Mother was stood on its head. The Mother as Creatrix
was replaced by a Father Creator; the essence of creativity was located
unnaturally in the paternal head, breath, or word rather than the natural and obvious maternal womb. Spirit was disembodied, no longer
infusing Nature but divorced from or opposing it. Unnatural images
(the birth of the goddess Athena from the head of her father Zeus;
the creation of Eve from Adam's rib; the Virgin Birth) and anti-body
practices (asceticism, celibacy) were seen as more spiritual than anything that partook of the life of the body and its natural cycles. The
archetypal Feminine, once imaged as the Mother of All, became assimilated to the Father, who claimed her supremacy and many of her
powers; she in turn became subordinate to him as wife or consort. The
primacy of Mother and Daughter gave way to Father and Son; officially, the divinity of the Mother was abolished altogether. Nature and
her cycles, life on earth and the life of the body, particularly the feminine body, became stripped of spirit, were renamed "carnal," "ani-

mal," "sinful," "material"—in the name of the male god and the male god's spirituality, they had to be conquered, made subordinate to masculine power, their temptations resisted and overcome.

Human life under patriarchy mirrored the values and hierarchies of the sky Father. Like the Mother turned wife and consort, women were subordinated to male dominance, authority, and value; they gained value and substance in the eyes of mainstream culture not from relationship to each other but via their connections to men. This bias in patriarchal culture has permeated the assignment of value in relationship; women's relationships with each other as mothers and daughters, sisters, friends, and lovers are still seen collectively as less vital in adulthood than are relationships between men and women. Women as lovers are still marginalized and seen as a threat to the "family values" of mainstream culture. Any relationship between women that does not include men is seen at best as less valuable than those that do, and at worst as a threat to male power.

Women's bodies, like Nature, have been de-spirited and subordinated to male pleasure, male conquest, and male standards of beauty. Despite the strength of the Women's Movement and its antipatriarchal message, this diabolization of the natural female body—its variety of shapes, sizes, smells, hairiness, and cycles—is a particularly entrenched aspect of patriarchy. Younger and younger girls are buying into the belief that their bodies are wrong and going on diets, resulting in an epidemic of health- and even life-threatening eating disorders among young women. While green politics and ecofeminism hearken back to the Goddess as Earth to stop the rape and destruction of Nature, the Goddess continues to be ravished by the ways young girls and women abuse and desubstantiate their bodies as they act out the patriarchal imperative to control and conquer what is natural.

If a relationship between women is fully infused with the Demeter-Persephone archetype, the entire mythic pattern is likely to unfold. But in a cultural setting that is already patriarchal, the sequence of the myth may be altered; there may be no original bond between women. The initial and most familiar bond may be with Hades, the shadow side of patriarchal emphasis on the primacy of relating to men. A matriarchal bond and the archetypal upperworld of the Feminine may be completely unknown to a woman, but she may know Hades well, through father or husband or simply the culture she lives in. If Hades is all she has known and the underworld is "home," she may not know consciously that there *is* anything else—yet unconsciously the woman who begins life in Hades may be driven to seek the Mother through whom both she and potentially her captor and his values may be released and transformed.

In these instances, a woman is unconsciously driven to live the myth backward, that is, she begins it not as a daughter of the Goddess but as Hades' wife (or daughter). This is her homeground, a given to her conscious psyche. Sometimes consciously, often unconsciously she experiences a sense of separation and loss that are the price of being identified with the realm of Hades. She is estranged from herself, lacks conscious grounding in a feminine matrix, both personally and archetypally, and exhibits symptoms of being in Hades: disembodiment, insubstantiality, lack of definition as a woman and person, and identification with patriarchal views and values. Lack and loss turn to longing: for embodiment, for value, for mothering, for feminine coherence. Finding the Mother as an alternative to and refuge from the patriarchal underworld becomes an unconscious if not conscious goal and is often achieved, at least in my experience in therapy, via a deep initiatory process, a symbolic death and rebirth. Through this initiation, the woman becomes a Demeterian Kore, a mother-nourished, one-in-herself person. From this process, a feminine identity is born, grounded in the transpersonal Mother and thus aligned with her, able now to better survive and creatively gestate the onslaughts of patriarchal shadow from within or without. It is these women, who live the myth backward and undergo such a difficult but fruitful transformation, that the rest of this chapter seeks to describe.

What follows is a kind of prototypic description of the woman who comes into therapy steeped psychologically in the patriarchal world of Hades and must live the myth backward, finding a bond with the Mother for the first time in order to be released from Hades' power. Becoming "at least for a time . . . woman-centered" takes place initially in therapy. A matriarchal bond is sought with the female therapist: this opens the door to (a) an encounter with the Goddess and attendant experiences of dissolution of the animus-identified and animus-ridden ego, (b) regression to and rescue of the nascent or wounded girl-child and her need for a Mother, and, finally, (c) re-formation and rebirth into a positive feminine ego grounded in the female Self. This process is both longed for and fought, embraced and resisted, by the woman whose only psychological home has been the patriarchal world of Hades.

161

The compensatory nature and meaning of the matriarchal bonding and the process of healing through living the myth backward is detailed and illustrated below. I have drawn from the therapeutic processes and unconscious material of several women in whom I have seen at least part of this pattern, but in particular from my work with two women: Joanna, a middle-aged lesbian, and Kara, a young married mother.

Women who begin in Hades and know no alternative have ingested patriarchal views of women, spirit, body, and feminine power. Their attitudes, histories, and even symptomatology mirror this world. They are likely to be identified with the collective values of patriarchal culture and usually have come from family backgrounds that have supported and embodied these values. Even women who have been exposed to feminist thinking and have tried to embrace it may struggle still with personal dynamics that resemble the patriarchal underworld with its predominance of unrelational masculine power-over; their mothers may have served such power (or even wielded it vis-à-vis their daughters), their fathers, husband, or lovers may have embodied it, or they may be involved in institutions that still at least covertly support it.

Joanna and Kara both came into therapy with past and current backgrounds that were steeped in patriarchal thinking. Joanna came from a family in which male dominance and preference were a given across generations; the imprint of this patriarchal pattern was stamped deeply into the lives of both her mother and herself. A shy, self-effacing, Victorian woman, Joanna's mother had, along with her sisters, worked for years as a schoolteacher to put their brother through college; none of the sisters ever went to college themselves. Male preference and male privilege extended into her life with her husband and her own children as well. Joanna's two brothers were the favorites of both parents and even as a young child, Joanna may have considered herself something of a co-mother to her brothers. Yet she had vivid and painful memories of longing for her mother's love and attention, which she received only when her brothers and father were not around; the moment they appeared, affection from her mother was sharply curtailed.

Joanna learned very early that her mother's allegiance was first and foremost to her father and only secondarily to her; since she experienced her father as exceptionally critical and cruel, she felt doubly estranged. Her mother's service as patriarchal wife left a deep imprint in Joanna's psyche. In a dream that came up early in our work, she dreamed that her mother was literally her father's appliance: she saw a washing machine shaped like a female figure that her father had made out of porcelain. It was a perfect likeness of her mother. In the dream, she was horrified and then realized she had seen this all her life.

As a man and a father, Joanna's father was much more like Hades than Zeus. Far from having the expansive, benevolent personality of Zeus, he was more like the god's underworld brother. At his job, Joanna's father was responsible for uncovering the errors of others, a mission that he brought home to his family life as well. Negative, narrow, rigid, and uncaring, he was quick to criticize his daughter but never to praise or support.

Only her intellect and intellectual achievements were valued—the abstract Logos world of the academic mind, one of patriarchy's more renowned achievements—though even this parental value, which Joanna met with straight A's in school, was more of an expectation than a support. Like Hades, Joanna's father was experienced as perpetually disrupting her connection with her mother and cutting off whatever was Kore-like: young, spontaneous, undeveloped, and, in his eyes, imperfect. In her dreams Joanna's father complex appeared as a male figure who crippled cats by cutting the tendons in each foot or set a deformed but still living baby out by the roadside as trash. Unlike Demeter, Joanna's mother had not protested the father's brutality and disruptiveness. By the time Joanna came to me, she had internalized, both consciously and unconsciously, this entire picture; it and the archetypal/historical dynamics behind it had shaped her wounds, defenses, values and fears, visions of evil and divinity, and relationship to both others and the Self.

Kara's background, though less overtly traditional in some ways than Joanna's (in that her mother worked outside the home), had some of the same patriarchal emphases. Her childhood was also characterized by more attention and care being given to the male members of the family and a paucity of feminine nurturance to the daughters. Her mother was a "banishing"[4] mother to Kara and her younger sister: extreme independence and practical competence were demanded of them at an inappropriately early age and all neediness, dependence, and emotional bonding were discouraged. The latter were reserved for their sickly brother who, in Kara's view, was the only one nurtured and "babied."

Even more damaging was the mother's deference to and support of

Kara's father in his continual disparaging and devaluing of his oldest daughter. Both her intense feeling nature and her body were the targets of his mockery and disdain. Thus when Kara suffered from early and extreme dysmenorrhea, he called her "Sarah Bernhardt," insisting her tears, complaints, and considerable pain were just a histrionic act. In his eyes, emotional intensity of any kind was hysteria. Her mother, who was critical of Kara's body in other ways and also demanded emotional containment, did nothing to protect her daughter from the father's onslaughts. Nor did she mirror a more positive image of Kara's feeling life or legitimate needs for care. Like Joanna, the only support Kara got from her parents was around academic prowess. She was seen as intellectually gifted at a young age and placed into accelerated programs; although she enjoyed some of the stimulation this tracking provided, the emphasis on her intellectual development both at school and at home left her even further estranged from her feelings. She learned at a very young age that passion and intensity in a woman were unacceptable and to be strongly controlled.

In my experience, the common threads in the families of women who begin the myth in Hades are effaced and relatively ineffective mothers, absent or repeatedly disrupted close and powerful mother-daughter bonds, and at a least tacit agreement that the lion's share of power and particularly of power-over lies in the hands of the father and other male members of the family. This carries over into the woman's marriage or partnerships as well; the husband or partner either is very power oriented and possesses (or is endowed with through projection) Hades- or Zeus-like qualities.

These family dynamics are a microcosm of the larger, collective arrangements and emphases that came into play historically and archetypally after the northern invasions. What was reflected then over millennia in shifting mythological images—the claiming of the Goddess's attributes and powers by an all-dominant sky God, the limiting of the supremacy of the Goddess as Creatrix and Mother of All to mere consort or wife in service to the Father, and in the Demeter and Persephone myth, the division of Mother and Daughter—now acts as an archetypal, unconscious backdrop infusing human arrangements in patriarchy. In a very real and profound sense, we could say that what happened to the Goddess as Deity and archetypal image has been repeated over and over politically, socially, and psychologically in the lives of women under patriarchy both collectively and individually.

164

We see it vividly in even this sampling: in Joanna's story, the service to the father and brothers threading across generations, the self-efface-ment of the women who are valued (and value themselves) only in terms of their service to the men, and the estrangement/disruption of the bond between mother and daughter in the context of this service. So too in Kara's family in which not only did the male members of the family receive more nurturing and exercise more power, but the mother fails to powerfully protect and protest the daughter's abuse by the fa-ther: she is not a Demeterian mother. Joanna's dream of her mother as an appliance created by her father embodies one of the many deep imprints of her patriarchal family life in her psychology and personal mythology: instead of mediating the archetypal Mother for her daughter as Creatrix and Source-ground, Joanna's mother is perceived to be merely a domestic machine created by and in service to her father.

In the myth, the child Kore remembered her mother and lan-guished in the underworld, crying out for her and refusing to eat; she was not separated from herself or the upperworld she came from. But women who have spent their lives in the underworld of Hades have no memory of being mothered; they may long for a mother but, at least in the beginning of therapy, are identified with their estrange-ment and attack themselves for wanting or needing care. They are separated not only from a mothering source-ground but from the daughter who longs for its nurturance. The child is lost or, more po-tently, hated and suppressed by the woman herself who turns a cold Hades eye on her own need for nurturance. (Some women even report wanting to kill the child self when they first become aware of it, even though it is often the healthiest part of them.) Then it becomes the task of the therapy to find the Kore child, allow her to emerge from the underworld, in which she has languished hated and rejected, and connect for the first time with the archetypal Mother and her fragrant world of nourishment and basic care. Here, as the case of Jenny in chapter 6 also illustrated, the relationship between therapist and cli-ent becomes pivotal and intense, the caldron of the transformative feminine aspect of the Mother archetype.

The precipitating event that had made Joanna seek out therapy at this time was a visit to a female massage therapist given to her as a Christmas gift; in the midst of the massage, she had felt a strong urge to "curl up in the fetal position," which had terrified her. Soon after the experience with the masseuse, she dreamed that she was in her childhood home and received an anonymous telegram that stated, "You must find the baby you gave up years ago." Wandering through the house, she came upon an unknown room and opened the door. She looked around and saw pictures of her mother and herself on the walls. Then she saw, lying in a bed, a hollow-eyed infant with its arms outstretched; she was not sure if it was alive or dead and fled the scene in horror.

Joanna came into therapy with many issues: considerable anger arising out of an early marriage, questions and conflicts regarding her Church and her vocation, relational problems with her grown stepdaughter, and dissatisfaction with her current relationships with women. Interfering with her capacity to commit to a partner were her fears of emotional neediness that had been tapped into when she saw the masseuse. She feared feeling "little" and dependent; the latter was especially unacceptable to her. "Being dependent means giving someone power over me," Joanna told me, and she was not about to do that. She felt she was always holding a great deal of herself back in her relationships but feared if she didn't, she'd be too needy and would collapse. She saw herself as responding strongly to the needs of others but found it very difficult to ask for anything for herself.

While she tended to idealize women, she saw men in general as cold, systematic thinkers, perfectionistic and demanding, exhibiting no passion, joy, spontaneity, or relationship to the moment. Men never apologized for anything, she asserted, for fear of losing face or authority. Men in general and her former husband and father in particular were seen as "preventers" and aggressors: "They make everything at hand into a weapon and the weapons have all been aimed at me." Once she recalled seeing pictures of Nazi tortures during World War II and being both shocked and fascinated; this seemed to her to be the paradigm of brutal masculinity. This description illustrated not only her experiences of her father and husband but was generalized to friends' husbands and most other men. It was also a part of her animus, though this was largely unconscious to her in the beginning of our work.

There were exceptions to her perceptions of men: a few men, both young and old, she knew through her church and valued for their wisdom and their humor. These were men she described as having some relationship with their "feminine side"; this link also appeared in her psyche during therapy in a dramatic and interesting way.

Both aspects—the brutal, Nazi-like man whose modus operandi is an authority rooted in perfectionism and power over others and a more

166

relational masculinity linked with the archetypal Feminine—reflect aspects of Hades and threaded through Joanna's outer and inner life. But, as her dream suggested, before these could be made more conscious and their influence confronted, the young, unmothered baby and girl in herself, the Kore child, would have to be found and nurtured.

In the first few sessions, Joanna presented herself as depressed, self-contained, and keeping her distance. Yet present and palpable was also her younger side, which I felt keenly and attempted to befriend and draw out a little. While holding me at bay with many questions and demands for immediate answers, Joanna also made an almost immediate attachment to me. Three weeks into the work, she went on vacation for a week but found it very hard to leave me; after the session just before her vacation, she called me and asked if I'd like her to drop off a copy of the lost baby dream detailed above. I felt the symbolic significance of this and welcomed her leaving her "baby" with me while she was away.

Our early sessions reflected her ambivalence. She vacillated between what I experienced as a keen but split-off intellect held captive to a passive-aggressive dynamic that peppered me with questions, demanding quick interpretations and answers, and a needy, inchoate, washed-over-with-feeling side that felt to me desperately hungry to be reached and valued but was unacceptable to her. I felt put on the spot by her demand for answers and discovered that when I tried to meet her on this level, she often felt wildly unsatisfied and would talk about feeling needy and fears of collapsing. At the same time, this more intellectual side afforded her the sense of having control, both over herself and the sessions.

It was not so much that this demand for answers was not a genuine need to understand herself and her dynamics; it was clear to me from the very beginning that she had a well-developed intellect, was widely read, and keenly interested in psychological and spiritual pursuits. But in the beginning of therapy, this "wanting to know" was infused with a sharply judgmental, controlling animus that constantly told her that her feelings and child needs were regressive and inappropriate and that any dependency meant letting someone else have power over her. Yet attempting to minister only to that side left the more inchoate, feeling side that needed to speak its "littleness" feeling abandoned and in despair. If I spoke to that side of her, encouraging the neediness to be expressed and accepted, she was touched and grateful but also frightened.

My task, I felt, was to administer to both and try to hold both sides of the split without losing either one. I met her animus with writing exercises that she asked for—topics drawn from the session or her dreams that she could reflect on and write to me about between the sessions. Each session at this point began with a focus on things she had written about herself or her dreams. Then at some point she'd begin to complain that she felt like collapsing; that became the signal to me that the session could now change levels and the younger side of her was pushing for expression even though she was scared. I met this side with simpler, feeling language, empathic companioning of the childhood memories that sometimes came up at this point, nonjudgmental acceptance of her expressions of attachment and dependence, and protective intervention when her animus voice interrupted to put her or her sense of connection with me down. She could only take such a feeling focus in small doses, though increasingly she sought and craved it and gradually allowed the dependence she so wanted and feared.

Longing for nurturance and comfort from a woman was a soul need for Joanna, an unconscious path back to what was missing with her own mother and to the archetypal realm of the Feminine that she had never experienced. One of her earliest dreams in therapy portrayed this as well as her attitude toward it. In the dream, her mother was part of a group that was praying for better relationships with their older children. Joanna was in a kitchen and there were individual boxes of cereal on the shelf. She picked up a bunch of pushpins and stuck them into the boxes.

Cereal, she told me in session, was the "staff of life" but she never ate it because it was "only for kids." She spoke of how she had never cooked breakfast for her stepdaughter; cereal was something kids could get for themselves. At the same time, cereal reminded her of the bread in the Christian communion; she told me what a deep experience communion was for her and of a prayer that affirmed the presence of Christ in all things. She herself understood the symbolic connection of cereal, grain, and access to divinity. But in the background here was not Christ but her own mother transformed from the woman who served the man into someone who was longing for a better connection with her adult daughter.

In reality, Joanna's mother had been dead for five years; she was

168

tearful in session as she spoke about her mother, of all that her mother had had to deny in herself and had denied her daughter. In the dream, her mother emerges as longing for a bond with her daughter, connected with Demeter as Ceres, the cereal goddess, and her food is available. But Joanna pokes holes in the food, just as consciously she related that it was just for kids, something they didn't need a mother for, and could get for themselves. This was exactly how she felt about her needs for nurturing. In the same session she spoke of feeling nurtured by a phone conversation with another woman friend, then feeling guilty because it was "so regressive."

This theme of refusing available food appeared in dreams periodically throughout the first few months of our work. Though she began to acknowledge more of an attachment to me as Mother on human and archetypal levels and to seek out more mirroring of her child self, her animus still tended to spoil our connection by suddenly shifting into a demand for answers when she got scared or embarrassed by how young she felt. Finally, a little over a year since we had begun to work, she had a dream so direct in its message about nurturance that she couldn't ignore it. Although this dream appeared in the writing she often brought to session and we did not get a chance to discuss it, she noted that it had made a very strong impact on her.

She recorded the dream as follows: *The birds cannot hear themselves sing. The very young require care by all the women all the time. There are some changes, like in the* I Ching, *which I had used the night before. To be fed then at this time under these circumstances is all right, correct. So allow it. Something about appropriateness, i.e., no shame, no blame. I was fascinated by the form of the dream—it seemed to be that the image was of the care of young bees in the hive. Connection with the Great Mother.*

The *I Ching* is a book of ancient Chinese oracles that can be used as a guide to a deeper understanding of oneself and one's situation. The form of Joanna's dream is like one of the oracles, offered as wisdom and guidance. Here she is told directly that the very young—the sprout life—require care by women all the time; consciously she despaired at how needy she felt herself to be, how much she wanted me and others around to help and guide her all the time. She was beginning to unearth and allow a dependency on a woman, on women, that she had never experienced or allowed before in a healthy way. The dream speaks with a voice and authority quite different from her animus judgment and conveys directly, objectively, "It's all right to be

169

fed, appropriate at this time, so let it be." Unlike what her spoiling animus told her, there was no blame or shame in this, nothing to be embarrassed about.

The image of the hive was striking to her. She had been in a study group focused on the archetypal Great Mother and connected the hive image and service to the Queen Bee with its archetypal core. The Queen Bee as Goddess also refers to Demeter, whose priestesses were called *mellisae*, honey bees. Here, in the structure of the dream itself, Joanna's neediness is archetypally framed within the service to the Mother, the queen of the hive. Here the young Kore child exists among the priestesses of the Great Mother.

In different versions of the myth of Demeter and Persephone, the Kore is of different ages; in some, a small girl, in others an older child or near adolescent. In both forms, she carries the archetypal child: a woman's potential, nascence, and capacity for self-renewal. But she is also Goddess, the Maiden form, the self-possessed, virginal, one-in-herself archetypal aspect of the Feminine. It was this latter aspect of Kore that was most prominently eclipsed into Hades' realm in Kara when she first came into therapy with me.

Despite a lack of parental support, Kara, unlike Joanna, had apparently had some sense of positive power as a woman and a particular feminine style before she got married. She had embraced the women's movement in the 1970s and constructed an image of her mother and grandmother as "strong, hard-working women," creating a "mother-line" in her mind from which she could draw. When she was asked to leave a conservative college because she had been caught sleeping outside of the dorm, she had felt a deep sense of failure and her family's disapproval, but she eventually rallied, moving to New York to take up art and lead a Bohemian lifestyle that she loved. Nevertheless, she often worried that her life, which was free and intense both emotionally and sexually, was out of control and sought to censure herself. She particularly feared power and anything irrational that she felt in herself at that time.

Secretly she still longed for her father's approval and still judged herself by her family's values. Finally she married a man her father especially liked: a bright and articulate academic named Mark who was ill at ease with intense feelings and had difficulties being close both emotionally and physically. Once again she reexperienced both her body and her feelings to be devalued by a man whose opinions and needs she readily gave authority over her own.

The reawakening of childhood issues and the practical arrangements of her marriage augmented her sense of being less valuable than her husband; despite the liberal views about women and parenting that both she and Mark espoused philosophically, they structured their marriage at this point along one particular traditional line. Although they shared a house with two other couples and their several children, Kara was the only adult who did not work outside of the home. She was the designated "housewife" and "mom," caring daily for all of the children and taking care of the home for them all. Financially supported by others, she felt less important and less valuable than the other adults.

When she first came to me, she was in her mid-thirties and at home with five little boys, three of her own and one from each of the other couples. She had not touched her artwork since her oldest child was born. She had virtually no time of her own, no space of her own, and felt she had no right to anything because she wasn't doing "real" work, as she put it. She felt she had to be superwoman—excel at all roles with no time off for her own development or even for illness. She was frequently ill, still suffered monthly from severe dysmenorrhea, but struggled against the needs of her body which she saw as her enemy.

In the first few months of our work, Kara came through to me as being profoundly "under," estranged from the life of her body, her passionate nature that was visible to me even then, and her own needs. The individual life she had begun to create for herself, grounded in her art and colorful style of being feminine before marriage, had gone under to a sense of what she "should" be. In this sense, her marriage at this point was a "death marriage." She was self-estranged, depressed, and angry, though she denied her anger and got extremely anxious when it was mirrored back to her. Though nurturant and tender with her sons and the other children in the household, she was unable to nurture herself or seek nurturance from others. For many women (as well as men), marriage and children usher in an eclipse of the personal, individual self in the face of collective expectations and images of what a wife and mother are and should be according to the culture. Despite her unusual living arrangement, once Kara married and became a mother, cultural representations of women at home as "just" housewives, "just" mothers enveloped her, unconsciously drawing up and merging with the more personal devaluation she had experienced in her family.

Like a shade in the underworld of Hades, Kara lacked a felt sense of substance and personal definition. When she first came to me, she had so little sense of individual self and felt so little right to have any kind of boundaries that separated her from the services she readily performed for others that each therapy session I felt as if I were metaphorically (and literally) taking her by the shoulders, looking into her face, and saying, "You, you, you!," trying to name her into herself. Therapy was literally the only time and space she had apart from the family and, like many women who are raising children, she had come into therapy only when she felt her capacity to carry her roles was threatened. She feared breaking down and becoming "irrational," and consciously wanted more order and energy to do even more and to do it all perfectly. She was indeed on the verge of breaking down, though not in the psychotic way she feared; more simply, she was overworking, profoundly undernurturing herself, and attempting to corset and contain her intensity.

Kara's inner life was dominated by harsh self-criticism that was representative of both her father's view of her and her projection of that onto her husband as well as the patriarchal devaluing of women that existed in both cultural attitudes surrounding the roles she carried and in her husband's shadow. This made up her animus, the "man" within her, and functioned like the mythological Hades; every time she felt her own needs, her hunger for value, for nurturance, for existence outside the masculine prerogative, this inner critic would rise up and pull her down into an underworld of self-hating and self-dissolution. She had no inner mother or solid feminine base from which to meet these onslaughts; she simply went under to the inner critic.

As was true with Joanna, a powerful initial dream cut through Kara's conscious defenses and set the course for the therapy. Right after our first session, she had what she described as "the most frightening dream of my life." In the dream she was sitting on her bed in a room. She decided to take advantage of the power of magic to get even with people in the next room who had devalued her feelings, as her father did. She took a light bulb and, using a wand or rod, tapped it into a flask. The circumference of the light bulb was greater than the flask but the magic allowed it to go in. Once the bulb went into the flask, its boundaries dissolved and it turned into a glowing substance. When she put the flask on the night table, she felt herself drawn into the power. She began to make increasingly weird noises as she was drawn more and more in. At that point, she woke up extremely frightened, as she was making the noises out loud.

In reality, on a rare weekend away, she had been at a Jungian conference with her husband and at first the room in the dream had seemed like the hotel room they stayed in. As she told the dream, however, the room seemed more like my office, which scared her. What scared her even more was her feeling in the dream that she wanted to "get even" with the other people. She said they had put her down, like her father used to when he called her hysterical and histrionic. Consciously, however, she was terrified of having negative feelings toward others and tried not to hurt anyone for fear she would be hurt in return. She also feared that if she did try to hurt other people, she might get pleasure from it, might enjoy getting back at them. She said she couldn't deal with other people's judgments of her because then she began to feel the same way and lost her perspective.

Light bulbs had been mentioned in a lecture she had heard at the conference. All she could remember of it was that the lecturer had talked about the goddess Artemis. Although neither Kara nor I could see the relevance of Artemis at this early point in our work, this goddess was clearly relevant to the dream content.

Artemis was a Greek goddess representing raw, untamed Nature, the original "wild woman," undomesticated and bivalent. She was neither wife nor mother but as guardian of the wild, she was called upon by women in the throes of childbirth, petitioned to bring either relief from pain and a safe delivery or a swift death. She was one of the Kores, a Maiden goddess who was essentially one-in-herself, connected to no man, and in some versions of the Persephone myth she was among the maidens picking flowers with Kore in the field.

In one of her Roman forms, she was also a light-bringer, Diana Lucifera, carrying the torch that signified the connection of the Goddess with both life and death. Although only implied in this dream via Kara's association, Artemis represents the opposite pole of the archetypal Feminine that Kara was attempting to embody: undomestic, unmothering, one-in-herself, raw and untamed, beholden to no man.

In addition she was a goddess of swift retribution when violated; when the hunter Actaeon dared to look upon her in her bath, she promptly changed him into a stag to be killed by his own hounds. Like Demeter Erinys who seeks revenge when she is violated, this raw, fierce, passionate aspect of the untamed Feminine existed in Kara's true nature, unknown and untapped, certainly unchanneled. It was Artemis' light that was to be discovered within the therapeutic container. The light bulb in the dream reminded me of the "bright ideas" that had been all that was valued in Kara by her parents; her intellectual brightness had been championed to the exclusion of her needs and her feelings. Here the light bulb form is tapped into the flask by the wand and dissolved; the light that had originally been in the bulb became a glowing substance, "like molten gold," she said.

The instrument she used to tap the light bulb into the flask was like a sculptural tool she had often used in her artwork, used to shape or trim away the clay. Here it trims away the symbol for intellectual brightness and releases the light into a new container. This is accomplished by magic but the instrument of magic is connected with Kara's art. It was only when she put the flask down, "lost connection with it," as she put it, that she got overpowered in the dream. She put it down, she said, because it was too intense. Then the power was no longer bound by the flask, took her over, and led to sounds she described as "guttural" and coming from deep inside her. I asked what was frightening about being drawn into the power. She said it was as though the usual body-mind separation dissolved.

The flask was central to this dream for it was both the new container of the light and what Kara needed to maintain connection with to keep from being overwhelmed. She said she had very strong feelings about the flask. I asked her to draw it and as she did, she said she kept visualizing the shape of a woman's body. The new container for the light was now feminine and embodied. All this took place in a room she associated with my office. It was a powerful vision of what "wanted" to come into the therapy and the shape it was to take, the shape that could hold it—a woman's body.

Thus the therapy began with her unconscious rage at being devalued and her desire for retribution. Intending to use her creative capacity to get back at the men in her life, she was instead faced with something overwhelming. The tables were turned—she was the one to be affected, to be taken over by the power her creativity had tapped into, she was the one who needed to maintain her connection with the woman vessel filled with power and light. Believing that she could control the process and use it for her own ends, she instead became the materia—as the transformative power embodied her and released a primitive expressiveness from deep within.

The dissolution of her brightness into the woman-shaped vessel (one thinks of Rosa's "womb-jar") foreshadowed a process in the therapy that neither of us could have predicted, a dissolution into the archetypal Feminine, a movement away from the Fathers and into all that they had devalued and pressed down. The relational space that grew between us made the woman-shaped vessel that could hold her process of transformation and at times even her sanity; returning to her art was the entrée to her feelings and her body. But at this time consciously she was frightened, constricted, and identified with being nothing. Instead of feeling her femininity as powerful, she spoke of "a fragile feminine inside me, like the hollow bone of a bird." It was that feminine that was the nascent Kore, insubstantial and devalued in the beginning: the bride of the patriarchal Fathers instead of Demeter's daughter. A pale and ghostly version of her real self, it was this Kore she was conscious of and this that needed to be mothered in the therapeutic process until her more self-contained and powerful Maiden aspect could emerge and be reclaimed.

Both Joanna and Kara knew nothing about Demeter's world; deprived of a basic bond with their personal mothers, both women were disembodied, feared incarnation and emotional expressiveness, and lacked grounding in a feminine archetypal Matrix both personally and transpersonally. As much as possible, they lived in their heads. As women, they were like shades in Hades' underworld: lacking substance, vitality, embodiment, and self-possession. Also like the shades, their way out of this insubstantial state was to be reborn through a woman. The vehicle of this rebirth was a kind of regressive process whose telos was not simply a corrective experience aimed at developing and strengthening the ego level—for example, allowing the unmothered child aspect of the client to experience mothering from the therapist so that it can gradually "grow up" and be integrated into the adult personality instead of obstructing it. The process had a deeper aim, to provide access to the archetypal Great Mother and a vision of Mother and Daughter as Self. A crucial element in this Demeter-Persephone constellation is also the presence of a negative, domineering Masculine that has pushed out or, in terms of its preeminence, stands in the place of the feminine Self in the woman's psyche. Thus the search is for the Mother who can stand against the patriarchal animus and eventually relativize and transform it. At first the archetypal dimension of the rebirthing Mother was carried through the transference and therapeutic process; later it would be recognized as coming through and existing in the clients' own psyches, psyches that ultimately mirrored the Goddess, the Mother of All.

As I understand and experience it, in the beginning of the myth the upperworld of Demeter is first and foremost a world of mother and child bondedness. It is a world close to Nature and instinct: below the Olympian realm of intellect and abstraction and above Hades' ghostly underworld of disembodied essences, Demeter's world is one in which the life of the body is primary and sensate. Psyche is incarnate; matter, including body, is magical and filled with spirit. This world is also an essentially relational world of permeable boundaries in which mother and child flow back and forth between each other, the mother lending both her body and her ego to the developing child and empathically tuning to the child's vicissitudes, the child embraced by and participating in a larger maternal wholeness. For a therapist who enjoys nurturing, the original Demeterian realm may seem ordinary, easy, even mundane; what is evoked by her client are maternal feelings, even maternal passions—the urge to nurture developing life; a receptiveness and enjoyment of spontaneity, play, bonding; an empathic concern for pain and grief; a fierce protectiveness. For an adult client for whom such maternal care is a new experience, however, what is ordinary in one sphere becomes in the container of the therapy extraordinary and charged with the full numinosity and transformative power of the archetype.

While it could be argued that many therapeutic processes call forth mothering from the therapist, not all do, and here there is a particular constellation of dynamics that mirror aspects of the Demeter and Persephone myth. The child self is cut off from nurturance, suppressed and thwarted; it appears in dreams and eventually more consciously as underground, held back, even threatened with inner death. An urgency surrounds this aspect of the Self; the therapist in the Mother position feels drawn to rescuing the child in her client. In the context of a constellation of the Demeterian Mother, this urge to rescue is part of the archetypal field. But the therapist must be conscious of it, separate it out from any personal predilection to inappropriately caretake or infantilize the client (in which case the urge to rescue might rob the client of the need to develop her own initiative),[5] and be able to hold it meditatively in image rather than acting it out; she must understand that this is a temporary constellation and part of an archetypal drama of death and rebirth. The client is not able to step into the realm of the archetypal Mother and nourish or rescue herself; she needs the therapist to help free the endangered child and supply not only maternal care but a Demeterian capacity to stand against and confront what seeks to prevent the younger self's expression, development, and integration.

The Preventer is present in masculine form, imaged as such in dreams or named as such by the woman herself; like Hades, this presence is forceful, unrelational, and repeatedly pulls the woman down, out of her access to maternal care, even out of the ordinary, sensate world into experiences of disembodiment or dissociation. In other words, the client does not feel herself to be in her body and may also have frightening experiences or anxieties around staying intact.

Despite the emphasis on the need for nurturing that appeared in Joanna's early dreams, she was much more frightened of the Demeterian upperworld than Kara. Full of suspicions, extremely indirect in her expression of needs and feelings, often imprisoned in all-or-none thinking, Joanna lurched painfully between terror and longing but as her process unfolded, it quickly became multilayered and emotionally profound. Her unconscious produced complex and detailed images not only in dreams but in powerful hypnagogic or hypnopompic images that came to her just before sleep or just after waking; often these were of archetypal content and frightened her but she reported them faithfully and in great detail.

The writing that she gave me evidenced a keen mind; she often reflected on books she had read, attempted to grapple with her dreams, and wrote insightful meditations focused on themes I had asked her to write about with regard to her own life. Yet she attributed her own capacities to me and spoke often of wanting to get rid of her head, of feeling separate from her body. Often she seemed to play dumb, insisting that I had all the answers and she knew nothing; I had the capacity to read and understand what I read while she did not, she maintained; I knew the "answers."

Her idealizing insistence that I had all the knowledge, insights, and interpretations allowed her to preserve yet separate from her head and get closer to her younger self. Several months into the therapy, she wrote to me: "If I were to stop asking you to interpret me, then I will

177

have to be older, I think, and then I cannot have the comfort and closeness I need for some much younger self. Or so it seems." Later in therapy, she gave another reason: "I want to get rid of my head because that's all anyone paid attention to—my body gets lost—I'm suspect of any admiration of my head and thinking because I immediately think, here it goes again, the rest of me is simply invisible." Projecting her intellectual capacity to me preserved an important part of herself while simultaneously allowing her a separation from the only thing her parents had ever valued about her.

She wanted her feelings and hurts to be seen and comforted, but her animus disdained these as infantile; the critical voice within her, so like her perfectionist father, dismissed these needs and cut them off. She dreamed of men interfering with or preventing bonds between women; one of these men was her former husband, who had always "prevented" her, she said. But as time went on, the imagery shifted. She dreamed she was in my house. Her former husband appeared, ordering her around as usual. But in my house he had no power. Here the relational space of the therapy served as matriarchal bond and the masculine critic was depotentiated.

Gradually her younger side gained courage and began to express itself without her cutting it off. She asked to hold my hands one session; this brought forth great feelings of awe and gratitude. Later, in a very moving moment, she put her head in my hands—an act of great trust for her, for as much as she sought to "lose" her head, she also had great anxiety about doing just that when she was in her more feeling side. Just as she allowed me to hold her head through projection of her considerable intellectual capacity onto me, so now she enacted this in bodily gesture.

When she felt safe enough in the maternal container of the therapy, the wall of words crumbled and she could risk the collapse she so feared. "Collapse" had always meant being able to cry when she was hurt or sad, something she rarely did even when alone. Being able to cry in the companioned space of the therapy released her frozen feelings and her spontaneity.

When she wrote about her child self, the picture she portrayed was of Kore-like innocence and freedom, so different from the way she presented herself in the beginning of each session. The child she remembered and longed for was sensuous, spontaneous, unselfconscious, fully in the present and connected with the timelessness that

earmarks the archetypal Child. The adult she presented and experienced was highly controlling, which she now began to become painfully aware of; she described it as short-circuiting her feeling
expression, preventing anything spontaneous from occurring during
the initial part of each session when she was still "in her head," full
of dread and self-consciousness and worries about the future. But as
she allowed herself to access the child and allowed her child to want
care, as she began to believe that I liked and wanted this part of her
to live, she began to expose herself to everything she feared, both the
Preventer and the Mother who could transform him.

Underneath her concern about staying intact were memories of what
had threatened her intactness and the bond she had wished for but
never had with her mother; these emerged slowly when she could feel
little and began to feel safe enough to speak from this younger self.
She had a particular terror that I would leave her, wouldn't like her
anymore, would drop her; over and over she needed reassurance that I
liked her enormously and would not abandon her. One day in the
midst of such an exchange, she suddenly had a vivid recollection of an
incident that had terrorized her when she was nine years old. It was
night and she'd been in bed when she heard some kind of commotion
outside. She looked out her window and saw her mother with a suit-
case, leaving; after some persuasion, her father managed to talk her
into coming back into the house. Joanna never told anyone that she had
witnessed this event, but she had remained terrified and devastated at
the thought that her mother might leave her without even telling her.

This pivotal moment as well as her mother's otherwise unwavering
patriarchal service to her father prevented the formation of an original,
solid bond between mother and daughter; faced with her father's cold
criticalness and later her husband's, Joanna had nothing to fall back
on, no matrix she could rely on and from which she could grow.

As was true also with Kara, a strong transference to me as "mother"
developed; this was one level of our work. But as Joanna came to trust
me and our bond deepened, its archetypal backdrop emerged; by
allowing herself, especially her child self, to be seen, she was also connecting directly with the Goddess. She spoke of "coming home," of
wanting to be inside me and lose herself in me. That this had a transpersonal context was clear, even to her. Her now intense feelings
danced between terror and awe. "I associate you somehow with the
Willendorf Venus," Joanna wrote to me. "When I first saw that in my

179

art history books, it blew my mind, more than any of the other figures from that time that I've seen. It seems to represent, were it not stone, what I wish to be lost in, engulfed by, rest in." Dissolution, so terrifying when she feared it meant dissolving into the body and losing her head, now became her deepest desire, an ecstatic merging with the Goddess. In her twilight visions, the Venus of Willendorf appeared surrounded by symbols of death and resurrection as her "animus ego" gave way to a journey through the matriarchal bond to the Mother as Source.

As both witness and receiver of this process, I too felt the numinosity; though I have experienced this with others as well, the sense of a transpersonal Third in the room was palpable during this phase of the therapy and this presence was female. Though Joanna at times attributed the Goddess's powers and knowledge to me, I was aware that an archetypal transference had taken place. The mantle of something much bigger than me was attributed to me and I took pains not to claim it but to watch and mirror it as its imagery played through the transference and the unconscious material that came up in fantasy and dreams.

Kara was more extraverted and less verbal than Joanna. The richest symbolic material came less through dreams, which she had difficulty writing down and relating to, than through her art and in dramatic enactments of her feelings in session. I experienced Kara almost immediately as gregarious, relational, imaginative, emotionally intense, sensual, and eminently likable. She had a strong physical presence and her gestures were more expressive than her words. But she did not experience herself this way. She kept her intensity under tight control, believing it to be a sign of craziness and seeing it through the eyes and the values she associated with her father and husband. She told me she was terrified to look inside for fear she was empty: "I'll look and find out there is nothing there." Her feeling life was so held back that at times she dissociated; anger and fear appeared in sudden outbursts that felt foreign to her and convinced her even more that she was falling apart. She felt disembodied and had recurring dreams of floating. She feared nothingness, intangibility. Though she told me she once had valued being a woman and saw women as strong, she now felt herself as weak, inferior to her far more articulate, rational husband, and fragile. She identified with however she was seen by masculine eyes, looked to her husband and father for validation of her feelings and value, and felt herself and especially her body to be bad, worthless, and insubstantial. Like Cyane, she could never stand her

180

ground in the face of a disapproving or dissenting male. In a self-portrait she drew early in therapy, she had no feet.

She was wary of me at first, particularly because I did not agree with her sense that she should always be rational and needed more order in her life. I saw nothing in her dreams or her presenting material that suggested this and felt concern and compassion for how frightened she was of expressing her feelings.

I was also concerned for how much she neglected and abused her body; she was frequently ill but couldn't allow herself to rest; she was physically stressed from overwork but felt she had no right to time off, and suffered debilitating pain with her periods that she dealt with by "toughing it out," though she did take painkillers (how much pain she suffered was something I became directly aware of once when we talked on the phone after she had just started her period; despite massive doses of codeine, she involuntarily whimpered throughout the conversation).

She was surprised that I was concerned instead of critical, poured out her history of menstrual problems and how often she had been ridiculed and disbelieved around her pain, and began to express a sense of identification with me as a woman. She took in my insistence that she needed to care for instead of continue to stress her body and asked me to help her begin to set boundaries around her energy and her time vis-à-vis the others in the house.

She also began to share how often her feelings were hurt by others, especially the men in the house, then told me more about her father's disparagement of her as a child, and finally confessed that something inside her consistently put her down and made her feel like nothing. She was surprised that I cared about this and encouraged her not to simply buy into the perspective of the devaluer; her tales of hurt elicited in me an imaginal and protective intervention, modeling the possibility of questioning whether what the inner or outer man said was really true about her and on what authority he claimed it. In this way she made me into a protective advocate, leaning on my ego capacity to cut through and confront until she could develop her own. Taking this in from me, she felt safer in bringing her hurt, assured that I wouldn't join the animus who ravaged her. In these simple ways, I functioned as a Demeter-like Mother, helping her nourish and take care of her body, encouraging the expression of feelings that made her feel young and vulnerable, and fiercely standing against the outer and inner other who repeatedly pulled her down and away from her own sense of value.

Insight and interpretation generally were not helpful to Kara; emotional release and movement, once she could trust me enough to allow them in session, opened up a transformative path and accessed the archetypal realm. What came out in these times often surprised us both. Thus, in the fourth month of therapy, she suddenly began crying deep tears and burst out with "I don't want to be a man, don't want to be a boy. I want to be a woman! I don't want to fight anymore, to argue with men!" She couldn't explain what she'd said, didn't know how she had felt herself to be a man, but felt "beautiful" after this outburst. She had a sudden vision of the Medusa, felt angry and pounded the floor, but in the middle of this, something shifted; becoming quiet, she rested her head on the floor, kneeling, and said she felt the presence of the Goddess.

Here again the other side of the ravished Kore broke through as it did in her initial dream; there the transpersonal connection was Artemis, the one-in-herself Maiden who avenges violation; here it is the darker side of Persephone, her connection with Medusa. Kara spoke of needing to "cleanse myself from the pollution of the Masculine." She began to spend more time with women and children and to actively claim and assert her value as a mother.

She also returned to her art; she told me that when she drew or sculpted, she felt herself to be in a particularly feminine place and wanted nothing masculine to interfere with it. This became the deepest and richest constellation of feminine grounding within her, interweaving with our relationship. Nearly a year into the therapy, she brought in a soft sculpture pillow she had made of two naked female figures with a vibrant green background of mountains and a yellow crescent moon. Strikingly, the figures were headless; like Joanna, Kara too had to "lose her head." As we looked at this pillow together, she told me how important being outdoors was to her, how connected she felt with her body and Nature when she used to hike in the mountains near her childhood home. She was taking better care of her body now and reclaiming her enjoyment of its strength. At one point during the therapy she joined an all-women's baseball team which she loved. This was a woman who particularly needed to be in her body to feel good about herself, who found pleasure and power in feeling physically vital.

But the pillow was also meant to convey a relational connection.

Shyly, she told me this also connected with me and our work. She was very tentative about putting this into words but she spoke of how connected she felt I was with my body and how physically present. She said she was fond of my body and loved my hands especially; as an artist, she was very aware of hands. She connected the colors in the pillow with the colors of my office and spoke of how much they meant to her (we both loved bright colors). She said she often wanted me to touch her but couldn't ask for it; saying this, she took my hands, much as Joanna had, and held them for a long time. She was embarrassed by her feeling and said she felt like an adolescent. At the end of the session, without making the connection to what she had said earlier, she told me for the first time that her mother was always critical of her body when she was an adolescent; only her head had been valued.

I was very moved by this session and could feel how the therapeutic vessel we made between us was being cast in the woman-form of the vessel filled with light in her initial dream. This emphasis on feminine embodiment continued. She dreamed I sent her to a play with my daughter. She didn't get to sit with my daughter as she had hoped but nevertheless went with her to the play. As she watched the play, a large black woman with huge breasts appeared on the stage and seemed to grow out into the audience. It was as if she had a message especially for Kara.

She imagined my daughter as someone who would have introverted values and thought that I would open up channels of introverted experience for her but not try to push her into a set path (this was the exact opposite of her animus's demand for a linear program in therapy, as I will discuss below); she felt my daughter would be free. In waking life, through the therapy and through her art, she was discovering her own interiority and it was leading her toward a new vision of Woman and Mother, as the dream suggested. She described the black woman as having a beautiful body but being somewhat scary too; she didn't know what message the black woman seemed to have for her. I commented on the maternal and nurturing qualities of the woman and tied this in with the mother-daughter motif in the dream.

She also connected the woman onstage with a figure she had drawn a few weeks before. I had asked her to try to draw the persistently critical male voice in her head and she'd produced a figure she called Rasputin after the charlatan Russian monk, a figure of sinister face and sharp angles.

183

But a female figure had come up as well, spontaneously, once she had given her critical animus form. This was a woman whose boundaries, though soft, could not be penetrated. She called the woman Oomphalla. I asked where the name came from; she had no idea. It was a critical image, for the *omphalos* was a powerful symbol in ancient times. "[Omphalos was a] Greek transliteration of Latin umbilicus," writes Barbara Walker in *The Woman's Encyclopedia of Myths and Secrets*. "[It was]the navel or hub of the world, center of the Goddess's body, source of all things. As every ancient nation regarded its version of the Great Mother as the cosmic spirit, so its own capital or chief temple was located at the center of the earth, marked by the stone omphalos that concentrated the Mother's essence."[6]

There was also an Omphale in Greek myth, a Lydian queen to whom Hercules was enslaved and had to serve for a year's time. Of her, Walker writes, "Omphale represented the Goddess as a consumer of sun-kings, each one annually killed and replaced by another who was born at the winter solstice."[7] During the year of his servitude, Hercules also wore the queen's robes and acted as deputy on her behalf which, according to Robert Graves, reflected a transition stage between a matriarchal and patriarchal vision of kingship.

I didn't know about Omphale then; I knew only that the *omphalos* was considered to be the navel of the earth, connected with the Goddess, and that some said it was also the entrance to the underworld. What strikes me now is the economy of symbolism condensed in Kara's image, a symbolism ungrasped by both of us at the time but telling and essential in retrospect.

Kara consciously experienced herself at the mercy of a critical animus and for much of her life felt disempowered in the presence of a critical man. Making this experience visible through her drawing and naming it (like giving a face to the faceless Hades) called up a powerful feminine counterpart as well, one deeply connected not only with the Goddess as Source but in her functions as Killer and Recycler as well—the Persephone/Erinyes/Medusa side of the helplessly ravished Kore.

This figure surfaced from a matriarchal layer in Kara's psyche, precisely compensatory to her conscious experience of being helplessly raped by her "mad monk" animus. Jung comments that Omphale represents "submission to the feminine principle that symbolizes the unconscious"[8] and the risk of a regressive enslavement to the woman from which the man cannot free himself and so becomes a child again.[9] But this is in masculine psychology. In the psychology of a woman, particularly a woman who has been eclipsed by the patriarchy as much as Kara was, the appearance of such a figure from a deep matriarchal layer of the psyche has a different meaning. It represents a kind of primitive compensation for the enslavement of her ego; faced with the critical and powerful animus, a more powerful woman who, unlike Kara, cannot be penetrated appears. Moreover she has her own power as Source (even of the man for whom the umbilicus also points to a feminine origin) and as Killer/Recycler, the Crone power to which he too must ultimately submit and serve.

I believe now that this was a Self figure for Kara, not the mythical Omphale but her own Oomphalla who through association with the big-breasted black woman on center stage stood for the Goddess as Source and as Killer/Recycler. Implied in this image and the contexts in which it evolved is the possibility of a transformed animus who, instead of wielding power over the human woman, can be in service to her feminine Self.

Though neither of us grasped the mythological symbolism at the time, Kara came to part of its meaning herself when she drew the black woman. She drew her as large and rounded, with prominent breasts and belly; again there were no facial features, as if emphasizing the nonpersonal layer this figure emerged from. She spoke of how this woman was both powerful and nurturing, commanding and maternal; the combination surprised her. Her conscious image of Mother did not include these qualities.

In this session she also drew a picture of herself, "me for me," she called it. Her self-portrait depicted a woman with soft, weak arms holding large, beautiful breasts (her breasts were small in reality) with a soft, substantial belly and no feet. Her ego, increasingly feminine instead of the animus ego she started out with, bore some resemblance to the Mother self now, and was in some ways her Daughter, but Kara still had difficulty standing her ground or reaching for what she needed and wanted. Before her ego could grow strong "arms" and "feet," her Hades animus would have to become even more visible and his power directly confronted. And before the animus would experience the transformative womb of the Self, Kara would experience it first more directly herself.

Both Kara and Joanna experienced being born at the height of their bonding with me and apperceptions of the Goddess as Source and as

Self. With Joanna I was more of a midwife; with Kara, simply a witness. Kara came into session one evening late in the therapy caught in an underworld state—blanked out, devalued, depressed. She felt this was somehow connected with having once again fallen into neglecting her body. She had barely begun talking when she started crying, saying how good it felt to be here, how safe. From what? I asked. Her father.

She kept crying, then said she felt like a baby, dumb and confused. She had a fantasy of crawling around the room and crying; I invited her to do it. She crawled around for awhile, then curled into a fetal position, sobbing. Then she got on her hands and knees again and started clawing the air, crying, "Let me out, let me out!" Her breathing became rapid, labored; she kept crying. As happened so often during these enactments, she suddenly shifted. No longer crying, she began hugging herself, touching herself all over, as if her body had come into being.

When she was calm and could talk about what she'd experienced, she said she had felt "borning"— she had felt herself coming through the birth canal and begin to breathe. Later she had heard a baby crying and realized it wanted her to mother it. She had a sense then of being both mother and child.

In the same session, she talked about how her hands came alive when she was with me. She had always hated her hands and envied other people's but now she experienced them as coming alive. This had happened first in therapy but now it was happening when she was with others as well. Her developing ego was beginning to find its full body.

Joanna's birth experience was more frightening and ambivalent. As we sat on the floor in one session, I mused about the recurrent emphasis on her head. I asked if she was willing to try an exercise I had just learned from a bodyworker in which the head is given over to the therapist's hands to see if its tension can be released. She was willing but had difficulty letting my hands carry the weight of her head as she lay on the floor. I set her head down gently and just held the top of it. She said she felt like she was being birthed but also being prevented; my hands felt like forceps. My hands were relaxed, barely touching her, and I told her I wasn't pulling her, that she could just stay right where she was. She suddenly connected with an image that had come up during one of her recent twilight visions, the image of a blind baby. She put her hands over her eyes and said she felt lost in blackness—

not entirely black but with stars. Then she felt that she couldn't see and identified with the baby in her vision and panicked. She curled up in a ball on the floor, crying and saying, "I can't be blind!" I assured her that she was all right, asked her to be aware of her body, to feel my hands on her head.

I was struck that she didn't realize that if she could see stars, as she described, she was not blind; only in lunar instead of solar consciousness. This is the night-sky consciousness of dreams and vision, a matriarchal consciousness that is more intuitive, less focused, less differentiated than what can be seen by the light of day. She had gone so far into her interior and regressed to the Origin but it had terrified her and perhaps echoed some kind of trauma surrounding her actual birth.

Still, at the end of the session, for the first time she could tolerate a prolonged silence. She sat quietly for a long time, eyes closed. When she spoke again, she said she had had the sense that she could hear a maternal heartbeat, "like the sea in a shell." She felt deeply moved by this, having traveled from her terror to the calming of the Mother's pulse.

During the most intense periods of therapy with these women, both experienced me in the archetypal transference as Mother and themselves in a daughter role. Both also sought to make this exclusive, to imaginally create what I have called a matriarchal bond—that is, for both Joanna and Kara, the mother-daughter bond was sought as a refuge from an invading Masculine they had formerly been identified with. They spoke not only of wanting to exclude men from their lives, wanting nothing masculine to invade them any more, but also of wanting to be hidden from the invader.

The theme of the hiding place came up in both processes; both women expressed wanting to be hidden, even wanting to hide in my body, from what frightened and threatened them, which was imaged in male form. I have experienced this with other women in deep work and understand it to be a regression to a matriarchal layer of the psyche in the service of relativizing and attempting to peripheralize the power of Hades and, collectively, of patriarchy. It is part of disidentifying from and dissolving the domination of the patriarchal eyes through which they have seen themselves as well as a protection of the sprout life they have now allowed themselves to become. The transpersonal, transformative womb here is transferred to the therapist; hiding imaginally in her body is felt to be both a refuge and a chance to gestate and be born anew, "unpolluted by the Masculine," as Kara put it.

But this is not entirely possible; the patriarchal rape cannot be denied or undone, it can only be confronted and transformed. In women who live the myth backward, the discovery of the Kore child held and cherished by the Mother is simultaneous with the awareness of having been raped and the task of disidentifying from the power of the Rapist. The female therapist must be in two places at once, must think and navigate paradoxically, carrying precisely the both/and tension of the myth. On the one hand, the therapist must contain the client in the matriarchal vessel of the therapy and protect it from rupture; on the other hand, she must stand against denial of the invasive animus and model the possibility of protesting and confronting it. In both functions, she embodies Demeter—first she nourishes the sprout life that appears after the animus identification is challenged and begins to break up, providing shelter, encouragement, and nurturance for the young, still inchoate feminine ego that is finding the Mother as Self for the very first time. In this function, she stands strongly against the Invader, taking issue with whatever attacks the developing ego, soothing the wounded woman, facilitating the healing regression as it develops; it is critical to neither collude with nor analyze the negative animus while the ego is still in its formative stage. But in her other function as Demeter, the therapist must gently convey that the wish for a matriarchal paradise, an original bond that envisions the Masculine only as negative and undoes the power of its shadow, is not possible. We cannot simply go back to and live in a matriarchal world; rather, we are to draw from that world as a base within ourselves from which to confront the sadistic patriarchal shadow, demand ourselves back from it, and transform that shadow's effect on our lives, collectively and individually.

This possibility was embodied in the work with Kara and Joanna. Once they encountered the Goddess in their dreams and waking visions and while they projected her also to me and felt themselves held in her care, then and only then could they also be helped to face the aggressors they had earlier only been victim to. Here I served as psychopomp, moving between worlds, closer to Hermes than to the goddesses, able to travel back and forth between the under- and upperworlds in the service of retrieving the Kore who would also become Persephone, having to gestate instead of deny the damage that had been done. With both women, the dominant Masculine in their psyches became more visible and more conscious the more they grew into substance as women, and though both sought to hide from what

188

had formerly overpowered them, they ultimately had to face it head on. As the myth suggests, this was no small task; what each had to face was formidable.

In the beginning of therapy, both Joanna and Kara were animus-identified. Their most conscious senses of themselves—their egos—were shaped in accordance with attitudes that had originally come from the men in their lives, both husbands and fathers, and reflected the biases of the patriarchal culture they grew up in as well. Like Hades, the patriarchal animus overpowers and dominates the ego, behaving just as tyrannically as a power-over man. The archetypal Feminine, which should provide the archetypal backdrop for the woman's ego and infuse the ego/Self relationship is instead in a subordinate role, defined by relationship to the animus. Thus the ego functions as the wife of the animus (or sometimes its daughter or lover or caretaker), taking its cues and directives from an inner masculine voice rather than from the Self. In other words, the woman's ego is not the daughter of the Self, does not function as the Self's representative in time and space. Instead, the woman unconsciously builds her life around a male script rather than struggling to realize the urgings of an inner, feminine Higher Power.

Consciously Joanna disdained patriarchal culture and the men who embodied it, yet her attempts to control both herself and, initially, the therapy expressed much of what she consciously labeled and denounced as masculine—a split-off power-over orientation that she had experienced and hated in both her father and her husband. At first she denied that this was part of herself; she saw it only in her father, husband, and brothers. When she dreamed that she was a man molesting a little girl, she was dumbfounded and horrified. Only later in the therapy and with great pain did she come to realize that she was identified with this oppressor and its target was especially the nascent girl child within herself who longed to express herself and develop.

Kara, on the other hand, was more of an animus victim in the beginning; she consciously identified not so much with the oppressor inside her as with his view of her. Her most conscious sense of self was as someone who was bad, inadequate, devalued, less than the man—the raped Kore position.

The Hades animus is often imaged in dreams and sometimes consciously as a male tyrant, robber, murderer, Nazi, rapist, or otherwise overpowering male, or it may exist as a voice inside the woman that functions in these ways. Kara reported the presence of a male voice within her that constantly criticized whatever she did or felt and plied her with "shoulds." Besides demanding that she be superwoman at home, this voice kept up a running commentary on how she should be in therapy as well. He made up rules and demanded to see a step-by-step program (which she projected to me in the beginning and also resisted) and linear progress. He had some respect for me—"you're the analyst," she said—but berated her constantly. He told her she wasn't good enough for Jungian therapy, hadn't read enough books, and the like.

Even when the therapy was visibly unfolding along its own path and she was more at ease with me and herself, this inner voice continually told her she wasn't making any progress in therapy, insisted she control her feelings (crying especially was not allowed) and even attacked her sense of continuity about the sessions. She had difficulty remembering what happened from one session to the next and at this point was completely estranged from any sense of organic order or rhythm about them. I asked if keeping a journal of what happened in session and what she felt might help, but this voice also attacked her writing: "I can't write," she said. "I'm not able to even stand my handwriting. If I write, it must be perfect, well said, and so forth. Writing is a terrible ordeal." For much of the therapy, she had difficulty even writing down her dreams. Fortunately she did not resist taking up her art again and it was here that she began to be able to actively struggle with this voice.

Nearly a year into our work, she reported a triumph. She had put her two youngest children into part-time daycare and convinced the others in her household to do the same with their children; this allowed her to keep the mothering role she valued but also to have time to herself for her sculpting. At first she could do nothing; the masculine voice told her she wasn't an artist, was no good at all, couldn't produce anything of value. Initially she dissolved, believed this, and gave up; she couldn't do a thing. But one day she responded by tricking him in a subtle and clever way. She spoke back to him and said, "Okay you're right; I'm not an artist, I can't do anything of value—but I still have an hour left until the kids come home, so I'll just play, okay? I'll just practice my skills." Then she sculpted her hand—her left hand—and what appeared in it as she worked with the clay was a tiny sprout. She felt the symbolism immediately, the young life that leapt up the first time she defended her space.

Hades as Rapist was much closer to consciousness in Kara's process than in Joanna's. Being aware of this animus voice that constantly cut her down, undermined her, and often left her voiceless was not difficult for Kara; what was harder was coming to see herself as a woman from a perspective other than his derogatory one and learning to cut through his euphemisms about progress and rationality and fight back. Hardest of all was uncovering and claiming the self he disdained that lay in her body, her feelings, her "irrationality." For Joanna, however, the rapist animus was more deeply entrenched, seen clearly in the "shadows" of the significant men in her life but largely unconscious and multilayered as an aspect of her own psyche. He appeared not only in behavior that continually undercut and disrupted her feeling expression and bondings with women but also in a series of deep dreams and visions. Like the god, these figures were multivalent and complex, revealing not only an angry aggression and her fear of it but also an essential ambivalence, loneliness, and suffering—and potential transformation.

During the second year of therapy, over a period of about nine months, Joanna had a series of dreams and twilight visions that centered on the image of a huge, powerful male head with distorted features. With one exception, the head appeared alone without a body. Work on this image was difficult, for she was frequently terrified by it and resisted looking at it. Only when she felt safe enough in the holding environment of the mother-child bond within the therapy, could she fully describe this image and consider with me what it might be about.

It appeared in various ways: as the still-living head of a murdered old man that she had to bury in the earth; a tortured head of Christ crowned with thorns and growing out of a plant; a triple-faced head with distorted features growing out of the ground and pushing up the limp body of a faceless woman; and finally, in full-bodied form, a man with a deformed face who was waiting his turn to see me for therapy. Sometimes the face appeared exhausted and tortured; more often it appeared threatening in a pronounced oral-aggressive way (open and scowling, screaming mouth, prominent teeth).

The image of the disembodied male head appeared during the deepest and most intense months of our work together, simultaneous with a deepening transference and a flowering of goddess images in her dreams and fantasies. It was as if her capacity to trust another woman with her younger, less rational self and to become increasingly woman-centered enabled the face of the unconscious Masculine in her life to become visible.

On a personal level, she connected these grotesque, distorted male heads with the "head trips," criticalness, and anger of her father, brothers, and husband. But these images were far more ambivalent than her views of the primary men in her life and also larger than personal images. With some of the heads, there was also an image of suffering, unredeemed isolation, and a connection with Christ. Moreover, in both her fantasies around these images and in her dreams there appeared to be the possibility of redemption through connection with the Feminine.

In the dream of the murdered old man, for example, she comes across his head—just his head—which is still alive and talking. But it needs to be buried and she realizes that she is the one who has to do it. The head is querulous, petulant, unspeakably weary yet frightened of being put in the earth. She looks for something to bury with it and chooses a translucent gemstone with the image of the crescent moon on it. Following this, on the same night, she dreamed she was painting without inhibition or self-conciousness a mandala in vibrant colors on a canvas that slowly moved in a circle. She woke exhilarated.

In another dream, she is leaving my office and sees a man—an ogre with a twisted, gaunt face—seated near the door, waiting to see me after the women had left. She glanced at him quickly, horrified at the sight of him. She wrote at length of the ogre and of what he might get from connection with me: "One side of his face was twisted. . . . I thought today of 'despised and rejected' and was jolted by that. If I felt I were not threatened by him, then maybe I could begin to pity him. If it were a disfigured woman, I would certainly feel sympathetic. . . . Perhaps he comes to Kathie because he knows she is kind and will accept him and listen to him. . . . Maybe the worst part of this man's life is his aloneness but if he comes to Kathie, he really must be trying to reach out."

There were also two related hypnagogic images that came to her just before sleep that terrified her. One was the image of the head of a tortured-looking Christ growing out of a plant, a grotesque kind of "blossom" emerging from the foliage. The other was more elaborate: a triple-faced male head with distorted features, also emerging from the earth and surrounded by foliage. His mouth was open and scowling and he had prominent teeth. Leaves exuded from his mouth while above him, draped over his head and completely limp and passive, was the body of a faceless woman. He had apparently pushed her up when he grew out of the ground.

These strange "flowers" terrified Joanna and though she described them in detail, she didn't want to talk about them, but we pondered them together. Her only comments were about the second one. She was struck by the passivity of the woman but thought perhaps if the woman woke up, she could reshape the man's features into a normal placement again. Alternatively, she said, perhaps the woman had been raped senseless by his anger.

The disembodied or decapitated head is an archetypal symbol that appeared prominently in alchemy, Celtic religion, and in the myth of Orpheus. In these contexts it was connected with prophecy, creativity/fertility, and transformation; it was considered to be the essence of the person—to capture the head and use it for ritual purposes was to have ultimate power over one's enemy or to possess the arcane substance in alchemy. In the latter context, Jung writes, "Beheading is an emancipation of the 'cogitatio' which is situated in the head, a freeing of the soul from the 'trammels of nature.' Its purpose is to bring about a unio mentalis 'in the overcoming of the body.' "[10]

But this again is a view for masculine psychology. In Joanna's process the body was not to be overcome but reclaimed; the "cogitatio" was not to be freed from nature but linked to it. Here creativity is released not via the possession of the head but by connecting it with a symbol of the transformative Feminine and burying it in the earth.

At the time I knew nothing about the image of the Green Man, but a year or so ago I came across this figure and recognized its relevance for Joanna's material. The Green Man was an archetypal image, pagan in origin but elaborated most profoundly in European church architecture during the Middle Ages. It appeared most frequently as the head of a man surrounded by foliage or exuding foliage from his mouth; at other times the Green Man's head appeared as the fruit or flower of vegetation.[11] The Green Man served the Goddess as lover, son, and guardian. In pagan mythology, Dionysos is "one of the chief precursors of the Green Man."[12] Thus the Green Man is linked to the most positive vision of Hades, his assimilation to the god Dionysos. "Dionysos, whether as a vegetation god, an inspirer of divine madness and intoxication, or the revealer of mysteries of the creative force of life and of the underworld,

193

was one of the most universal manifestations of the archetypal common cause of the Green Man."[13] This common cause was the essence of Goddess religion, the basic underlying motif: death and renewal.

My sense is that the imagery in Joanna's dreams and waking visions represents both a distortion of this archetypal image and the dying and resurrecting god—a god who is part of and serves the cycles of the Feminine—and its potential redemption. Its features are distorted and in one case, tripled like the patriarchal god himself, but even this can be linked with the Green Man, for in a twelfth-century image he appears as three-headed; according to some interpretations, this form is considered demonic, connected with Satan or demons. Hence he is also linked with the Evil One and the underworld he rules.

In Joanna's imagery he is intensely bivalent, on the one hand grotesque and most often threatening, oral-aggressive, a figure who rapes through the savagery of words perhaps. At best, he is querulous and petulant. Like the god of the underworld in the Persephone myth, he is also set apart, feared, and hated, even lonely. And in his loneliness, he too seeks therapy and compassion from a woman.

Underlying the figure of the Green Man is the archetypal motif of death and renewal—not Hades' form of death, fixed and unnatural, but rather death and renewal as they are played out in Nature, perpetually recycling and held by the Maiden-turned-Crone. All of Joanna's imagery appeared to have the intention to reconnect this split-off masculinity with a feminine cycling. In the dream of the old man, Joanna buries his head with an image of the moon, the Mistress of night vision and lunar consciousness, sacred to the Crone side of the Goddess. The moon was also the receptacle of the dead, the keeper of souls.[14] In the dream, Joanna buries the head in the earth like a seed, linking him with the ever recycling death and resurrection of the moon. The burial is fertile; what is born from its meeting with the earth is the release of Joanna's creativity in an image of wholeness.

In the visions of her flowering heads, the connection with the Feminine is even more obvious. Here the male head is connected directly with the earth, sprouts from it; it is linked with the Green Man who represents the underworld male who serves the Goddess instead of overpowering her. Moreover, it is the faceless and perhaps raped woman herself who possibly can reshape the Masculine and re-create it in a less distorted form. And finally, in more personal form, the "despised and rejected" aspect of the animus, not only Christ-like

194

but profoundly reminiscent of the isolated, hated Hades, reaches out for the Feminine himself and submits himself to the therapy. In each instance, the head finds its way back to the transformative Feminine—the old man's head is buried in the earth, surely to rise again like the moon; the flowering heads spring from the earth, already connected with Demeter's vegetative realm. The tormented head undergoes gestative transformation in the belly of the Mother. And the most human of these figures, the ogre, comes to therapy; here the deformed male becomes self-conscious, is no longer a rapist, and seeks out solace and comfort for his loneliness.

Most of this was far beyond Joanna's consciousness and by the end of the therapy had been only partially realized in her life. Insofar as these related to the patriarchal shadow in her animus and personal psychology, there appeared to be some sense in which the formerly power-oriented animus became better integrated with her growing feminine ego and now became its tool instead of its suppressor or defense. As our work went on, Joanna's intellect was no longer used to cut off her child or relationship; then her creativity flourished—her feelings no longer held back, she wrote poetry, music, essays, and meditations. She became more assertive about her needs, moving out of the essentially passive-aggressive position she had been in at the beginning of therapy and into a recognition that she was in charge of her life.

Her relationships with women deepened. Once her child self was known to her and accepted, it no longer overweighted her connections with other women. Although each new love relationship was initially numinous, each one a sense of coming Home, they were also fully human relationships and, as she had not adequately been able to do before, Joanna learned to navigate the joys and disappointments of human partnerships. Particularly significant was her newborn capacity to confront conflicts and even in one instance end a relationship that was not adequately meeting her needs; her previous difficulties in expressing her needs and in separating from women were overcome once she developed a more grounded and proactive ego.

Though she had several male friends whom she valued, men she saw as particularly in touch with their feminine sides, relationships with men remained a peripheral part of her life. During the course of therapy, she became aware of her enormous anger at men, at her brothers, father, and husband in particular, but also at patriarchal culture in general. With pain and courage, she had recognized and con-

195

fronted the ogre within her. The imperative to see that what she had experienced "out there" was also within required her not to run away from these figures who frightened her. When she dreamed that she was a man who molested a child, she was horrified. But she understood that not only had her child self been the target of abusive men in her life, she had also introjected their energies and continued to suppress and deny her younger, more feeling side. In a heartfelt meditation written during the Church's commemoration of the Holy Innocents (the children killed by Herod in his attempt to eradicate the Christ) she wrote, "The horror of the children murdered, always the children, always the innocent. . . . Thinking that if I had any confession, it would be the killing of the child, of all my head full of children, of all my possibilities. Herod's massacre really a suicide. Of all the murders of the innocent which diminish us—-but if we know that, the sheer magnitude of it can make larger and larger wells of life in us, the numbness becoming enlarged feeling."

This enlarged feeling born out of being able to take responsibility for the patriarchal shadow that was also in her opened out to embrace the world. Thus her anger at men and at patriarchy became honed, at least at times, into an articulate, powerful voice expressed in the creative writing that now went out into the world around her, advocating on behalf of women's rights, gay and lesbian issues, and inclusion within the church. Her spirituality, although always thoughtful and deep, became vastly expanded through her personal connection with the Goddess and she became a perceptive critic of the Church as well as of patriarchal institutions in general.

Kara also experienced an animus transformation as her ego capacities developed. As she developed more confidence in the validity of her feelings and needs, she was able to assert herself more often against the masculine critics, both inner and outer, in her life. She learned to question their claims to authority and to check their views against her own experience of herself. She developed from a depressed, devalued, disembodied "shade" into a woman who took care of and tuned to her body and in so doing extended that to the whole of herself.

Although at times she withdrew her energies from the men in her life in the service of restoring and renewing herself (she used to joke about how nice it would be if our culture provided a "menstrual hut" where women retreated once a month to be with each other), she also became a more active, vital partner, developing a life that could hold its own with her husband but also included him. In her dreams, a man appeared who instead of ridiculing her writing, encouraged and appreciated it as did the dream image of a positive, sensual male artist who valued her work. Near the end of our work, she decided that she wanted to work outside the home and began training in a field that was almost entirely dominated by men. Although nervous at first, she fielded both the competitiveness and resistance to her as a woman with humor and hard work, eventually winning the respect and camaraderie of her coworkers. When I last spoke to Kara, several years after our therapy had ended, she was working in a supervisory capacity with several men under her.

As each woman developed an ego capacity to actively mother herself and her animus became more often creative than destructive, the matriarchal bond that had characterized the therapeutic relationships dissolved. The archetypal energies returned to their Source and became part of an inner vision that each woman now carried and drew from for comfort and grounding instead of projecting onto me. The experience of Mother and Daughter was now an internal base and functioned like the original bond between the goddesses. Faced with an inner or outer Hades-like attack, the women could now live the myth forward, drawing from protective maternal energies and the Daughter's capacity to survive and transform the experience. As Joanna and Kara carried more of these energies into the fullness of their outer lives, the therapy organically ended.

In summary, for women who live the myth backward in the therapeutic process with a female therapist, the starting point is characterized by conscious or unconscious identification with a patriarchal perspective and its values; the woman is the captive of Hades and has known no other archetypal home. Her identity is an animus ego, merged with patriarchal judgments and "shoulds," and serves the negative Masculine against herself. Unconsciously, however, a compensatory picture presents itself in images, dreams, and desires that appear to strive toward the manifestation of aspects of the Demeterian upperworld. Matriarchal bonding that provides a grounding in relationship with the archetypal Mother is sought through the therapy as a shelter from the negative Masculine until a new ego base can be forged. This ego develops as a feminine matrix is established and enables the woman to stand up to the Hades-like animus; then it too

197

can undergo transformation and become integrated into the feminine psyche, no longer opposing but serving the Self.

This is the process I have observed in women who encounter the Hades Masculine in themselves, in men, and in patriarchal culture. When a man must confront Hades in himself and in patriarchy, the process is different, as the next chapter will show.

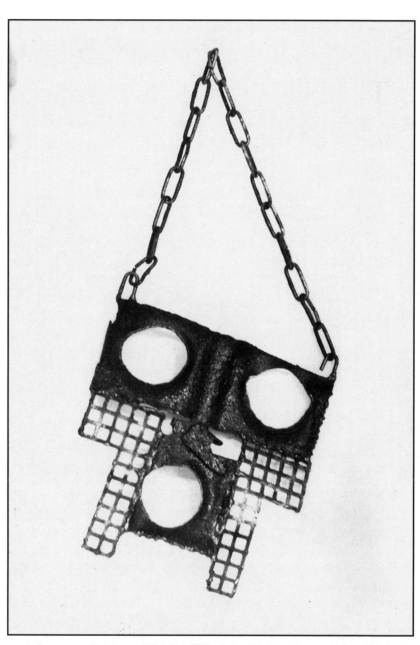

Suzanne Benton, *The One Who Dies*, Holocaust series, 1983.

8

The Hades-Identified Man:

Shadow and Transformation of the Masculine

> . . . the male initiate, as we can see from many
> particulars in the accounts, sought to identify him-
> self with Demeter, i.e., with his own feminine as-
> pect. Here it should be stressed that in Eleusis, as
> in all mysteries, the experience was predomi-
> nantly emotional and unconscious, so that even in
> a late epoch, when the male consciousness had
> long become patriarchal, such a prepatriarchal ex-
> perience was possible in a mystery. And another
> essential factor seems to be that in the mysteries
> the male was enabled, through his experience of
> the creatively transforming and rebearing power
> of the Great Mother, to experience himself as her
> son—i.e., to identify himself both with the new-
> born, divine spirit son, as child of the Great God-
> dess, and with Triptolemus, the son invested by
> her with the golden ear of grain.
>
> —ERICH NEUMANN,
> *The Great Mother*[1]

IN DESCRIBING THE "HADES MAN," I am not describing men in general but rather imagining the archetypal dynamics of Hades in

human form; some men might fit the pattern quite fully and well, in others it might just be an aspect of their personalities. I have tried to keep in mind that Hades is a god, that we are dealing not just with a political reality (i.e., an aspect of patriarchy) or human predilections alone but rather a larger-than-human dimension of power that sometimes constellates in collective and individual psychology, just as Demeter and Persephone do. I also speak as a woman observing this aspect in men and here from a matriarchal perspective only in which Hades is valenced negatively. Zeus and his cronies would see Hades quite differently, as would men who still identify with and champion patriarchal arrangements.

Hades-infused masculinity is, first of all, characterized by an intense power drive and concern with power dynamics. The Hades man may not have a lot of power but he is very power oriented; he seeks to dominate and overpower and may be especially concerned about who's in control and who's "on top." He seeks power over others; concomitantly, he tries to undercut the power of others, desubstantiating those around him whenever possible.

His concept of maleness is identified with patriarchal values and stereotypes: male supremacy; female subordination; emotional containment; hierarchical power arrangements; conquest through physical or psychological strength and violence. Following traditional masculine conditioning in our culture, his sense of self is defined in terms of separateness from others instead of within a matrix of relationships. Such a man may embody these premises of patriarchy directly and model his conscious ego in their image; like Zeus, he appears to be and sees himself as being an expansive, dominant, benevolent patriarch. In such a case, the Hades archetype may appear as shadow, as a hidden possessiveness or unacknowledged lethal power drive. Alternatively, this archetype may dominate the personality completely, resulting in an inferior Zeus, that is, the man may see himself and be seen by others as unable to measure up to the patriarchal conception of manhood. Like the god Hades relative to his more revered brother, the Hades man may be set apart and even reviled by others, failing to achieve and enjoy the privileges and spoils of patriarchal manhood.

Unlike his successful, promiscuous, gregarious brother, the Hades man is particularly unrelated to others. He tends to be emotionally distant and remote, a "loner" among men. Even if he has some connections with other men, he has a poor relationship to the Feminine, both in terms of relating to women and to the Feminine in himself.

202

His is a masculinity without feminine connection; alternatively, he may have sentimental and stereotyped images of women, especially those that allow him to see himself as dominant and a conqueror. His view is essentially narcissistic: women exist to serve him, as objects to be possessed and used or—more darkly—"killed" so that he can revitalize himself with their power. But Hades' power drive is hidden; the Hades man, like the god, may surround himself with euphemisms, a charming persona, an excellent capacity to con a woman, a protestation of his modesty/his liberalness/ his feminism, all covering a core of absolute possessiveness. He may even believe the illusions, denying his ruthlessness and the unrelatedness of his power drive to himself as well as to those he seeks to conquer.

In my experience, the Feminine looms large in the unconscious of such a man; unconsciously, women are perceived as a threat, particularly if they are more related to themselves (virginal in the old sense of the word) or each other than to him. Unconsciously, this man sees women as having potential power over him, power to dominate, control, and castrate him. He frames the world in power-over terms and attributes such motivation to women as well. He may also envy women on a deeply unconscious level. Women have what he has not, are allowed what he is not, all the things that have had to be discarded from himself to maintain the ideal of patriarchal masculinity: softness, nurturance, feeling, relatedness, connection with Nature. He may even envy women's capacity to get pregnant and give birth—the one power he can never claim as his own (though patriarchal religion and mythology achieved even this power by creating unnatural or supernatural images of creation and birth through the sky god alone). But the form his envy takes is wanting to overpower, wanting to take away whatever the woman has; in a way, he wants to take her into himself or put himself into her and overpower her from within in order to own her, possess her qualities and powers as his own. (Thus the patriarchal gods gradually claimed and assimilated the titles and powers of the Goddess.)

My hypothesis is that this primitive attempt at possession actually masks a genuine need in the man infused with the Hades archetype, a need buried deep in his psyche, to compensate an overly remote hypermasculinity or masculine ideal and reconnect himself with the world of Nature, relationship, and the Feminine. At some deep level, he knows what he needs; he truly needs qualities from the Feminine to be whole, to be connected to life, but cannot conceive of any way of getting them without raping them away. Anything that stands outside of his power

203

and excludes him threatens the Hades man. Thus he may be especially attracted to and seek to penetrate and disrupt the matriarchal unit. He is particularly threatened by women's relationships with each other, even more so if they exclude him. This may manifest outwardly in a father who continually disrupts his daughter's relationship with her mother or a husband who is jealous of and tries to prevent his wife's relationships with her women friends. It may also appear as an intrapsychic dynamic (as in the case of Oliver I present below). Matriarchal bonds are seen as both tantalizing and a challenge to a Hades-identified man; underneath is a fear of having no power at all in relation to women, being relegated to the periphery and seen as irrelevant.

Another striking characteristic of the Hades man is his refusal to serve. Not only will he not subject himself to women but often his need for power is so great that he will not subject himself to a god-image either. Like Erysichthon who honors no gods and arrogantly chops down Demeter's sacred oak, the Hades man acknowledges no power greater than himself. In Jungian terms, this man's power-ridden ego is not relativized in the service of the Self; instead, the god-image is brought down to the human realm. His ego is aggrandized—he sees himself as the real power in his world or possibly worships power but not in a related way (as would be the case if he experienced himself as humanly "small" and in service to a Power greater than himself); rather, he seeks to become that Power, to appropriate it for himself. He may be extremely arrogant; his opinion is the only worthy one, whatever he says goes. He may also envision himself (and perhaps men in general) as the conqueror of women and of the power of the Goddess. Psychologically, of course, this leaves him vulnerable to terrible backlashes from the archetypal realm of the gods to whom hubris is a most serious offense that cannot go unpunished. Men who see women and the Goddess as that which they have conquered must constantly be fortifying themselves against real or imagined uprisings; thus the power of the oppressed is reflected in ever greater defenses and power-over posturings.

Psychologically and spiritually there is something indeed to fear: oppression engenders resentment and rage, which sooner or later rise up to counterattack. And in mythology, the banished, dishonored Feminine returns demonic, like Lilith threatening particularly the man who is home alone without his wife, like Demeter Erinys avenging the raping of both herself and her daughter. Unrelated power-over and its motivation to dominate and control others eventually elicit a backlash, no less among individuals than between groups and even intrapsychically.

Finally, the Hades man lives in a world of abstracts instead of concretes, is removed from everyday practical life, natural cycles (including the aging of his body), and upperworld values. He may seek to be outside his body altogether, identifying only with his head or his penis, or alternatively, attempt to mightily control his body through extreme athletics or muscle building. He may himself become something of an abstraction, depersonalized, ghostly, split off and depressed, like the shades in the underworld. Unrelated even to himself, his life is barren, sterile; his creative efforts—unlike those of his sky god brother—lack life force and do not bear fruit. Unconsciously, like the shades who long to feel real again, he yearns for rebirth, for transformation; he is drawn precisely to what he is most outside of and most disdains: the Mother and Crone who hold the link between life and death and can recycle even him into new and more viable form.

The male initiates in the Eleusinian mysteries understood that the path to rebirth through the Mother as Queen of the Dead had requirements: a voluntary sacrifice of destructive, patriarchal aggression, an entering into and feeling with the Mother who mourns for what patriarchy has savaged, and finally, a voluntary service to the Goddess as seed bearer and son. The Hades man, however, will not bend his knee to the Feminine. Instead he attempts to appropriate her (albeit through the tacit consent of the sky god Zeus), to grab her for himself, to become her and thus assimilate her powers. She in turn throws him down until he learns that her power is outside his capacity to appropriate and possess.

There are many ways in which these dynamics may constellate, both personally and collectively. To illustrate their inner workings, I have chosen the vivid and unusual story of an older man I saw in my practice when I first moved East years ago. While extreme, his psychology affords an in-depth look at one way in which the Hades archetype may infuse masculine psychology and also, in this case, get stuck there, unable to move through the full drama of the myth to its transformative initiation.

Oliver was a retired scientist who came into therapy because he felt there was something "dangerous" inside of him. He had problems with his wife and was concerned that his creativity was stifled.

205

Throughout his adulthood, he had been enormously identified with his work and work persona and was suffering a late-life identity crisis in the wake of his recent retirement. Dry, pedantic, and repetitive when he spoke, he was nonetheless drawn to creative and spiritual issues but not generally creative or spiritual himself. He was disdainful of his colleagues, extremely unrelated and distant emotionally, and had virtually no close friends.

His only ongoing relationship was with his wife of fifty years. They had no children. His marriage, as it came through to me in the several years we worked together, appeared to be something of a horror show of power play, rage, and mutual disdain. Underneath were the tiniest occasional flickers of affection as well as a profound interdependence.

Oliver had been in a study group in Jungian psychology that had grown out of a workshop he had attended in the town he lived in outside of New York. He had some spiritual interests as well as a longing for creativity that could not be realized. Once he launched a creative endeavor, as he had years before when he had managed to produce and self-publish a book of poems, he used it to see others as "less"; this power drive and the grandiosity that accompanied it repeatedly killed whatever spark there was in him of genuine creative experience or feeling.

He complained of being dominated by his wife, who did indeed harass and nag him constantly. But even by his own admission, this was only half the picture; he agreed with her accusations that he lacked feelings and spoke of a kind of ruthlessness about himself, especially with her.

Yet he felt a real contrast between who he was at home and his career persona. He presented his career alternately as a string of failures and as an aggrandized vision of the importance of his point of view and accomplishments. Despite this swinging back and forth, he felt he had been fairly successful at his work and attributed this to his ability to be detached. When he could be completely detached, he told me, "as in writing letters," he felt most successful.

He spoke of being particularly concerned about being controlled by others and felt that his mother—a powerful and histrionic woman who had dominated both his father and his three brothers as well as himself—had controlled and manipulated him throughout his early years. Feelings and expression of feelings had made him vulnerable in his early years, he felt, and he presented himself in therapy as having spent a lifetime trying not to feel. This was so extreme that in one period of his life he stopped reading novels and going to movies because they stirred him up too much. Major effort was put into, as he put it, "reducing feelings into harmless rationality."

Feeling was also connected with women, and his attempt not to feel anything was synonymous with his attempt to be a man. He had always felt inadequate in relation to the masculine conditioning of his day, was continually exhorted to "be a man, learn to take it," to be tough, unemotional, and athletic. Feelings and sentiment were reserved for women, and even as a young boy he both envied and disdained this. Throughout his life he had struggled to cut off his feelings and control his moods. His was a masculinity extreme in its patriarchal imprint; except for his relationship with his wife, he was cut off from anything feminine and from both relatedness and feeling—as remote from Demeter's upperworld values as was Hades in his underworld.

But in Oliver's case, tragically in some ways, he was also remote from a positive masculine identity. He felt himself to be inadequate as a man, struggled mightily to embody some aspects of patriarchal power but never had managed to get the benefits enjoyed by the masterful, strong-egoed Zeus-like man who was the ideal of his environment and his times. Like Hades, he experienced himself as set apart, hated by those who gave homage to this ideal—unathletic and fearful of other, more aggressive boys, he had been teased and bullied as a child and judged as never measuring up. Like the underworld god, he was cast into the role of inferior shadow of the "real" man Zeus. Here his father, who had presented himself to his son as helpless before the mother's manipulations, had particularly failed to mediate a positive and grounded masculinity. These feelings of inferiority made up part of Oliver's sense of being insubstantial as a person, which was also extreme, although this was evident only later in the therapy.

The extent of his detachment in our sessions was remarkable. He presented himself as a series of insights, all of which were written down ahead of time and to which he was not attached emotionally. Depersonalized to an extreme, he saw himself as a case, a history of events and interpretations. For the first three years of our work, our sessions consisted of his reading the insights he had written in his diary to me.

The ruthlessness he attributed to himself was indeed there in the form of an enormous power drive and came through in his attitude toward me in the early months of our work. Pedantic, disdainful, and very power oriented, he often lectured me about Jung, as if I were a particularly dumb student of his, putting down any suggestion, idea, or comment I happened to make. It was as if he had to wipe me out, appropriate any power he felt I might have, every time he came to session.

This need to repeatedly overpower women is typical of the Hades-dominated man, I think, though outside of therapy we don't often get to see his underlying fear of being overpowered by women or by what appear to him to be feminine qualities. The Hades man "lords it over" women, tries to dazzle them with his superior knowledge but has to shut them up. In extreme, nothing a woman has to say is given any credence, and whatever she stands for is disdained—yet he may keep a woman around to preach to or correct or as an audience to whom he can continually display himself.

Dreamwork was particularly difficult with Oliver, and this was one place in which Hades' euphemistic masking was evident. Oliver presented himself as extremely interested in Jung and Jungian work and at times got very inflated with the idea that he was doing Jungian therapy; this proved how "progressed" he was compared to others. But he controlled the process as completely as possible. He would bring in dreams along with quick and extremely reductive interpretations. He resisted association and was even more resistant to any kind of imagination (though part of him also longed for this). He would commit himself to nothing that went beyond his own perspective. He assigned no value to anything but presented everything as hypothetical; pressed to make a connection with any particular aspect of a dream or interpretation, he would say, "Well, it *might* be that." Often even the dream ego was detached, cast in the role of an observer. Although I have worked with many people with schizoid and narcissistic defenses over the years, Oliver's remoteness was truly extreme for a nonpsychotic process. Like Hades, he was cut off from life and anything life-giving, cut off from any kind of development or process, flow, feeling, or relationship even within himself.

An early dream gave me a picture of his psychic situation and the archetypal field we were in. In the dream he was in a Victorian house with a group of people who were involved in witchcraft. He was sitting next to a young woman "who didn't look very bright" (his unconscious devaluation of me at the time!). The group wasn't meeting in one room but in two. There was a wall between the two rooms so that the room on the left, where the chairman was, could not be seen by Oliver.

To Victorian, he associated an emphasis on morality. He also spoke of the gingerbread on Victorian houses. So in this dream there is the outer persona of moral rightness, a favorite persona of a drive to power, as well as a lot of "decoration." (I was reminded of the witch's house in Hansel and Gretel that was literally made of gingerbread—a euphemism in image form.) Things are not what they seem to be. Here is part of the covering over that Hades is so good at: the outer appearance makes invisible what's underneath or inside.

Witchcraft he described tellingly as "having power over others" (this is witchcraft from a patriarchal perspective). To the chairman, he associated the Devil, which takes us into the archetypal dimension. The power drive that appeared in sessions was fueled by an archetypal dimension of evil that later appeared in our work as a personality dynamic that he described as the Torturer or Nazi. In this later work, he described the Nazi's qualities (and the Nazi phenomenon is an excellent example of Hades-like detachment and drive to power): lacking compassion, insensitivity to others' pain, suspicion that everyone's out to get him (i.e., assuming that everyone else is driven by the same power-over motivation), and dominating others. While in reality Oliver did not literally act out his aggression toward others in a physical way, his split-off shadow carried all of these psychological ingredients, which he himself recognized. He was very resistant to seeing the piece of himself that was like this with me or his wife or with others. He paid lip service to admitting "ruthlessness" toward his wife but rationalized that by saying she dominated him or that this was part of his image of respectable masculinity. His desire and control wore the gingerbread of "the right way to be a man."

His wife at this point was probably alcoholic (which he colluded with by continually supplying her with liquor) and extremely depressed. She came through to me in his descriptions as a raging bitch of a woman but with some capacity for life. Thus he reported that once she had held out her hands to newly opening flowers and exclaimed, "Oh you blessed things!" and that years before, she'd expressed her most fervent desire: to have a child. She had even tried to adopt a little boy. All this was most strongly refused by Oliver; he consistently tried to kill this off in her. Later in therapy, he admitted that he had wanted her all to himself and more deeply, had envied her capacity to have a child. By depriving her, he later admitted, she was "more like me." He was also eventually able to acknowledge that she was right when she claimed he had ruthlessly used her to further his own ends; she had given countless hours over to augmenting his scientific work, typing his notes, helping him organize his data, for which he had never expressed either gratitude or recognition of her considerable contribution to his life and well-being.

For much of the early work, our sessions were pedantic and sterile; though ostensibly wanting therapy, Oliver was unable to get beyond a power orientation and having to be right. Everything shifted when he brought in what he called his "lesbian fantasies." In the basic fantasy, he imagined becoming involved with a mother-daughter pair. One of them dresses him as a woman and he becomes sexually involved with both of them. There were hundreds of variants of this fantasy, some very elaborate. Much of Oliver's fantasy life focused on disrupting and also seeking to become part of the matriarchal unit. He also imaginally invented what he called a "milking machine." This was a costume that enabled him to simulate breast-feeding; in his eyes, it enabled him to conquer his envy of and distance from the upperworld Feminine and literally become a mother. As these fantasies began to pour out of him, he also revealed that sometimes, when his wife was away, he liked to dress up in feminine clothes.

When he spoke of these fantasies, he became softer, more receptive, more relational. Even more striking was his demeanor when he described what it was like for him when he put on feminine clothes. He went into a kind of reverie as he spoke, becoming very relaxed, even physically (as compared to the rather stiff and tight deportment he usually maintained), gentle, with more access to his feelings. An aesthetic dimension also emerged at these times, which expressed itself in a sensitivity to color and texture. He was also closer to the creativity he so coveted.

Wearing women's clothes apparently enabled Oliver to access some of what his rigid masculinity had banished to the realm of women only. This has an archetypal dimension as well. In many ancient and even some modern cultures that worshiped the Goddess, male priests sometimes practiced ritual transvestism in her service. This has also been true in some cultures whose religious practices include a strong tradition of shamanism. Such an act, set in the context of high ritual, becomes a vehicle for connection with and relating to a higher female Power.

Oliver, however, was too power-driven to relate to a higher power and see himself as serving it. At one point as we explored his experience of being in women's clothes, he spoke of literally becoming the Goddess at these times. He believed that he could possess the Goddess, become a woman and not only that, could serve as the Goddess for another woman as well (as if Hades not only appropriated her titles but claimed to be Demeter, replacing the Mother instead of just snatching away her daughter). Witnessing this in Oliver's psychology was like being able to observe that intersect of archetype and history in which patriarchal peoples appropriated the Goddess mythology of those they conquered, investing their gods with titles, attributes, and powers that had formerly belonged to the Goddess. But, though even the early Christian church claimed that the position of the man in the family was analogous to the position of the Father to the church, the line differentiating human from divine was not (at least officially) blurred. Oliver, however, did cross this line. He saw his cross-dressing and immersion in his fantasies not as a way to *connect* with the Goddess but as a way of *becoming* her and appropriating her power. Then he would become hugely inflated again.

In myth this appropriation of divine power is represented as the sin of hubris and harshly punished. Such was also the case with Oliver, for each appropriation of the Goddess was followed by psychic backlashes—nightmares and terror fantasies of being engulfed by women or castrated. Though he wrote of these in his diary or in the notes on his dreams that he presented to me, he would also deny them; yet he was thrown into these terrors every time his arrogance crossed the boundary and he attempted to appropriate transpersonal feminine power. Defending against his terror, he'd become hypermasculine again: unfeeling, detached, rational, defensive.

What struck me most was that when he appropriated the Feminine, there was no sense of fear of a Deity, no deference in him. He knew of my interest in the Goddess from having heard me lecture once and even spoke of wanting to be the Goddess for me. I was surprised and instructed by the depth of rage that I felt at this. While I could tolerate his disdain, feel empathic toward the small sparks of longing for growth and creativity that existed in him, and stay with an extremely slow and difficult process, this pushed my buttons. I was willing to help him relate to the Feminine, if that was what the Self seemed to push him toward, but not to ultimately take her over—and certainly not to mediate the Goddess for me in this way.

Partly my rage (which I did not express to him) was grounded in my own personal history of having experienced my father continually asserting himself as the only true "mother" available despite my need and profound longing to be connected with a woman as mother, but I also sensed a collective layer of my rage—the rage of women or even of the Goddess herself at being appropriated in patriarchal history. I have also worked with men who were genuinely related to a transpersonal dimension, through whom Spirit was powerfully manifest at times, but these men were aware of their own relativity with respect to the Deity they worshiped and served it with deference and respect; with these men, I was open to their mediating Spirit to me. But Oliver's aggrandizement would not let him become a genuine instrument or vessel of the transpersonal Goddess; in his mind, he became her, possessed her, then suffered the difficult but inevitable consequences of such inflation. It seemed that the only way he could experience the bigness of the archetype and his own relativity and smallness compared to it was when he was terrorized by images of the terrible side of her. I wondered what would happen if he ever came to recognize his humanness in the face of her power and to open to the possibility that he had been called to serve her, like her seed bearer Triptolemus, instead of believing that he or any human being was big enough to take her over.

Why would a man seek to become the Goddess rather than relate to her? Certainly on a personal level, Oliver's cross-dressing and his beliefs concerning it represented an attempt to appropriate and overcome through identification the power his mother had always held over both him and his father. Archetypally, however, we can understand his motivation by considering again the characteristics of Hades, the god who also sought to break into the mother-daughter relationship and appropriate their realm.

Hades was cut off from the upperworld of relationship and natural process, including the downgoing phase of Nature in which everything decays, dies, and decomposes. In Demeter's realm, seed gives rise to plant, plant to flower and fruit, then the fruit decays and dies but contains within it the seeds of the next generation, the Crone power that receives death and endlessly recycles it. In the versions of the Demeter and Persephone myth most available to us, it appears that the goddesses have lost touch with their Crone aspect; she appears only in Hecate whose power is effaced and who is assigned only a minor role in the mythic drama. Without a goddess of the underworld, Hades has replaced the Crone and her version of death; death was no longer part of the natural cycle but cut off from life, became repetition and stasis, the eternity of heaven or hell rather than just one stage in an ever recycling process.

Thus we might expect that a man identified with Hades and seeking to overpower the Goddess would have a disturbed relationship to the natural cycle of aging and death. Such was the case with Oliver. For him, believing he could become the Goddess and appropriate her powers by wearing feminine clothes was connected with a flight from aging and the inevitability of death.

This became evident only late in the therapy when I once made a remark about cross-dressing that he interpreted as critical and as telling him he should stop doing it. The dream and associations that followed were extremely revealing, making visible another terror from which his cross-dressing attempted to protect him. In the dream, he was on a bus filled with old women that descended into the earth. Walking about the shoddy, decrepit town they came to that he consciously associated with hell, he met a woman colleague who in reality had committed suicide several years before.

Barbara Walker in her book *The Crone* hypothesizes that part of woman hating is connected with an avoidance of the inevitability of natural death. Because women outlive men, there are more old women around, and because it is most often women who tend the dying in our culture, old women serve as reminders of death to men. Because patriarchal spirituality separates natural life from spirituality and preaches human dominion over whatever is natural, men tried to conquer death by inventing an artificially controlled version of it—the waging of war. A man who dies in battle becomes heroic and glorious, while natural death is felt as his defeat and, by association, women are connected with natural death, old women in particular; thus they too are to be devalued and disappeared from their roles in patriarchal society (Walker makes a strong case for this as the basis of misogyny against older women in our culture).[2] The connection between old women and death appeared to be strong in Oliver's psychology. Asked to associate to parts of the dream, he spoke of old women as sad creatures in nursing homes, waiting to die. The reality trigger for his association was his wife's having undergone a cataract operation and his

213

fear that she might have to go into a nursing home when she had another. (He had not been able to let her have life—the child she wanted, her spontaneous joy at the flowers—but was also afraid of her reminding him of death.)

Of the woman who had committed suicide, he was vehemently judgmental. She was a coward, he said, couldn't take it (remember his being exhorted to "take it like a man"), "couldn't face the diabolical in herself." Deprived by my untimely intervention of the comfort of the Good Mother that he got through cross-dressing, faced with the need to protect himself from the Terrible Mother who (from a patriarchal perspective) brings castration and death, he was led into his fears of old age and death. At this point in therapy, a profound underlying depression surfaced; I had sensed this depression in him all along in our work but it had not overtly emerged until this point.

As his wife prepared for another surgery, Oliver's dreams continued to bring up images of old age and death. He consistently split off from these images whenever possible, maintaining his defensive stance that he could take it (here again was another example of his persona of arrogance; faced with death—which is transpersonal as well as personal and against which no human power can ultimately triumph—he continued to refuse to acknowledge human relativity and appropriate fear, as if he were equal to Death as well as to the gods). He spoke of being a Stoic, unfeeling and detached, though at this point he also admitted at times that this was his way of keeping himself from being swallowed by the abyss.

As we worked with this, at times the Stoic image would crumble and another would come up: of being a ghost man or wraith who had no attachments to anyone or anything. This image, reminiscent of the shades in Hades, would be accompanied by the threat of deep depression which would send him back into either the Stoic or his feminine fantasies. In sessions he alternated between arrogance and inflation and feeling flat and depressed. He was moved by what he experienced as my seeing and accepting the "sad old man" in him but to get this close to it was simply too threatening.

Oliver's psychological situation was extreme and difficult to work with. There were moments of real connection and an ability to face into himself, moments of hunger for relationship to himself, to other people, and to a spiritual realm, but all were ultimately interfered with and swallowed by his arrogance. There were glimmers of hope (that

214

was in part what held me in my work with him through several years, that and my compassion for his depression); at times he could talk about his fears of aging and death. He even began to be able to admit that he had used people and at times wanted to hurt others and had hurt them. There was also, now and then, the faint spark of related-ness that came up as he was increasingly able to take in my compas-sion and my care.

He focused most of his sessions on his immersion in the archetypal Feminine or on his defenses. But one day, after a dream of my own had paired Oliver with a little boy who brought healing to him, I com-mented with compassion on his father's failure to be really there for him, to bond with his son and initiate him into a more substantial man-hood than the culture permitted or than he himself had ever been able to find. This evoked a rush of tears and began a tenuous but significant new development in him. Over time Oliver was able to connect more genuinely with masculine experience, even masculine sexuality, and occasionally his dreams and fantasies reflected this. Thus he reported one fantasy in which he debated strongly with another man, won the debate, and then his penis grew big. Once he watched women on tele-vision whoop it up at a male strip show and was amazed that women could be so turned on at the sight of a male body.

As time went on, his relationship to cross-dressing and to his fanta-sies of women changed slightly. Occasionally he could hold his femi-nine imagery as a fantasy that he could relate to rather than become. And once, late in the therapy, he imagined being reborn through the Mother rather than appropriating her powers as his own. This came up in the context of a particularly moving session.

He seemed more reflective than usual this day. He began the ses-sion as usual, speaking about some of his fantasies but then stopped and started to talk about black Madonnas, asking what their meaning was; he seemed genuinely curious about what in the psyche might create such a figure. He slipped in that he had had a fantasy of me as his wife accompanying him to one of the churches that held a black Madonna. (He rarely brought fantasies of me directly, so I picked up on this, asking him to go into it and imagine it further.) After some hesitation, he got easily into the fantasy, which became quite pow-erful.

He imagined that we went to the church. He wasn't sure if we were married or if I was the goddess Athena (the chaste warrior maiden of

215

the Father!). He described the church, which was one he had been to in reality, as a place of great spiritual integrity in spite of the number of tourists who pass through it. We entered the church in his fantasy and looked at the Madonna. Then Oliver imagined taking me up to the black Madonna. She reached out to give us each a blessing. Then he kissed me and touched my breasts as I touched his. The Madonna oversaw this. Afterward he was naked and I saw him and he saw my breasts and we had intercourse. The Madonna watched us and he had a picture of all the saints gathering round. Then I went up to the Madonna; with her bent over me, I gave birth to a child. I broke in here to ask if it was his child and he said it was a boy and that it was *him* being born.

I imagined all of this with him, trying to follow his feeling which was unusually present. The fantasy flowed from him; I could feel the power and saw the near-ecstasy on his face as he continued. Then, after seeing me as the Virgin with Child, he experienced a mandala of darkness filled with light and saw me with the child. He experienced himself as far away, moving further and further into the distance. I thought this to be either the rising up of a matriarchal exclusion of him as a man or his splitting off from what he'd experienced. But this was not the meaning of this image; he said it was instead as if his spectator self, the one who was always on the outside and detached (even in his night dreams) was disappearing, the way a caterpillar does in a chrysalis. I was deeply moved: this suggested that if he could be reborn through the Feminine, through relatedness to me and to the Goddess, the observer stance could fall away. At the end of the session he started to cry and spoke with great feeling about how much I carry for the people I work with and said that he prayed for me every day.

This was a late and unusual session in our work, uncharacteristically more personally and archetypally relational and full of feeling. It was from this session that I first perceived that it is through the Mystery baby Brimos that Hades is reborn as son of the Mother and once again reconnected to Life. Like the shades in his underworld who longed to inhabit a bean or a fish, be eaten by a woman, and be born again into the upperworld of the body, of Nature, of relatedness, Hades the wraith-man can only become substantial again if he is united with the Goddess. Then the death that he carries transforms and he too participates in the cycle of life, redeemed forever through the Maiden-turned-Mother-turned-Crone.

Near the end of our work there were small but significant changes in Oliver. He became less defensive, more able to acknowledge his fears and tolerate the anxiety they generated without fleeing either into a hypermasculine stance or identification with the Feminine. Thus he dreamed of a stream of water coursing down stairs into the darkness; when I asked him to go into the dream, for the first time he acknowledged directly that he was afraid. The dark, unknown depths suggested death to him and he was afraid to get too close to them. He also became more able to genuinely acknowledge that some of his shadow was dark. When the Torturer/Nazi appeared again in his dreams, he was able to speak directly of times in his life when he deliberately tried to hurt people. He was also able to risk more genuine relatedness. When I finally asked him to speak more directly to me in session instead of hiding behind his pages of insights, he readily acknowledged his fear that I'd be bored and wouldn't want to see him anymore yet was able to take in my reassurance that the person was less boring to me than the distancing. From this point on, he related more directly, tolerating well the anxiety of being without this habitual mechanism of keeping both himself and the other at bay.

Dressing up in feminine clothes also faded; he reported that, to his surprise, the fantasy of dressing up was now more powerful than its enactment. Consciously he began to link feminine and masculine a little more instead of excluding either. Here he moved beyond the lysis of the Demeter and Persephone myth and his dreams began to picture both male and female resources for his psychological growth. Thus, near the end of our work, he dreamed he was in a clinic for therapy. There were several implements he had been working with, among them a ball and a stick. Then he overheard a group of doctors talking about an operation he had to have (the work he had done with the implements apparently was not enough)—he thinks the operation will be on his genitals or his brain and he is afraid. He feels the need for protection and thinks he must get his wife to sign a consent form. But then he realizes that this is inadequate and thinks of contacting the young male priest in his parish and me; we would help him through this.

The ball and stick reminded him of a ball and bat and he spoke of how poorly he played baseball as a boy; more and more his early experiences of being a boy among other boys were coming back to him and we had been talking more about his image of what it took to be a "real man." In the dream the superficial, collective solution ("become more athletic") was inadequate. More drastic steps must be taken: a transformation of both his sexuality and his thinking. Of this he was afraid and wanted to flee to his wife for consent but strikingly her approval was no longer enough to protect him from his fear (as it sometimes was in the past). Instead he turned to a spiritual young man whom he liked in reality and who liked him and to the inner therapist, at last bringing together in balance and on a more personal level the spiritual Masculine and Feminine. Through this connection, he could undergo the healing transformations his psyche was urging upon him.

The image of initiation for men into the Eleusinian mysteries is radical for our times and probably abhorrent to many, for it involves a "feminization." Both men and women were asked to enter into the Goddess, to feel for and with the grieving Mother's experience, move into her loss, her grieving, her rage, her longing for life that has been ravaged and lost, and gradually move from the "witlessness" that Demeter denounces in Metanira and all human beings to the enlightenment that she models for us: the transforming power of passionate care that protests violation, stands against ravaging power-over, and through this care and protest reconnects with the power to bring forth new life from the holocaust. For women, this means identifying, at least for a time, with a female-centered experience, reconnecting with transpersonal female power. But for men, this involves renunciation of the "lust" of the runaway patriarchal Masculine and voluntarily entering into what is most fully Other—the Mother-Daughter relationship—not by conquering the Mother but by feeling with her, seeing the consequences of patriarchal raping through her eyes. It means disidentifying with the patriarchal image of what it means to be a man, disavowing violence and the spoils of power-over, giving up the illusion of conquering Nature, aging, and death. It means entering the service of the civilizing Goddess who nourishes, sustains, and recycles and, in exchange for delusions of eternity or terror of death as finality, becoming reintegrated with the Matrix who takes back what she births but also brings it forth again in perpetual renewal.

This is not just a modern interpretation of what it meant for a man to undergo the Eleusinian initiation. Carl Kerényi writes at length about this in his essay on Kore:

> Anyone could be initiated into the mysteries of Eleusis who spoke Greek and was not guilty of the shedding of blood, men and women alike. Men, too, entered into the figure of Demeter and became one

with the *goddess*. To recognize this is the first step toward an understanding of what went on in Eleusis. There is historical evidence to show that the initiate regarded himself as a goddess and not as a god— the coins of the [Roman] Emperor Gallienus [Augustus], which give him the title of Galliena Augusta. The explanation of this official title is to be found in the fact that Gallienus attached particular weight to his having been initiated into the Mysteries of Eleusis. There are other proofs that men incarnated themselves in the goddess of the Demeter religion. In Syracuse, at the shrine of Demeter and Persephone, men took the great oath clad in the purple robe of the goddess and with her burning torch in their hands. From Plutarch's Dion it appears that in Syracuse this was the garb of the mystagogos, master of the initiation. The same mysteries existed in the Arcadian Pheneos as in Eleusis, and there the priest wore the mask of Demeter Kidaria in the "greatest mystery." It was a far from friendly face, more like some ghastly apparition which one can only imagine as Gorgonesque.[3]

This latter detail is also of interest for it mirrors a man who instead of trying to slay the Gorgon face of the Goddess's rage, takes it on, presumably in empathy for what she and her values have suffered at the hands of the patriarchal hero mentality.

So Gallienus regrounded his majesty in the Feminine after his initiation. This is precisely the matriarchal vision of human life and, if we believe the intent of the Mysteries, its hope: male and female alike, we are held by a Matrix, stronger than we are, more powerful, that ultimately holds us in her ever recycling hands. Like seeds we are planted and flower and die but like seeds when we fall to the earth, we go back into her and will rise again and be reborn. What if Oliver had grasped this, had ever understood the profound archetypal role he was pulled to enact in his wearing of feminine clothes? What if he had sought to relate instead of to conquer, had submitted his ruthlessness, sadness, and terror of aging and of death to the power of the transformative womb he so longed to have for himself? What if he had allowed himself to be born through the Goddess, born back from his spectator distance into engagement again with all the vicissitudes of being human, the pain and the suffering, the joy and connections and vulnerabilities, all part of what compels us to search for meaning in relationship with the Ultimate and each other? Only at the end of our work did the tiniest glimmers of these possibilities begin to emerge in this contemporary man.

219

Anita Soos, *Pomegranates—Study*. 1996.

Conclusion

> . . . it is not just this one initiand who is trans-
> formed; the entire world is remade as a result of
> her initiation.
>
> —Bruce Lincoln,
> *"The Rape of Persephone"*[1]

DEATH THREATENS US in many forms before we die. Hades is but one imaginal vision of death and this book only one of many perspectives on a deeply layered, multifaceted myth that includes a confrontation with Hades. To compensate the literature already exist-ing on this myth, I have chosen to look at Hades through a matriarchal accent that stands firm in the vision of the Old Religion of the God-dess and sees Hades as the shadow side of the patriarchal interloper whose influence on the fate of the archetypal Feminine in Western culture has been profound and far-reaching. The unrelational lust, sudden ungrounding, and fixating yet desubstantiating realm that the image of Hades represents are powerful metaphors for the death forces threatening our planet and our individual lives today—as per-sonal as abuse and its consequences within the family, as collective as the power politics behind the appropriation and destruction of indige-nous cultures, the ravaging of Earth's resources, and the "genocidal mentality" that through the glorification and stockpiling of nuclear weapons threatens the entirety of life as we know it.[2]

For the ancient Greeks, as far as we know, Hades was not viewed through a psychological or political lens. They knew him as represen-tative of a certain kind of death, a death that meant an eternity of repetitive activity, desubstantiation, fruitlessness, and profound de-spair. (Recall Martin Nilsson's comment in chapter 5 about the shades, "[They] are not of a nature to enjoy anything; they are feeble, impotent wraiths, mere semblances of men, all doomed to the same

221

miserable travesty of life; the bodies from which they are now severed were their real selves, and there remain now only impalpable, joyless phantoms.")[3] The Greeks pictured death through Hades as the sudden, unwanted rapist of life, and in their minds the kind of life he ravaged was like a budding young woman deeply bonded with her grain-giving Mother, on whom they all depended not only for subsistence but for civilization. Yet through the mythology of rape and reunion and the Mysteries that grew out of it and were offered first for the salvation of Greece and then to the world, the Greeks revisioned death. The destruction of life by its rapist was transformed and superseded by a vision of death as reunion with the Mother who could protest stultification effectively and gestate it back into her endless recycling of death into new birth.

This vision of literal death as heuresis, reunion with and transformation through the Mother, was not limited to the Greeks or their times. Nor is it limited to women. Perhaps it is simply human instinct—the homing instinct articulated so poignantly in the cases of Jenny and Joanna—that envisions return to a feminine Source as the outcome of death. We see it in the comments of psychiatrist Robert Jay Lifton, writing about survivors in Hiroshima. Noting the tale of one survivor who had a vision of his mother's face as he lay trapped underneath a collapsed building, Lifton writes, "This kind of maternal image was reminiscent of reports about Japanese soldiers in World War II; trained to go to their deaths with the phrase 'Long live the Emperor' on their lips, they instead called out 'Mother!' Both cases suggest an effort to reassert the ultimate human relationship in the face of death's severance, along with . . . a protest against what is perceived as premature death."[4]

So too the female protagonist in Eva Figes's novel *Waking*. Picturing herself on the seashore, washed over with waves as she's dying, the woman experiences the following:

> Everything has been washed away in the last tide, no more pain, now my body has been swept away I am light as a bird, no more trying to find bits of myself, the ache of effort with each breath, holding myself, pulling myself together like my poor old dislocated doll, how many years now, finding an arm, now a numb foot, pulling on aching muscles and stiff hot joints on first waking? Admit it, the hollow head, the mechanism for making the eyes open and shut could no longer be con-

nected to the rest of it. The illusion was shattered. And now it has been washed away by the tide and I can float freely on the black waves, though I still hear the plaintive cry, mamma, each time it was tipped back, feeble but constant, unvarying in its timbre. And though the night is cool and the tide is creeping silently along the damp dark sand and I am not afraid, no, though the moon is rising over the dark horizon, the small voice in my head is crying mamma, why do you not come, why have you left me alone on the seashore with night coming in all round? But now I see a small light bobbing in the dark, it quivers, trembles, is it a spirit, no, the light of a fishing boat putting out to sea on the far horizon, no, perhaps a single star, the north star, rising in the sky, but no, it is coming nearer, she has come for me, she has not forgotten, she holds a torch in her hand, mamma, she has come back to the seashore and I am safe, now that she has come to fetch me, pick me up and carry me home.[5]

The woman with the torch, Demeter-Persephone-Hekate, the Triple Goddess of old, affords a kindly face to death, brings to its dark embrace a maternal promise: that death is a return to the Origin for man and woman alike, a return to the Source, both human and divine, a dying into her transformative womb, only to sprout again in her ancient, holy, never-ending cycle. Every one of our deaths on every level becomes thus a regression to the Source and even the most destructive and traumatic experience becomes her fruit, carrying within it her seeds not of eternity, not of unending life or fixated death, but of vibrant, perpetual renewal.

Notes

PREFACE

1. M. Esther Harding, *The Way of All Women* (New York: G. P. Putnam's Sons, 1970), 91–119. This book was first published in 1933. While Harding's chapter on friendship reflects some thinking we would now consider outmoded (particularly her discussion of homosexuality), hers was an early, significant voice in the Jungian literature on feminine psychology. In this particular chapter, she asserted the value of women's friendships not only for women themselves but for the psychological development of the world at large.

2. M. Esther Harding, *Women's Mysteries, Ancient and Modern* (Boston: Shambhala Publications, 1990.)

3. Irene Claremont de Castillejo, *Knowing Woman* (New York: G.P. Putnam's Sons, 1973), 165–82.

4. Erich Neumann, *The Great Mother* (Princeton: Princeton University Press, 1955, 1983).

5. Compare, for example, Neumann's discussions of the ornamentation and schematization of the body in ancient Goddess sculptures in his chapter "The Primordial Goddess" (*Great Mother*, 94ff.) with Marija Gimbutas's far more sophisticated explication in her work *The Goddesses and Gods of Old Europe* (Berkeley and Los Angeles: University of California Press, 1974), 89ff., and in *The Language of the Goddess* (San Francisco: Harper and Row, 1989). Given the early date of Neumann's writing, however, and the relative lack of archaeological scholarship on these figures available to him, the breadth and depth of his consideration of these early Goddess figures are remarkable.

6. So Robert Graves writes in his postscript to *The White Goddess* (New York: Farrar, Straus, and Giroux, 1966, 490–92) about women who mediate the Goddess as Muse and thus inspire male poets. Neumann rather categorically states that women, "fashioned in the likeness of the Great Goddess," experience themselves "first and foremost as the source of life" (*Great Mother*, 305). Both seem to assume that the woman readily embodies and is cognizant of embodying the Goddess—as if the suppression of the female Divinity during nearly 5500 years has had no effect on woman's experience of herself!

7. Neumann, *Great Mother*, 24ff.
8. Kathie Carlson, *In Her Image: The Unhealed Daughter's Search for Her Mother* (Boston: Shambhala Publications, 1989), 93–113.

CHAPTER 1. APPROACHING THE MYTH

1. Carl Kerényi, "Kore," in C. G. Jung and Carl Kerényi, *Essays on a Science of Mythology: The Myths of the Divine Child and the Divine Maiden* (New York: Harper and Row, 1963), 155.
2. *The I Ching or Book of Changes: The Richard Wilhelm Translation*, trans. Cary F. Baynes (Princeton: Princeton University Press, 1950), 194.
3. *The Homeric Hymns*, trans. Charles Boer (Chicago: The Swallow Press, 1970), 133.
4. Carl Kerényi, *Eleusis: Archetypal Image of Mother and Daughter* (New York: Bollingen Foundation, 1967), 12.
5. C. G. Jung, "Archetypes of the Collective Unconscious" and "The Concept of the Collective Unconscious," in *The Archetypes and the Collective Unconscious*, vol.9i of *The Collected Works* (Princeton: Princeton University Press, 1969), 3–53.
6. Rudolf Otto, *The Idea of the Holy* (New York: Oxford University Press, 1958), 5–7.
7. Kerényi, *Eleusis*, xx. Compare Jane Harrison, *Prolegomena to the Study of Greek Religion* (London: Merlin Press, 1962), vii.
8. *The Oxford Classical Dictionary*, 2d ed., s.v. "Demeter."
9. Harrison, *Prolegomena*, 164.
10. See Erich Neumann, "The Moon and Matriarchal Consciousness," in *Fathers and Mothers* (Zurich: Spring Publications, 1973), 40–63.
11. Notable exceptions include the treatment of the Demeter-Persephone myth in Nathan Schwartz-Salant, *Narcissism and Character Transformation* (Toronto: Inner City Books, 1982) (although Schwartz-Salant sees Demeter as being in the "depressive position" he also grasps that losing Persephone is a loss of an original wholeness in the Goddess herself) and in Virginia Beane-Rutter, *Woman Changing Woman* (San Francisco: Harper Collins, 1993).
12. See especially Patricia Berry, "The Rape of Demeter/Persephone and Neurosis," in *Spring* (New York, 1975), 186–98. Excerpted in Christine Downing, ed., *The Long Journey Home: Revisioning the Myth of Demeter and Persephone for Our Time.* (Boston: Shambhala Publications, 1994), 197–205.
13. The myth clearly depicts Demeter as depressed, but many commentators see her emotional state as neurotic psychopathology rather than as appropriate reaction to the circumstances (see Berry, "The Rape," for a

representation of this view). Even if divine behavior is reduced to human dimensions, this point of view has always seemed remarkable to me—as if it is unreasonable and excessive for a mother to become extremely depressed when her daughter has been abducted and raped out of life.

14. See Downing, *Long Journey*, p. 141; Vera Bushe, "Cycles of Being," in Downing, ed., *Long Journey*, 178; and Helen Luke, "Mother and Daughter Mysteries," in Downing, ed., *Long Journey*, 190–96, for examples of depictions of Demeter as overpossessive of Kore.

15. See especially Bushe, "Cycles of Being," 173–85. Bushe writes, "[Demeter] does not consider the suggestion that this relationship might be good for Persephone. She never considers that her daughter may be ready for something different in life. She does not support her daughter to take an independent step" (176). This kind of commentary boggles me; Kore resists the abduction, screams that she is being raped, and cries out in terror for help. But apparently there is enough of a bias in our culture against mothers and for men, regardless of how brutal their behavior, that such distortions of the myth can go unchallenged.

16. This view is depicted most clearly in Polly Young-Eisendrath, "Demeter's Folly: Experiencing Loss in Middle Life," *Psychological Perspectives*, (Spring 1984): 39–43. Although I disagree with Young-Eisendrath's interpretation of Demeter, I found this otherwise to be a very valuable paper on midlife dynamics.

17. See Berry, "The Rape"; see also Downing, "Puberty Rites," in *Long Journey*, 163–65.

18. A representative sample of sources for this viewpoint includes Jean Bolen's chapter on Persephone in her *Goddesses in Everywoman* (San Francisco: Harper and Row, 1984), 187–223, and Downing, *Long Journey*, "The Return to the Mother," 144, "Puberty Rites," 163–65.

19. Bolen, *Goddesses in Everywoman*; Bushe, "Cycles of Being," 166–85.

20. See James Hillman, *The Dream and the Underworld* (New York: Harper and Row, 1979), especially 48, and Christine Downing's chapter on Persephone in *The Goddess* (New York: Crossroad, 1984), 30ff. In *Long Journey*, Downing writes, "Persephone's 'true savior' is Hades, not Zeus" (163ff.). Compare this position to Bruce Lincoln's assertion that "Kore's defloration changes her utterly. She has, in effect, been initiated by rape, a pattern found in a number of male-centered, misogynistically inclined cultures and strongly suggested in numerous Greek myths. . . . Hades is no tender bridegroom who lovingly takes his bride to bed, but rather, is the male oppressor who forces his will upon a young girl for the first time, thus teaching her proper submission to all members of his sex" ("The Rape of Persephone," in Downing, *Long Journey*. 171.) Downing's reframing of Hades' violence is so extreme that at one point she even

227

suggests that Demeter is responsible for her daughter's rape; see "Mid-life Passage," in *Long Journey*, 187. Compare Berry, "The Rape," in the same, 202ff.

21. See Carol Gilligan, *In a Different Voice* (Cambridge, Mass.: Harvard University Press, 1982) as well as Carol Gilligan, Nona P. Lyons, and Trudy J. Hanmer, eds., *Making Connections* (Cambridge, Mass: Harvard University Press, 1990). See also Terri Apter, *Altered Loves: Mothers and Daughters During Adolescence* (New York: St. Martin's Press, 1990). The work of Jean Baker Miller and her research group at Wellesley College's Stone Center is also exploring the relational paradigm that appears to be at the heart of feminine psychology.

22. Adrienne Rich held this point of view back in the 1970s in her comments on this myth in her book *Of Woman Born* (New York: W. W. Norton and Co., 1976), 237ff. See also Beatrice Bruteau, "The Unknown Goddess," in Shirley Nicholson, *The Goddess Re-awakening* (Wheaton, Ill.: The Theosophical Publishing House, 1989), 68–79; Eleanor Gadon, *The Once and Future Goddess* (San Francisco: Harper and Row, 1989), 143–66; Laura Simms, "Long Journey Home: A Retelling of the Myth of Demeter and Persephone" in Downing, ed., *Long Journey*, 71–90; Bruce Lincoln, *Emerging from the Chrysalis* (Cambridge, Mass.: Harvard University Press, 1981), 71–90; Virginia Beane-Rutter, *Woman Changing Woman* (San Francisco: Harper Collins, 1993); and Nathan Schwartz-Salant, *Narcissism and Character Transformation* (Toronto: Inner City Books, 1982), for more positive views on Demeter and Persephone. In addition, I recommend a particularly well-conceived paper that was unknown to me when I wrote this manuscript and that looks at the Demeter-Persephone myth in terms of lesbian relationships: Karen Loftus Carrington's paper, "The Alchemy of Women Loving Women," *Psychological Perspectives*, 23(1990), 64–82. Several newer works show other feminine figures in the Demeter-Persephone myth in positive terms as well: Clarissa Pinkola Estes' classic *Women Who Run with the Wolves* (New York: Ballantine Books, 1992), 336–40, and Winifred Milius Lubell's *The Metamorphoses of Baubo* (Nashville and London: Vanderbilt University Press, 1994) offer unique and provocative interpretations of Baubo, while Downing's chapter "Hekate, Rhea, and Baubo: Perspectives on Menopause," in *Long Journey*, 233–242, is a particularly rich study of these three female figures in this myth.

23. Downing, *Long Journey*, p. 5.

CHAPTER 2. THE MYTH, ITS VARIANTS, AND ITS MYSTERIES

1. The epigraph is from Laura Simms, "Long Journey Home: A Retelling of the Myth of Demeter and Persephone," in Christine Downing, *The*

Long Journey Home: Revisioning the Myth of Demeter and Persephone for Our Time (Boston: Shambhala Publications, 1994), 275.

2. The date of the Homeric hymn to Demeter is found in Paul Friedrich, *The Meaning of Aphrodite* (Chicago: University of Chicago Press, 1978), 163, while the dating of Genesis appears and is discussed at length in Gerda Lerner, *The Creation of Patriarchy* (Oxford: Oxford University Press, 1986), 161–67.

3. Robert Graves, *The Greek Myths*, vol. 1 (Middlesex, England: Penguin Books, 1955), 17.

4. Lerner, *Creation of Patriarchy*, 202.

5. Friedrich, *Meaning of Aphrodite*, 163.

6. Ibid., 164.

7. Graves, *Greek Myths*, 90.

8. See Friedrich's discussion of the word *parthenos* in *Meaning of Aphrodite*, 168. Compare with M. Esther Harding's explication of the "virgin" as "one-in-herself" in *Women's Mysteries, Ancient and Modern* (Boston: Shambhala Publications, 1990), 103–4, 125.

9. "The Rape of Proserpine," in *The Metamorphoses of Ovid*, trans. Mary M. Innes (Middlesex, England: Penguin Books, 1955), 125–31.

10. Graves, *Greek Myths*, 93.

11. See, for example, Nathan Schwartz-Salant, *Narcissism and Character Transformation* (Toronto: Inner City Books, 1982), 138–40.

12. Friedrich, *Meaning of Aphrodite*, 164.

13. Graves, *Greek Myths*, 96.

14. *The Homeric Hymns*, trans. Charles Boer (Chicago: Swallow Press, 1970), 98.

15. Barbara Walker, *The Crone: Woman of Age, Wisdom, and Power* (San Francisco: Harper and Row, 1985), 13.

16. Friedrich, *Meaning of Aphrodite*, 167–68.

17. *Homeric Hymns*, trans. Boer, 100.

18. Graves, *Greek Myths*, 95.

19. Carl Kerényi, *Eleusis: Archetypal Image of Mother and Daughter* (New York: Bollingen Foundation, 1967), 36.

20. Ibid., 23.

21. Ibid., 43.

22. Jane Harrison, *Prolegomena to the Study of Greek Religion* (London: Merlin Press, 1962), 152–153.

23. Friedrich, *Meaning of Aphrodite*, 169.

24. Ibid.

25. Ibid., 28.

26. Kerényi, *Eleusis*, 31.

27. Friedrich, *Meaning of Aphrodite*, 171.

28. Ibid., 172.
29. Kerényi, *Eleusis*, 40. Cf. Graves, *Greek Myths*, 90d.
30. Friedrich, *Meaning of Aphrodite*, 173.
31. *Homeric Hymns*, trans. Boer, 113.
32. Barbara Black Koltuv, personal communication.
33. Graves, *Greek Myths*, 91.
34. For an interesting psychological exposition of Persephone's self-starving in the underworld, see Angelyn Spignesi, *Starving Women: A Psychology of Anorexia Nervosa* (Dallas: Spring Publications, 1983).
35. Graves, *Greek Myths*, 91.
36. Kerényi, *Eleusis*, 134 ff.
37. Ibid., 139.
38. Graves, *Greek Myths*, 93.
39. Ibid., 95.
40. Friedrich, *Meaning of Aphrodite*, 177.
41. Ibid.
42. Ibid.
43. Ibid., 178.
44. Kerényi, *Eleusis*, 126.
45. For an extensive description of the Mystery celebrations, see Kerényi, *Eleusis*, 105–74, from which much of the material in this section of chap. 2 is derived. See also Goblet D'Alviella, *The Mysteries of Eleusis* (Wellingborough, Northamptonshire: The Aquarian Press, 1981).
46. Harrison, *Prolegomena*, 543.
47. Kerényi, *Eleusis*, 82.
48. Ibid., 92–93.
49. Ibid., 94.
50. This entire story can be found in John C. Lawson, *Modern Greek Folklore and Ancient Greek Religion* (New York: University Books, 1964), 79–84.
51. Ibid., 81.
52. Ibid.
53. Ibid., 83.
54. This is in keeping with Christianity's preservation of an effaced form of Maiden and Mother in the image of the Virgin Mary but obliteration of the Crone altogether. See Walker, *The Crone*, 13.
55. Poseidon overcomes the mourning Demeter in the shape of a stallion; Zeus takes the shape of a swan in order to violate Leda. Shape shifting in Greek mythology is often a prelude to rape.
56. Loring Danforth, *The Death Rituals of Rural Greece* (Princeton: Princeton University Press, 1982).
57. Ibid., 141–143.
58. Ibid., 143.

59. Ibid.
60. Lawson, *Modern Greek Folklore*, 101.
61. Ibid., 105.
62. Ibid.
63. Ibid., 99.
64. Ibid.
65. Ibid., 107–108.
66. Danforth, *Death Rituals*, 129.
67. Ibid., 82. See also 74–82 and 85ff. for more on the death-marriage theme.
68. Ibid., 96.
69. Ibid., 98–99.
70. Ibid., 100.
71. Ibid., 103–104.
72. Ibid., 106.
73. Ibid., 97ff.
74. Ibid.
75. Ibid. See also Alesander Tsiaris's photo essay at the end of Danforth's book.

Chapter 3. "Seed for the Planting Shall Not Be Ground Up!"

1. Elisabeth Kübler-Ross, *Death: The Final Stage of Growth* (Englewood Cliffs, N.J.: Prentice-Hall, 1975), 120.
2. Mina C. Klein and H. Arthur Klein, *Käthe Kollwitz: Life in Art* (New York: Schocken Books, 1975), 151.
3. Kübler-Ross, *Death: The Final Stage of Growth*, 120.
4. Robert Graves, *The Greek Myths*, vol. 1 (Middlesex, England: Penguin Books, 1955), 92.
5. Louis Richard Farnell, *The Cults of the Greek States*, vol. 3 (Oxford: Clarendon Press, 1907), 33ff.
6. *The Metamorphoses of Ovid*, trans. Mary M. Innes (Middlesex, England: Penguin Books, 1955), 125–133.
7. Graves, *Greek Myths*, 89.
8. Sir James George Frazer, *Spirits of the Corn and the Wild*, vol. 7 of *The Golden Bough* (New York: Macmillan, 1935), 43.
9. Erich Neumann, *The Great Mother* (Princeton: Princeton University Press, 1955, 1983), 24ff.
10. With regard to the latter, compare Angelyn Spignesi, *Starving Women: A Psychology of Anorexia Nervosa* (Dallas: Spring Publications, 1983).
11. For one of Jung's discussions of the instinctual versus spiritual dimensions of the archetype, see his essay "On the Nature of the Psyche," in

The Structure and Dynamics of the Psyche, vol. 8 of *The Collected Works* (Princeton: Princeton University Press, 1959), 159–234.

12. See Kathie Carlson, *In Her Image: The Unhealed Daughter's Search for Her Mother* (Boston: Shambhala Publications, 1989), especially chaps. 7 and 8.

13. *People*, 3 July 1989, 39–40.

14. Farnell, *Cults*, 49.

15. *Metamorphoses of Ovid*, trans. Innes, 200.

16. Ibid., 198–202.

17. Carl Kerényi, *Eleusis: Archetypal Image of Mother and Daughter* (New York: Bollingen Foundation, 1967), 31.

18. Jane Harrison, *Prolegomena to the Study of Greek Religion* (London: Merlin Press, 1962) 214.

19. Ibid., 215–217.

20. Ibid., 216.

21. Robert Graves, *The Greek Myths*, vol. 2 (Middlesex, England: Penguin Books, 1955), 72.

22. Ibid., 71.

23. Graves, *Greek Myths*, vol.1, 174–75.

24. Thanks to Sara de Beer, Connecticut storyteller, for making me aware of this tale; the story appears in Edward L. Keithan, *Alaskan Igloo Tales* (Seattle: Alaska Northwest Books, 1990), 80–83.

25. Carl Kerényi, "Kore," in C. G. Jung and Carl Kerényi, *Essays on a Science of Mythology: The Myths of the Divine Child and the Divine Maiden* (New York: Harper and Row, 1963), 122–129, 137.

26. Ibid., 123.

27. Ibid., 137.

CHAPTER 4. GESTATIVE TRANSFORMATION

1. River Malcolm, "The Two Goddesses—Persephone," in Christine Downing, *The Long Journey Home: Revisioning the Myth of Demeter and Persephone for Our Time* (Boston: Shambhala Publications, 1994), 155–160.

2. Kerenyi, "Kore," in C. G. Jung and Carl Kerényi *Essays on a Science of Mythology: The Myths of the Divine Child and the Divine Maiden* (New York: Harper and Row, 1963), 104.

3. Ibid., 107.

4. Christine Downing, *The Goddess*,(New York: Crossroad, 1984), 49.

5. Ibid., 37.

6. For a deeper consideration of the symbol of the narcissus flower, see Nathan Schwartz-Salant, *Narcissism and Character Transformation* (Toronto: Inner City Books, 1982), 138ff.

7. Robert Graves, *The Greek Myths,* vol.1 (Middlesex, England: Penguin Books, 1955), 121.
8. C. G. Jung, "The Psychology of the Child Archetype," in Jung and Kerényi, *Essays,* 79–84.
9. Ibid., 80.
10. William Ernest Henley, "Invictus," in Oscar Williams, ed., *Immortal Poems of the English Language* (New York: Pocket Books, 1952), 475–76.
11. Zsuzsanna Budapest, *The Grandmother of Time* (San Francisco: Harper and Row, 1989).
12. Barbara Walker, *The Woman's Encyclopedia of Myths and Secrets* (New York: Harper and Row, 1983), 39.
13. Ibid.
14. Kerényi, "Kore," 102ff.
15. Robert Jay Lifton notes that parents frequently attribute to and experience through their children a "symbolic immortality" of themselves. Through their children and their children's children and the ensuing numinous vision of infinite generations, parents have the sense that something of themselves will live on, even after their deaths. For fathers, at least in our culture, this archetypal vision is often attached to the handing down of a surname to a son. But for mothers, this sense of being carried forward into infinite time attaches most often to a daughter. See Robert Jay Lifton, *The Broken Connection* (New York: Simon and Schuster, 1979), 18ff.
16. These lines are from Sandra Hochman's poem "Thoughts About My Daughter before Sleep," in Lyn Lifshin, ed., *Tangled Vines: A Collection of Mother and Daughter Poems* (Boston: Beacon Press, 1978), 4–5.
17. Paul Friedrich, *The Meaning of Aphrodite* (Chicago: University of Chicago Press, 1978), 159.
18. Loring Danforth, *The Death Rituals of Ancient Greece* (Princeton: Princeton University Press, 1982), 75.
19. Ibid., 74ff. (for further discussion of death-marriage parallels).
20. Ibid., 83.
21. I believe this emphasis on separation reflects a tendency in masculine conditioning in our culture to see development and maturation in terms of separateness from rather than interconnectedness and ongoing relationships with others. Jean Baker Miller first noted this tendency in her classic *Toward a New Psychology of Women,* 2d ed. (Boston: Beacon Press, 1986), xxi. Baker Miller and her associates at Wellesley College's Stone Center are now in the process of reformulating developmental theory according to a more relational paradigm. So, too, newer investigations into the mother-daughter relationship have revealed that daughters tend to place a greater value on maintaining and developing the bond with

their mothers as they mature rather than breaking away in some defini-
tive sense. See Sharon Rich, "Daughters' Views of Their Relationships
With Their Mothers," in Carol Gilligan, Nona P. Lyons, and Trudy J.
Hanmer, eds., *Making Connections* (Cambridge, Mass.: Harvard University
Press, 1989), 258–73, and Terri Apter, *Altered Loves: Mothers and Daughters
During Adolescence* (New York: St. Martin's Press, 1990), to name but two
examples of this developing research.

22. Graves, *Greek Myths*, 122.
23. Ibid., 93.
24. See Kerényi's discussion of Persephone's link with Medusa in "Kore,"
    125–128.
25. Ibid.,127.
26. See all of Robert Jay Lifton's seminal work, especially *The Life of the Self*
    (New York: Basic Books, 1976). See also Judith Herman, *Trauma and
    Recovery* (San Francisco: Harper Collins, 1992).
27. Starhawk, *Dreaming the Dark* (Boston: Beacon Press, 1982), 226.
28. Judy Grahn, *She Who* (Oakland, California: Diana Press, 1972, 1977), 33.

CHAPTER 5. THE SHADOW OF PATRIARCHY

1. Jennifer Barr, *Within a Dark Wood: The Personal Story of a Rape Victim*
   (Garden City, New York: Doubleday, 1979), 47.
2. Louis Richard Farnell, *The Cults of the Greek States*, vol. 3 (Oxford: Clarendon Press, 1907), 281.
3. Ibid.
4. Robert Garland, *The Greek Way of Death* (Ithaca: Cornell University Press,
   1985), 1–2ff.
5. Martin Nilsson, *A History of Greek Religion* (Oxford: Clarendon Press,
   1949), 517.
6. Robert Graves, *The Greek Myths*, vol. 1 (Middlesex, England: Penguin
   Books, 1955), 121.
7. Carl Kerényi, "Kore," in C. G. Jung and Carl Kerényi, *Essays on a Science
   of Mythology: The Myths of the Divine Child and the Divine Maiden* (New York:
   Harper and Row, 1963), 124.
8. Graves, *Greek Myths*, 120–21, 123.
9. See Jane Harrison, *Prolegomena to the Study of Greek Religion*, (London:
   Merlin Press, 1962), chap. 1, for a complete discussion of rites of "ten-
   dence" vs. rites of "aversion" in Greek religious ritual.
10. Carl Kerényi, *The Gods of the Greeks* (London: Thames and Hudson,
    1951), 230.
11. Ibid., 231.
12. Graves, *Greek Myths*, 121–22.

13. Farnell, *Cults*, 281.
14. Graves, *Greek Myths*, 122.
15. Ibid., 121.
16. Harrison, *Prolegomena*, 15–17ff.
17. Farnell, *Cults*, 283.
18. Robert Graves, *The White Goddess* (New York: Farrar, Straus, and Giroux, 1966), 62.
19. Graves, *Greek Myths*, 93.
20. Ibid., 17.
21. See Graves, *White Goddess*, 62ff., and *Greek Myths*, 17ff.
22. Graves, *Greek Myths*, 94.
23. Farnell, *Cults*, 280.
24. *The Homeric Hymns*, trans. Charles Boer (Chicago: Swallow Press, 1970), 134.
25. Farnell, *Cults*, 282.
26. One of Dionysos's many names was "Bromios." Harrison describes this name as being synonymous with "Demetrios, son of Demeter the Corn-Mother before he becomes god of the grape and son by adoption of Olympian Zeus" (see *Prolegomena*, 416).
27. See Harrison's extensive discussion of the evolution of the god Dionysos in *Prolegomena*, 363ff.
28. *The Metamorphoses of Ovid*, trans. Mary M. Innes (Middlesex, England: Penguin Books, 1955), 127.
29. Ibid.
30. Ibid., 128.
31. Anne Sexton, *The Book of Folly* (Boston: Houghton Mifflin, 1972), 24–25.
32. See Diane Wood Middlebrook, *Anne Sexton: A Biography* (Boston: Houghton Mifflin, 1991), 14–16.

CHAPTER 6. THE INTRAPSYCHIC EXPERIENCE

1. James Hillman, "Senex and Puer: An Aspect of the Historical and Psychological Present," in *Eranos Jahrbuch* 36 (Zurich: Rhein-Verlag, 1967), 338.
2. Erich Neumann, *The Great Mother* (Princeton: Princeton University Press, 1955, 1983), 336.
3. Kathie Carlson, "Prayer," words and music published in *The Beltane Papers* 2, nos. 2–3 (1985): 45.
4. Jung called this "synchronicity." See his essay, "Synchronicity: An Acausal Connecting Principle," in *The Structure and Dynamics of the Psyche*, vol. 8 of *The Collected Works* (Princeton: Princeton University Press, 1959), 417–531.

5. For a very readable explication of Jung's concept of the Self, see Edward C. Whitmont, *The Symbolic Quest* (New York: G. P. Putnam's Sons, 1969), 216ff.
6. Ibid., 253.
7. Ibid., 225.
8. C. G. Jung, "The Structure and Dynamics of the Self," in *Aion*, vol. 9ii of *The Collected Works* (New York: Pantheon Books, 1959), 225.
9. All of this material on the lunar and chthonic aspects of the Neolithic Great Goddess is drawn from a summary of her functions and images in Marija Gimbutas's *The Language of the Goddess* (San Francisco: Harper and Row, 1989), 328–29.
10. Kathie Carlson, *In Her Image: The Unhealed Daughter's Search for Her Mother* (Boston: Shambhala Publications, 1989), 106–107.
11. From the artist's writing about the etching.
12. See Barbara Walker, *The Crone: Woman of Age, Wisdom, and Power* (San Francisco: Harper and Row, 1985). "Diabolized" is Walker's word describing the patriarchal tendency to designate as 'evil' all that was sacred in the Goddess religion. A good example of this is the snake, sacred to the Goddess as a symbol of regeneration, reappearing in the Old Testament as the animal cursed by God for bringing about the fall of man.
13. These temples existed on the isle of Malta. See Cristina Biaggi's *Habitations of the Great Goddess* (Manchester, Conn.: KIT Publications, 1994).
14. See Gimbutas, "Power of Two," in *Language of the Goddess*, 161–72
15. Carlson, *In Her Image*, 45–47.
16. For information on and photos of corn dollies, see Michael Dames's *The Avebury Cycle* (London: Thames and Hudson, 1977), 24–26, and *The Silbury Treasure* (London: Thames and Hudson, 1976), 149–51. The photo on p. 151 of *The Silbury Treasure* is particularly stunning.

CHAPTER 7. RELATIONAL DYNAMICS

1. Gerda Lerner, *The Creation of Patriarchy* (Oxford: Oxford University Press, 1986) 227–28.
2. For a different view on how this myth can be constellated between female client and female therapist, see Virginia Beane-Rutter, *Woman Changing Woman* (San Francisco: Harper Collins, 1993).
3. As far as I know, the term "animus ego" was coined by Sylvia Perera and used throughout her *Descent to the Goddess* (Toronto: Inner City Books, 1981).
4. See my discussion of the banishing mother in *In Her Image: The Unhealed Daughter's Search for Her Mother* (Boston: Shambhala Publications, 1989) 24–37.

5. Thanks to Sylvia Perera for pointing this out to me in a personal communication, 1996.

6. Barbara Walker, *The Woman's Encyclopedia of Myths and Secrets* (New York: Harper and Row, 1983), 740.

7. Ibid.

8. C. G. Jung, "A Study in the Process of Individuation," in *The Archetype and the Collective Unconscious*, vol. 9i of *The Collected Works* (New York: Pantheon Books, 1959), 324.

9. C. G. Jung, *Symbols of Transformation*, vol. 5 of *The Collected Works* (Princeton: Princeton University Press, 1956), 300.

10. C. G. Jung, *Mysterium Coniunctionis*, vol. 14 of *The Collected Works* (New York: Pantheon Press, 1963), 513.

11. William Anderson, *Green Man* (San Francisco: Harper Collins, 1990), 14.

12. Ibid., 33.

13. Ibid., 34.

14. Walker, *Woman's Encyclopedia*, 671–72.

CHAPTER 8. THE HADES-IDENTIFIED MAN

1. Erich Neumann, *The Great Mother* (Princeton: Princeton University Press, 1955, 1983), 323.

2. Barbara Walker, *The Crone: Woman of Age, Wisdom, and Power* (San Francisco: Harper and Row, 1985), especially chap. 8, 171ff.

3. Carl Kerényi, "Kore," in C. G. Jung and Carl Kerényi, *Essays on a Science of Mythology: The Myths of the Divine Child and the Divine Maiden* (New York: Harper and Row, 1963), 138.

CONCLUSION

1. Bruce Lincoln, "The Rape of Persephone," in *Emerging from the Chrysalis* (Cambridge, Mass.: Harvard University Press, 1981), 90.

2. See Robert Jay Lifton and Eric Markusen, *The Genocidal Mentality: Nazi Holocaust and Nuclear Threat* (New York: Basic Books, 1990).

3. Martin Nilsson, *A History of Greek Religion* (Oxford: Clarendon Press, 1949), 517.

4. Robert Jay Lifton, *Death in Life* (New York: Vintage Books, 1969), 22.

5. Eva Figes, *Waking* (New York: Pantheon Books, 1981), 87–88.

Bibliography

Anderson, William. *Green Man*. San Francisco: Harper Collins, 1990.

Apter, Terri. *Altered Loves: Mothers and Daughters During Adolescence*. New York: St. Martin's Press, 1990.

Barr, Jennifer. *Within a Dark Wood: The Personal Story of a Rape Victim*. Garden City, N.Y.: Doubleday, 1979.

Beane-Rutter, Virginia. *Woman Changing Woman*. San Francisco: Harper Collins, 1993.

Benjamin, Enos. *Dearest Goddess*. Arlington, Va.: Current Nine Publishing, 1985.

Berry, Patricia. "The Rape of Demeter/Persephone and Neurosis." *Spring* (1975): 186–98.

Bertreau, Bernice. "The Unknown Goddess." In *The Goddess Re-awakening*, edited by Shirley Nicholson. Wheaton, Ill.: The Theosophical Publishing House, 1989.

Biaggi, Cristina. *Habitations of the Great Goddess*. Manchester, Conn.: KIT Publications, 1994.

Bolen, Jean Shinoda. *Goddesses in Everywoman*. San Francisco: Harper and Row, 1984.

Budapest, Zsuzsanna. *The Grandmother of Time*. San Francisco: Harper and Row, 1989.

Bushe, Vera. "Cycles of Being." In *The Long Journey Home: Revisioning the Myth of Demeter and Persephone for Our Time*, edited by Christine Downing, 173–85. Boston: Shambhala Publications, 1994.

Carlson, Kathie. *In Her Image: The Unhealed Daughter's Search for Her Mother*. Boston: Shambhala Publications, 1989.

———. "Prayer" (words and music). *The Beltane Papers* 2, nos. 2–3 (1985): 45.

Carrington, Karen Lofthus. "The Alchemy of Women Loving Women." In *Psychological Perspectives* 23 (1990): 64–82.

Christ, Carol. *Diving Deep and Surfacing: Women Writers and Spiritual Quest*. 2d ed. Boston: Beacon Press, 1986.

———. *Laughter of Aphrodite*. San Francisco: Harper Collins, 1987.

Christ, Carol, and Judith Plaskow, eds. *Womanspirit Rising: A Feminist Reader on Religion*. San Francisco: Harper and Row, 1979.

D'Alviella, Goblet. *The Mysteries of Eleusis*. Wellingborough, Northhampton-shire: The Aquarian Press, 1981.

Dames, Michael. *The Avebury Cycle*. London: Thames and Hudson, 1979.

———. *The Silbury Treasure: The Great Goddess Rediscovered*. London: Thames and Hudson, 1976

Danforth, Loring. *The Death Rituals of Rural Greece*. Princeton: Princeton University Press, 1982.

de Castillejo, Irene Claremont. *Knowing Woman*. New York: G. P. Putnam's Sons, 1973.

Dinnerstein, Dorothy. *The Mermaid and the Minotaur*. New York: Harper and Row, 1976.

Downing, Christine. *The Goddess*. New York: Crossroad, 1984.

———. "Hekate, Rhea, and Baubo: Perspectives on Menopause." In *The Long Journey Home: Revisioning the Myth of Demeter and Persephone for Our Time*, edited by Christine Downing, 233–42. Boston: Shambhala Publications, 1994.

Downing, Christine, ed. *The Long Journey Home: Revisioning the Myth of Demeter and Persephone for Our Time*. Boston: Shambhala Publications, 1994.

Estes, Clarissa Pinkola. *Women Who Run with the Wolves*. New York: Ballantine Books, 1992.

Farnell, Louis Richard. *The Cults of the Greek States*. Vol. 3. Oxford: Clarendon Press, 1907.

Figes, Eva. *Waking*. New York: Pantheon Books, 1981.

Frazer, Sir James George. *Spirits of the Corn and of the Wild*. Vol. 7 of *The Golden Bough*. New York: Macmillan, 1935.

Friedrich, Paul. *The Meaning of Aphrodite*. Chicago: University of Chicago Press, 1978.

Gadon, Eleanor. *The Once and Future Goddess*. San Francisco: Harper and Row, 1989.

Garland, Robert. *The Greek Way of Death*. Ithaca: Cornell University Press, 1985.

Gilligan, Carol. *In a Different Voice*. Cambridge, Mass.: Harvard University Press, 1982.

Gilligan, Carol, Nona P. Lyons, and Trudy J. Hanmer, eds. *Making Connections*. Cambridge, Mass.: Harvard University Press, 1990.

Gimbutas, Marija. *The Goddesses and Gods of Old Europe*. Berkeley and Los Angeles: University of California Press, 1974.

———. *The Language of the Goddess*. San Francisco: Harper and Row, 1989.

The Gospel of Sri Ramakrishna. New York: Ramakrishna-Vivekananda Center, 1952.

Grahn, Judy. *She Who*. Oakland, Calif.: Diana Press, 1972, 1977.

Graves, Robert. *The Greek Myths*. Vol. 1. Middlesex, England: Penguin Books, 1955.

————. *The Greek Myths.* Vol.2. Middlesex, England: Penguin Books, 1955.

————. *The White Goddess.* New York: Farrar, Straus, and Giroux, 1966.

Haddon, Genia Pauli. *Body Metaphors: Releasing God-Feminine in Us All.* New York: Crossroad, 1988. Reissued as *Uniting Sex, Self, and Spirit.* Scotland, Conn.: Plus Publications, 1993.

Harding, M. Esther. *The Way of All Women.* New York: G. P. Putnam's Sons, 1970.

————. *Women's Mysteries, Ancient and Modern.* Boston: Shambhala Publications, 1990.

Harrison, Jane. *Prolegomena to the Study of Greek Religion.* London: Merlin Press, 1962.

Herman, Judith. *Trauma and Recovery.* San Francisco: Harper Collins, 1992.

Hillman, James. *The Dream and the Underworld.* New York: Harper and Row, 1979.

————. "Senex and Puer: An Aspect of the Historical and Psychological Present." In *Eranos Jahrbuch 36.* Zurich: Rhein-Verlag, 1967.

Hixon, Lex. *Great Swan: Meetings with Ramakrishna.* Boston: Shambhala Publications, 1992.

————. *Mother of the Universe.* Wheaton, Ill.: The Theosophical Publishing House, 1994.

The Homeric Hymns. Translated by Charles Boer. Chicago: The Swallow Press, 1970.

The I Ching or Book of Changes: The Richard Wilhelm Translation. Translated by Cary F. Baynes. Princeton: Princeton University Press, 1950.

Jung, C. G. *Aion.* Vol. 9ii of *The Collected Works.* New York: Pantheon Books, 1959.

————. *The Archetypes and the Collective Unconscious.* Vol. 9i of *The Collected Works.* Princeton: Princeton University Press, 1969.

————. *Mysterium Conunctionis.* Vol. 14 of *The Collected Works.* New York: Pantheon Press, 1963.

————. *The Structure and Dynamics of the Psyche.* Vol. 8 of *The Collected Works.* Princeton: Princeton University Press, 1959.

————. *Symbols of Transformation.* Vol. 5 of *The Collected Works.* Princeton: Princeton University Press, 1956.

Jung, C. G., and Carl Kerényi. *Essays on a Science of Mythology: The Myths of the Divine Child and the Divine Maiden.* New York: Harper and Row, 1963.

Keithan, Edward L. *Alaskan Igloo Tales.* Seattle: Alaska Northwest Books, 1990.

Kerényi, Carl. *Eleusis: Archetypal Image of Mother and Daughter.* New York: Bollingen Foundation, 1967.

————. "Kore." In *Essays on a Science of Mythology: The Myths of the Divine Child and the Divine Maiden,* by C. G. Jung and Carl Kerényi, 101–55. New York: Harper and Row, 1963.

————. *The Gods of the Greeks.* London: Thames and Hudson, 1951.

Kintsler, Clysta. *The Moon Under Her Feet.* San Francisco: Harper and Row, 1989.

Klein, Mina C., and Arthur H. Klein. *Käthe Kollwitz: Life in Art.* New York: Holt, Rinehart, and Winston, 1972.

Kübler-Ross, Elisabeth. *Death: The Final Stage of Growth.* Englewood Cliffs, N.J.: Prentice-Hall, 1975.

Lawson, John C. *Modern Greek Folklore and Ancient Greek Religion.* New York: University Books, 1964.

Lerner, Gerda. *The Creation of Patriarchy.* Oxford: Oxford University Press, 1986.

Lifshin, Lyn, ed. *Tangled Vines: A Collection of Mother and Daughter Poems.* Boston: Beacon Press, 1978.

Lifton, Robert Jay. *The Broken Connection.* New York: Simon and Schuster, 1979.

————. *Death in Life: Survivors of Hiroshima.* New York: Vintage Books, 1969.

————. *The Life of the Self.* New York: Basic Books, 1976.

Lifton, Robert Jay, and Eric Markusen. *The Genocidal Mentality: Nazi Holocaust and Nuclear Threat.* New York: Basic Books, 1990.

Lincoln, Bruce. *Emerging from the Chrysalis.* Cambridge, Mass.: Harvard University Press, 1981.

Lubell, Winifred Milius. *The Metamorphoses of Baubo.* Nashville: Vanderbilt University Press, 1994.

Luke, Helen. "Mother and Daughter Mysteries." In *The Long Journey Home: Revisioning the Myth of Demeter and Persephone for Our Time,* edited by Christine Downing, 190–96. Boston: Shambhala Publications, 1994.

Malcolm, River. "The Two Goddesses—Persephone." In *The Long Journey Home: Revisioning the Myth of Demeter and Persephone for Our Time,* edited by Christine Downing, 155–60. Boston: Shambhala Publications, 1994.

The Metamorphoses of Ovid. Translated by Mary M. Innes. Middlesex, England: Penguin Books, 1955.

Middlebrook, Diane Wood. *Anne Sexton: A Biography.* Boston: Houghton Mifflin, 1991.

Miller, Jean Baker. *Toward a New Psychology of Women.* 2d ed. Boston: Beacon Press, 1986.

Mookerjee, Ajit. *Kali the Feminine Force.* Rochester, Vt: Destiny Books, 1988.

Neumann, Erich. *The Great Mother.* Princeton: Princeton University Press, 1972, 1983.

————. "The Moon and Matriarchal Consciousness." In *Fathers and Mothers.* Zurich: Spring Publications, 1973.

Nilsson, Martin. *A History of Greek Religion.* Oxford: Clarendon Press, 1949.

Otto, Rudolf. *The Idea of the Holy.* New York: Oxford University Press, 1958.

Perera, Sylvia Brinton. *Descent to the Goddess: A Way of Initiation for Women*. Toronto: Inner City Books, 1981.

Rich, Adrienne. *Of Woman Born*. New York: W. W. Norton, 1976.

Rich, Sharon. "Daughters' Views of Their Relationships with Their Mothers." In *Making Connections*, edited by Carol Gilligan, Nona P. Lyons, and Trudy J. Hanmer, 258–73. Cambridge, Mass.: Harvard University Press, 1989.

Schwartz-Salant, Nathan. *Narcissism and Character Transformation*. Toronto: Inner City Books, 1982.

Sexton, Anne. *The Book of Folly*. Boston: Houghton Mifflin, 1972.

Simms, Laura. "Long Journey Home: A Retelling of the Myth of Demeter and Persephone" In *The Long Journey Home: Revisioning the Myth of Demeter and Persephone for Our Time*, edited by Christine Downing, 71–90. Boston: Shambhala Publications, 1994.

Spignesi, Angelyn. *Starving Women: A Psychology of Anorexia Nervosa*. Dallas: Spring Publications, 1983.

Starhawk. *Dreaming the Dark*. Boston: Beacon Press, 1982.

Stone, Merlin. *When God Was a Woman*. New York: Harcourt Brace Jovanovich, 1976.

Walker, Barbara. *The Crone: Woman of Age, Wisdom, and Power*. San Francisco: Harper and Row, 1985.

———. *The Woman's Encyclopedia of Myths and Secrets*. New York: Harper and Row, 1983.

Whitmont, Edward C. *The Symbolic Quest*. New York: G. P. Putnam's Sons, 1969.

Williams, Oscar ed. *Immortal Poems of the English Language*. New York: Pocket Books, 1952.

Young-Eisendrath, Polly. "Demeter's Folly: Experiencing Loss in Middle Life." *Psychological Perspectives* 15 (Spring 1984): 39–63.

Credits

ART

Anderson, Judith. *As I Am So Shall You Be.* 1990. Etching in blue-black ink. 18″ × 24″. Courtesy of the artist. Photo by Jim Colando.

Benton, Suzanne. *Persephone.* 1985. Mask and tale. Bronze and steel. 14″×8″×3½″. Courtesy of the artist. Photo by Lori Grinker.

Benton, Suzanne. *The One Who Dies.* Holocaust series, 1983. Steel. Chain 35″, body of mask 10¼″×9″×2″. Courtesy of the artist.

de Barolet, Anne-Marie. *The Rape of Kore.* 1983. Paper collage. 18″ × 22″. Courtesy of the artist.

de Barolet, Anne-Marie. *Hades and Kore: The Myth Rewritten.* 1989. Paper collage. 15″ × 18″. Courtesy of the artist.

Käthe Kollwitz. *"Seed for the Planting Shall Not Be Grounded Up!".* 1942. Lithograph. 14⅝″ × 15½″. © 1997 Artists Rights Society (ARS), New York/ VG Bild-Kunst, Bonn.

MacDougall, Sue. *Searching for Persephone.* Demeter Series #1, 1986. Graphite. 19″ × 25″. Courtesy of the artist.

MacDougall, Sue. *Demeter Still Searching.* Demeter Series #2, 1987. Graphite. 13″ × 18″. Courtesy of the artist.

MacDougall, Sue. *Persephone: Guardian of the Underworld.* Demeter Series #6, 1987. Graphite. 13″ × 18″. Courtesy of the artist.

Soos, Anita. *Pomegranates.* 1996. Etching. Ink. 38″ × 50″. Courtesy of the artist.

Soos, Anita. *Pomegranates—Study.* 1996. Etching. Ink. 24″ × 18″. Courtesy of the artist.

Plate 1. Demeter, Persephone, and Triptolemus. Greek votive relief, 5th century, BCE. National Archaeological Museum, Athens, Greece. Courtesy of Erich Lessing/Art Resource, NY.

Plate 2. Head of Demeter. Terra-cotta decorative panel. Museo Nazionale Romano delle Terme, Rome, Italy. Courtesy of Alinari/Art Resource, NY.

Plate 3. Imperial period marble statuette depicting the goddess Demeter holding her daughter, the Kore, on her lap. (Inv. 76-460). Courtesy of Dr.

Donald White, Director, University of Pennsylvania Museum of Archaeology and Anthropology's Expedition to Cyrene, and Dr. Susan Kane, Oberlin College.

Plate 4. Kore. Greek, Archaic Period, Acropolis Museum, Athens, Greece. Courtesy of Nimatallah/Art Resource, NY.

Plate 5. Demeter and Core, "Exaltation of the Flower" (470–460 BCE), Louvre, Paris, France. Courtesy of Erich Lessing/Art Resource, NY.

Plate 6. Panel from container with relief depicting Persephone and Pluto enthroned. Museo Archeologico Naz., Reggio Calabria, Italy. Courtesy of Scala/Art Resource, NY.

Plate 7. Demeter and Kore. Votive relief, 5th century BCE. Archaeological Museum, Eleusis, Greece. Courtesy of Alinari/Art Resource, NY.

Plate 8. G. Gatti. *Persephone as Queen of the Dead*, drawing from an Etruscan tomb in Tarquinia, 4th century BCE, Museo Archeologico, Florence, Italy. Courtesy of Alinari/Art Resource, NY.

TEXT

The author would like to thank the following publishers, authors, and agents for permission to reprint material copyrighted or controlled by them:

River Malcolm for lines from her poem "The Two Goddesses" in her book *No Goddess Dances to a Mortal Tune*, self-published, Del Mar, Calif., copyright © 1992. Reprinted by permission of River Malcolm.

The Crossing Press for lines from "She Who" by Judy Grahn, reprinted with permission from "She Who," pp. 84–85 in *The Work of a Common Woman* by Judy Grahn. Copyright © 1978. Published by The Crossing Press, Freedom, Calif.

Princeton University Press for excerpts from Loring Danforth, *The Death Rituals of Rural Greece*. Copyright © 1982 by Princeton University Press. Reprinted by permission of Princeton University Press.

Lines from "Thoughts about My Daughter Before Sleep" by Sandra Hochman in *Earthworks* (Viking Press, 1974). Reprinted by permission of Curtis Brown, Ltd. Copyright © 1974 by Sandra Hochman.

Every effort has been made to contact copyright holders.

Index